USING AND ABUSING
THE HOLOCAUST

JEWISH LITERATURE AND CULTURE

SERIES EDITOR, ALVIN H. ROSENFELD

USING AND
ABUSING THE
HOLOCAUST

Lawrence L. Langer

Indiana University Press
Bloomington & Indianapolis
OCM 622904 77

PUBLISHED WITH THE ASSISTANCE OF THE JEWISH STUDIES FUND, INDIANA UNIVERSITY PRESS.

THIS BOOK IS A PUBLICATION OF

INDIANA UNIVERSITY PRESS
601 NORTH MORTON STREET
BLOOMINGTON, IN 47404-3797 USA

HTTP://IUPRESS.INDIANA.EDU

Telephone orders   800-842-6796
Fax orders   812-855-7931
Orders by e-mail   IUPORDER@INDIANA.EDU

MANUFACTURED IN THE UNITED STATES OF AMERICA

THE TRANSLATION OF ABRAHAM SUTZKEVER'S "FOR MY CHILD" ON PAGES 79–80 APPEARS COURTESY OF SEYMOUR MAYNE AND WAS ORIGINALLY PUBLISHED IN THE VOLUME, *BURNT PEARLS: GHETTO POEMS OF ABRAHAM SUTZKEVER* (1981).

LIBRARY OF CONGRESS CATALOGING-IN-PUBLICATION DATA

LANGER, LAWRENCE L.
USING AND ABUSING THE HOLOCAUST / LAWRENCE L. LANGER.
P. CM. — (JEWISH LITERATURE AND CULTURE)
INCLUDES BIBLIOGRAPHICAL REFERENCES AND INDEX.
ISBN 0-253-34745-9 (CLOTH : ALK. PAPER)
1. HOLOCAUST, JEWISH (1939–1945) — PERSONAL NARRATIVES — HISTORY AND CRITICISM.
2. HOLOCAUST, JEWISH (1939–1945) — INFLUENCE. 3. HOLOCAUST, JEWISH (1939–1945), IN LITERATURE. 4. HOLOCAUST SURVIVORS — BIOGRAPHY — HISTORY AND CRITICISM.
I. TITLE. II. SERIES.

D804.195.L357 2006
940.53'18 — DC22

2005031635

1   2   3   4   5   11   10   09   08   07   06

FOR SANDY

WHOM AGE CANNOT WITHER

NOR CUSTOM STALE.

Human beings are human only insofar as they bear witness to the inhuman.

GIORGIO AGAMBEN

CONTENTS

PREFACE

The ghastly details of the Holocaust are a constant reminder of the abyss separating the lived experience of those who endured it from the language that seeks to describe it. To ignore this menacing chasm by bridging it with a brittle rhetoric of consolation only increases the risk of plunging into the uncertainty churning in its depths. But yielding to its magnetic pull creates dilemmas of its own, and the essays in this volume try to address some of them. Visitors to the realm of Holocaust anguish are met by the threat of death at every turn, not only as the end of an ordeal of misery but also as a partner to the challenge of staying alive. As the event recedes in time, it grows more and more difficult to recapture the way it was for those who faced it: everything has come to depend on who tells the tale, and how. History resembles narrative as we speak or write about it, or in the case of art, find shapes to represent its reality. Summoning versions of the Holocaust past requires a verbal or — in the case of film or painting — visual agility that returns us to the problem of choosing an apt vocabulary to confront the atrocity we call the Holocaust. We soon learn, however, that such a vocabulary involves more than words or images.

Deflective texts about the Holocaust experience continue to proliferate, their titles often barely concealing their programmatic intent. One recent example is called *Hidden from the Holocaust: Stories of Resilient Children Who Survived and Thrived.* Surely the subtitle "Stories of Children Who Survived" would have been enough. The addition of "resilient" and "thrived" shifts the prospective reader's attention from the implicit death scenario, which is the main focus of accounts of the destruction of European Jewry, to the attractive auxiliary idea that one could emerge from the universe of extermination virtually intact, unscathed by the murder of so many others, including in many instances one's own parents. Whether the same hopeful impulse that drove the American publishers of Primo Levi's *If This Is a Man* to change its title to *Survival in Auschwitz* and of its sequel *The Truce* to *The*

Reawakening is operative here we cannot know. All of these titles misleadingly identify the Holocaust as a healable offense, and leave us wondering whether those who bore its torments but failed to prosper afterward were somehow guilty of willfully rejecting a self-administered antidote called "resilience."[1]

As several of the following essays show, there is considerable evidence for a complex form of necrotic consciousness, which I call *deathlife*, that is a neglected legacy of the Holocaust experience — and indeed of many other subsequent national catastrophes. When Primo Levi told his biographer in 1986, a year before his demise, that after the camp ordeal "I had the sensation that I was living but without being alive,"[2] he was not describing a neurotic or disabling post-Holocaust disorder but a not uncommon attitude among many who had endured the lethal universe of Nazi oppression. Novelist and Buchenwald survivor Jorge Semprun voiced a similar feeling when he admitted "that I have not escaped death, but passed through it. Rather: that it has passed through me. That I have, in a way, lived through it."[3] Though not widely shared, this notion surfaces often enough in witness testimony and literature to require some careful reflection about how we can best admit it to the pantheon of possible modern responses to atrocity. There it would join other pedestals of remembrance with more familiar titles like amnesia, evasion, denial, indifference, healing, "working through," resistance and transcendence. Semprun calls his approach "despairing memory," and if the insights it offers into the domain of Holocaust dying seem bleaker than the attitudes of its above-named companions, this response may turn out to be more a commentary on *their* limitations rather than on his.

Certainly two of the works I examine in this volume, Roberto Benigni's film *Life Is Beautiful* and Anne Frank's *Diary*, have little to do with despairing memory. Both are marked by an absence of pain, a muting of anguish, a neglect of death. It is hard to discount these qualities as major sources of their appeal, though Anne Frank is innocent of the calculation that inspired the popularity of Benigni's cinematic exploitation of his theme. Yet her audience is guilty of canonizing her adolescent musings in a way that I doubt she would have embraced. Both she and Semprun recognized the crucial role of writing in mastering reality, but unlike him she never had a chance to apply this belief to the lived experience of the camp world. The sequel to her *Diary*, in which she would have recorded her reaction to her "deathlife" after Auschwitz and Bergen-Belsen, remains one of the much-missed unwritten books of Holocaust literature. Her legacy has been fashioned less by the substance of her entries than by her audiences' delight with her manageable narrative. And this is even truer of Benigni's film, which insulates the viewer from the onslaught of despairing memory up to its final moment of reunion.

Yet the same cannot be said of Binjamin Wilkomirski's false memoir, *Fragments*, which does nothing to protect the reader from pain, anguish, or death. Wilkomirski's popularity in America, especially in critical and academic circles, remains one of the most puzzling episodes in recent Holocaust inquiry, and my only explanation is that this response was not so much to his work (which did not sell noticeably well, here or abroad) as to his personality. Audiences usually celebrate survival more easily than they absorb what has been survived, and in his American lectures Wilkomirski was sufficiently prudent to concentrate on his sessions with other child survivors rather than on his own ordeal. One is left to wonder how carefully readers had studied the text of his memoir, since, as we shall see, it is full of so many logical and historical flaws that anyone familiar with the techniques of literary narrative and the history of the camps should have been instantly suspicious. It appears that when the Holocaust is the subject, misdirected popular enthusiasms form easily, especially when they deflect us from the task of tackling the authenticity of unbearable truths.

As someone who has outlived the camps, the survivor moves further from death; but as someone who has returned to the realm of the living, he or she moves closer to it. This paradox remains unresolved in most Holocaust commentary, but it is an issue we cannot afford to ignore. When eagerness to hear more about the Holocaust is combined with a failure to learn enough about it in advance, audiences have trouble separating remembered from invented reality. This was clearly the case with the reception of Wilkomirski's *Fragments*. And not only outsiders are vulnerable to this lapse. I have interviewed two women survivors of Auschwitz who, upon entering a small chamber shortly after their arrival in the camp, said they were relieved to see that the Germans had "turned on the water instead of the gas." I assume charitably that a notorious episode from *Schindler's List* has unconsciously infiltrated their narrative, and one hopes it does not signify an alarming trend that would allow Hollywood and other entertainment venues to reshape our recall of the details of this atrocity. Although the film's emotional moment in the showers of Auschwitz may rouse a quiver of actual horror in the general viewer, it remains a fusion of melodrama and myth for anyone who knows that the gas chambers contained no plumbing, and the real showers no gas.

Gabriel Garcia Márquez begins the first volume of his memoirs, *Living to Tell the Tale,* with the cautionary reminder that "Life is not what one lived, but what one remembers and how one remembers it in order to recount it." His title, of course, has nothing to do with the Holocaust and his words seem valid for anyone recording memories of childhood, youth, and early experiences. But there is a difference between narratives driven by a desire to explain how one got from "there and then" to "here and now" and darker stories inspired by Semprun's idea of "despairing memory." There would be a grave dimension, beyond the obvious punning, to an autobiographical volume by Márquez — if he had written one — called *Dying to Tell the Tale.* Deathlife as a theme, though it flourishes in works of major writers like

Charlotte Delbo and Piotr Rawicz, has yet to receive the attention it deserves in the universe of Holocaust discourse. Witnessing it through "despairing memory" requires us to amend or supplement Márquez's sentiment to read: "*Death* is not what one lived, but what one remembers and how one remembers it in order to recount it." Before the grim magnitude of the Holocaust was known, Albert Camus had written with a prophetic thrust few were aware of at the time: "There is but one freedom: to put oneself right with death." The abstract tinge to his words receives more precise shading in W. G. Sebald's post-Holocaust version, born of despairing memory: "a proper understanding of the catastrophes we are always setting off is the first prerequisite for the social organization of happiness." Roberto Benigni's *Life is Beautiful* seems consciously designed to reverse Sebald's position. The rivalry between these outlooks, and the implications of avoiding or embracing them, surface repeatedly in the following essays as central thematic concerns.

The Book of Common Prayer reminds us that "in the midst of life we are in death," though modern history has forced a radical shift to our understanding of that sentiment. A sober cue to the human spirit about its brief earthly sojourn has grown into a shattering secular vision of global slaughter for which Auschwitz has become an archetypal center. If, as Susan Neiman argues in *Evil in Modern Thought*, rather than "asking why this particular event [the Holocaust] produced the sense of unique devastation that heralds the violent end of an era, we should look more closely at what conceptual resources were destroyed,"[4] then one is left dismayed by how little intellectual energy has been spent (prior to her study) in searching for new "conceptual resources" to explain with philosophical conviction the existence of an Auschwitz (to say nothing of subsequent atrocities of equal impact if lesser scope).[5] Indeed, we do not even have reliable statistics for how widely the "sense of unique devastation" she speaks of is shared, nor have we identified which "conceptual resources" (if any) were destroyed. On the front jacket of her book, Neiman reproduces Francisco Goya's etching and aquatint *The Sleep [or Dream] of Reason Produces Monsters*, a fitting caution to the late eighteenth century for what happens when reason is allowed to slumber — but perhaps also an ironic reminder of the nightmares that an active reason can conjure. For if the Holocaust has taught us anything, it is that *waking* reason produces monsters too, making reason itself one of those "conceptual resources" needing revisitation. A study of the role of reason in the creation of Auschwitz could lead to some audacious conclusions about the unwarranted significance ceded to terms like *meaning* and *sense* in discussions of this bleak topic.

Neiman states the issue clearly: "What seemed devastated — nay, entirely thwarted — by Auschwitz was the possibility of intellectual response itself. Thought stood still, for the tools of civilization seemed as helpless in coping with the event as they were in preventing it."[6] Thought may have stood still after Auschwitz, but it was not permanently immobilized. Few appeared willing to embrace the disquieting option that by the twentieth century mass murder in various forms had *become* one of the tools of civilization, and that a major problem for its heirs was how to absorb rather than evade this dismal fact. The current popularity of "forgiveness" and "reconciliation" as fruitful responses to the agents of atrocity only confirms how little we have advanced in our journey to appreciate the nature of the beast. The inclination in some circles to regard some evils of apartheid or the slaughter in Rwanda as pardonable offenses may be seen as a desperate refusal to admit that certain "tools of civilization," whether we call them Christian vision or restorative justice, failed miserably to forestall the criminals they are now seeking to rehabilitate. Despairing memory may not seem a sanguine replacement, but it merits consideration as a psychologically helpful means, as Semprun puts it, "to make peace with all that death." At least it provides a beginning to our search for a suitable discourse to encompass our culture of atrocity.

Not much thought is required to understand why the author of *Fragments* — surrendered by his unwed mother as an infant and later adopted — should have sought to solve his personal identity crisis by inventing as a new persona a Jewish child named Binjamin Wilkomirski who had survived several Nazi deathcamps. He must have known that audiences were primed, both emotionally and morally, to embrace in advance the suffering of an innocent child. Both Dostoevsky in *The Brothers Karamazov* and Albert Camus in *The Plague* had explored this theme at crucial moments in their novels. The dilemma is not addressed intellectually in *Fragments,* but it remains implicit in the text. Indeed, by focusing on the imagination rather than the mind, Holocaust literature gives access to a realm of experience alien to established conceptual frameworks. The thought that stood still after Auschwitz, when translated into artistic vision, stirs into action a kind of consciousness that boldly pushes back the frontiers of understanding. After witnessing the ruthless destruction of the Warsaw ghetto from the safety of the Christian side, poet Czesław Miłosz was prompted to ask "what it means to bear such an experience inside oneself." It may not be too extreme to state that art is one of the few disciplines able to stimulate conceptual resources for facing this question. But Miłosz knew that the terms of the confrontation would have to be radically changed: "horror is the law of the world of living creatures and civilization is concerned with masking that truth. Literature and art refine and beautify, and if they were to depict reality naked, just as everyone suspects it is (although we defend ourselves against that knowledge), no one would be able to stand it."[7] This is not an Adorno-like statement about the barbarism of art after Auschwitz but an invitation to literature and art to incorporate barbarism into its conscious resources without flinching, knowing that the harmony of the world would have to pay a steep price for such inclusion.

I end this volume with an essay on the remarkable sequence of paintings based on the Book of Genesis by the artist Samuel Bak, a survivor of the Vilna ghetto. In Dostoevsky and Camus the suffering of little children remained a question of theodicy—why a benevolent God allows evil to prosper—though their motives for asking were utterly different. Bak's visual universe replaces that question with a more unsettling inquiry by wondering whether in a post-Holocaust world any bond is still possible between the human and the divine. His sober amendments to Michelangelo's *Creation of Adam* on the ceiling of the Sistine Chapel daringly revise the familiar iconography that once joined the Creator with His creation. In Bak's paintings Adam appears in the tattered garments of a soldier or survivor and God as a mere silhouette, the vacancy forming a stark contrast to Michelangelo's powerful anthropomorphic figure. God's animating finger seems to have gone astray, rarely meeting the extended digit of his quiescent creature. Bak thus adds to modern consciousness a conceptual framework for balancing the traditional spiritual harmony of scriptural precedents with the destructive impulses of an age of atrocity. He paints numerous versions of biblical narratives formerly designed to strengthen human communion with the sacred in which Eve, the patriarchs, Noah, and even angelic messengers appear weary and bereft, in search of a language and gesture to animate their quest. In redefining the role of art, scripture, belief, and hope for the future in human endeavor, Bak addresses directly the issue of finding new conceptual resources for confronting the Holocaust, the subject of most of the essays in this volume.

The Holocaust has forced us to add to Roman comic dramatist Terence's famous maxim, "I am human. Nothing human is alien to me," a fellow sentiment reading "I am human. Nothing inhuman is alien to me"—inhuman through someone else's nature, if not through one's own. Though this may sound like a summons to gloom, it is really a call to clarity, to what Camus called lucidity, a viewing of the world through a lens that reveals the paradoxical legacy of atrocity. Charlotte Delbo prefaces *None of Us Will Return,* the first volume of her Auschwitz trilogy, with the statement that "Today, I am not certain that what I wrote is true [*vrai*]. I am certain it is truthful [*véridique*]." Philosopher Giorgio Agamben calls such apparent contradictions the "aporia of Auschwitz, indeed the very aporia of historical knowledge: a non-coincidence between facts and truth, between verification and comprehension." This is the fundamental challenge to all Holocaust commentary, which Agamben defines as bearing witness to "what it is impossible to bear witness to." Old facts meet new truths in a clash between form and chaos, and the result is a fresh creation that includes destruction as part of our vision for the future. To find a rough parallel, one would have to imagine Adam and Eve in Eden knowing death *before* the Fall. They did not, so somehow the innocent language of Eden survived the expulsion, and must now die another death. Agamben calls for "certain words to be left

behind and others to be understood in a different sense. This is also a way—
perhaps the only way—to listen to what is unsaid."[8] The current daily reminders that life is not beautiful do not mean that we cannot learn to live
fruitfully within the limits of the possible, without pretense or illusion. The
conceptual resources we surrender in order to get there will determine the
extent of our success.

NOTES

1. Other volumes determined to extract an affirmative core from the murder of
European Jewry include William Helmreich's *Against All Odds: Holocaust Survivors
and the Successful Lives They Made in America* (New York: Simon and Schuster, 1992),
Tzvetan Todorov's *Facing the Extreme: Moral Life in the Concentration Camps* (New York:
Henry Holt, 1996), and Nechama Tec's *Resilience and Courage: Women, and Men, and
the Holocaust* (New Haven, Conn.: Yale University Press, 2003).

2. Ian Thomson, *Primo Levi: A Life* (New York: Henry Holt, 2002), 208.

3. Jorge Semprun, *Literature or Life,* trans. L. Coverdale (New York: Viking, 1997),
14–15.

4. Susan Neiman, *Evil in Modern Thought: An Alternative History of Philosophy* (Princeton, N.J.: Princeton University Press, 2002), 256.

5. Writers like Jean-François Leotard, Maurice Blanchot, and Giorgio Agamben
have shared Neiman's concern, though with a greater emphasis on linguistic rather
than conceptual resources.

6. Neiman, 256.

7. Czesław Miłosz, "Anus Mundi," in *To Begin Where I Am: Selected Essays,* ed. Bog-
dana Carpenter and Madeline G. Levine (New York: Farrar, Straus and Giroux,
2001), 371, 372.

8. Giorgio Agamben, *Remnants of Auschwitz: The Witness and the Archive,* trans.
Daniel Heller-Roazen (New York: Zone Books, 1999), 12, 13, 14.

ACKNOWLEDGMENTS

Four of the essays in this volume — "Anne Frank Revisited," "Life Is Not Beautiful," "Memory and Justice after the Holocaust and Apartheid," and "Witnessing Atrocity: The Testimonial Evidence" — have never appeared in print before. "Wounded Families in Holocaust Discourse" is a revised and much expanded version of "Damaged Childhood in Fact and Fiction," which appeared in *Humanity at the Limit: The Impact of the Holocaust Experience on Jews and Christians,* edited by Michael A. Signer (University of Notre Dame Press, 2000). "Fragments of Memory: A Myth of Past Time" grew out of a brief review of Binjamin Wilkomirski's *Fragments* in *Congress Monthly* (March/April 2000). It is essentially a new essay. "Moralizing and Demoralizing the Holocaust" began as a short essay called "Moralizing the Holocaust" that was published in *Dimensions: A Journal of Holocaust Studies* 12, no. 1 (1998). The present version is about twice as long, and the second half is entirely new material. "Representing the Holocaust" first appeared as a review essay in *Holocaust and Genocide Studies* 16, no.1 (Spring 2002). The section on Berel Lang's *Holocaust Representation: Art within the Limits of History and Ethics* has been completely rewritten. "The Book of Genesis in the Art of Samuel Bak" is a condensed version of a much longer essay that was part of the volume *In a Different Light: The Book of Genesis in the Art of Samuel Bak* (Pucker Art Publications, 2001). I thank Bernard Pucker for permission to reproduce several of Bak's paintings.

The only essay with very minor revisions is "The Pursuit of Death in Holocaust Narrative" from *Partisan Review* 68, no. 3 (Summer 2001), reprinted in *Narrative and Consciousness: Literature, Psychology and the Brain,* edited by Gary D. Fireman et al. (Oxford University Press, 2003).

I am especially grateful to the director and staff of the Rockefeller Foundation Study and Conference Center in Bellagio, Italy, whose unprecedented support created an idyllic atmosphere for scholarly endeavor that enabled me to complete several of the essays in this volume.

USING AND ABUSING
THE HOLOCAUST

1

THE PURSUIT OF DEATH IN
HOLOCAUST NARRATIVE

Autobiographical narrative by its very nature explores a journey that has not yet reached its end. One study of the genre by James Olney is called *Memory and Narrative: The Weave of Life-Writing*. It occurs to me that a study of Holocaust memory and narrative might justifiably be subtitled "The Weave of Death-Writing." Although Holocaust testimonies and memoirs are of course concerned with how one went on living in the midst of German atrocities, their subtexts offer us a theme that is more difficult to express or to understand: how, under those minimal conditions, slowly but inexorably, one went on dying — every day, every hour, every minute of one's agonizing existence. We are forced to redefine the meaning of survival, as the assertive idea of staying alive is offset by the reactive one of fending off death. The impact on consciousness of this dilemma is a neglected but important legacy of the experience we call the Holocaust.

The Holocaust survivors I am speaking of do not merely recover their lives in their narratives. Through complex associations with their murdered comrades, family members, and communities they also recover what I call their missed destiny of death. Because the logic of existence in places such as Auschwitz dictated that one should die, witnesses often feel that survival was an *abnormal* result of their ordeal in the camps, a violation of the expected outcome of their detention. They were not meant to return. Charlotte Delbo calls the first volume of her Auschwitz memoir *Aucun de nous ne reviendra* (*None of Us Will Return*). This response has nothing to do with guilt or what some label a death wish but with a stubborn intuition that unlike the others, through accident or luck, those who held out somehow mistakenly eluded their intended end. In many instances the sensation of being dead while alive reflects a dual thrust of their present being: in chronological time they seek their future while in durational time, those isolated moments of dreadful memories do not dissipate but congeal into dense claws of tenacious consciousness. A lethal past relentlessly pursues them.

According to Auschwitz survivor Jean Améry, mass murder in the form of genocide forced its victims to live not next door to but in the same room as death. Distinguishing between the violence of war and the rigid milieu of the camps, Améry observed: "The soldier was driven into the fire, and it is true his life was not worth much. Still, the state did not order him to die, but to survive. The final duty of the prisoner, however, was death"[1] In other words, the *necessity* of dying replaced the possibility of dying, even as many inmates struggled to stay alive — which is different from resolving to survive. Their surroundings, rather than some internal system of values inherited from normal life, infiltrated the mental content of their days. What this meant can be illustrated by two brief excerpts from witness testimonies. Renee H., who was little more than ten years old at the time, recalls a scene from Bergen-Belsen:

> Right across from us was a charnel house filled with corpses, not just inside but overflowing all over. There were corpses all over. I lived, walked beside dead people. After a while it just got to be so that no one noticed, and one had to say to oneself, "I am not going to see who it is. I am not going to recognize anyone in this person who is lying there." It got to a point where I realized that I had to close my eyes to a number of things. Otherwise I would not have survived even at that time, because I saw people around me going mad. I was not only having to live with all things, but with madness.[2]

We need to imagine how such imagery imprints itself on consciousness, despite efforts to avoid the unavoidable; but even more, we need to acknowledge the impact of such imagery on the unfolding of Holocaust narrative as memory stumbles repeatedly over death while seeking to recount episodes of life in the camps under conditions of atrocity.

The second example is both more vivid and more graphic. It documents with uncanny if unintended precision a moment of failed purgation, as if the *body* were seeking to expel what memory could not cast out from consciousness:

> I got a job carrying people's waste out from the barrack at night. . . . I was very sick. I got diarrhea. That was already recuperating a little bit from the

malaria. I walked out with two pails of human waste and I was going toward the dump. I walked out, and between the barracks was a mountain of people as high as myself. The people died at night, they were just taken out on the dump — you know, a big pile of people. And I said to myself "O God. Must I walk by?" But in the meanwhile, I couldn't hold back, and I just put down the two pails and I sit down because I had a sick stomach. And the rats were standing and eating the people's faces — eating, you know, they were having a . . . [*long silence*]. Anyway, I had to do my job. I was just looking, what's happening to a human being. That could have been my mother. That could have been my father. That could have been my sister or my brother.[3]

The sheer physicality of Hanna F.'s description would dampen the ardor of those who insist on the triumph of the spirit even in Auschwitz, which is the locale of this remembered episode. The fusion of excrement, corpses, and predatory rats creates a cluster of images that forces us to redefine our notion of dying. At that moment the witness seemed to be trapped by a cycle of decay from which there was no escape. The cherished idea of the family as an intimate unit succumbed momentarily to the horrible alternative of the family as prey for hungry rodents. We are left numbed by the challenge of absorbing into our hopes for a human future this grim heritage of unnatural death.

I said that the witness succumbed *momentarily* to a new and unprecedented vision of her family's fate, but this was more a charitable concession than a discovered truth. Such images may lurk in consciousness undeciphered, but they inspire insight only after being filtered through a mind determined to wrestle with the implications of the harsh burden that the Germans imposed on their victims. Jean Améry spent his post-camp life, which ended in suicide, unsuccessfully trying to placate the ghost of unnatural death that plagued him after his survival. In his now classic work, *At the Mind's Limits*, he reported:

There was once a conversation in the camp about an SS man who had slit open a prisoner's belly and filled it with sand. It is obvious that in view of such possibilities one was hardly concerned with whether, or *that*, one had to die, but with *how* it would happen. Inmates carried on conversations about how long it probably takes for the gas in the gas chambers to do its job. One speculated on the painfulness of death by phenol injections. Were you to wish yourself a blow to the skull or a slow death through exhaustion in the infirmary? It was characteristic for the situation of the prisoner in regard to death that only a few decided to "run to the wire," as one said, that is, to commit suicide through contact with the highly electrified barbed wire. The wire was after all a good and rather certain thing, but it was possible that in the attempt to approach it one would be caught first and thrown into the bunker, and that led to a more difficult and more painful dying. Dying was omnipresent, death vanished from sight. (17)

Améry's variations on a theme of dying in Auschwitz leave little space for consolation. "These were the conditions under which the intellectual collided with death," he concluded. "Death lay before him, and in him the spirit was still stirring; the latter confronted the former and tried—in vain, to say it straight off—to exemplify its dignity" (16).

Dying among the living, even when it is abrupt and painful, is a termination, and for those left behind society provides rituals of closure, including grief for the departed—we even have an appropriate vocabulary of solace—to ease the separation. But dying among the dying leaves us with no analogy to help us imagine the ordeal and find a suitable place in consciousness to lodge it. We have few narratives that portray such dying and its effect on traditional versions of the self. Améry's prisoners who discuss their possible doom bear no agency for their fate. They are left with a permanent uncertainty about the responsibility for their anguish, unable to blame a gas chamber or a hypodermic needle or the crushing force of a club. The absence of an identifiable human killer that allows one to trace a clear path from cause to effect is joined by another important hiatus that afflicts the memory of survivors, and that is the missing ritual of mourning. This is complicated by the foreknowledge that their own dying, when it occurs, will preclude a similar ritual for themselves. Permanently barred from details of how members of their families died, witnesses often seem less distressed by the illogic of those early deaths than by the "illogic" of their own continued lives. The psychic discontinuity implicit in such experience prevents the death of others—really, the murder of others—from being integrated into the natural rhythms of existence, leaving the survivor vainly groping for some tie between consequential living and inconsequential dying. The former is the text, the latter the subtext of numerous Holocaust narratives, oral and written, leading to a constant tension between pursuit and escape as divided consciousness seeks to integrate what cannot be reconciled—except perhaps in the ambiguous landscape of art.

The rift in time and memory that separates the unnatural death of others from one's own staying alive cries out for a bridge, but continuity is not its name. The vision of decay that reminds Hanna F. of her family's wretched end spreads its sway over the surrounding narrative terrain, contaminating efforts to soothe the transition from past to present or to free one to enter tranquilly into the future. The view that Holocaust survivors should be able to generalize their anguish in order to leave behind them the aura of death derives from unfamiliarity with how durational time assails the memory of so many witnesses. On the deepest level, a large number of their life stories are also death stories, which include the partial death of the self in ways that still need to be interpreted. The quest for a rebirth of that part of the self is as futile as would be any effort to transform Hanna F.'s pile of corpses into a sacred community of the dead. This may be a dark view, but there is overwhelming evidence from Holocaust narratives that it is a realistic one, from which we have much to learn. The effect of atrocity, and not only Holocaust atrocity, on the modern sensibility is a virgin territory into which few analysts have yet ventured.

One of the many victims of these narratives is the very notion that we can expel from consciousness, and hence from being, zones of memory that threaten our intact spirits. Unnatural death creates an inversion of normality that we cannot easily dismiss. In her Auschwitz trilogy, Charlotte Delbo crafts a monologue by a fellow survivor named Mado that, because of its stylized intensity, approaches the level of art, but nonetheless conveys the despair of a woman who is denied the remission of amnesia. She begins: "It seems to me I'm not alive. Since all are dead, it seems impossible that I shouldn't be also. All dead. . . . All the others, all the others. How could those stronger and more determined than I be dead, and I remain alive? Can one come out of there alive? No, it wasn't possible. . . . I'm not alive. I see myself from outside this self pretending to be alive. I'm not alive. I know this with an intimate, solitary knowledge."[4]

Mado's paradoxical refrain — "I'm not alive" — accents the need for a narrative form to capture the post-war effects of the daily rule during her imprisonment that to be alive was to be a candidate for death. Delbo has taken the liberty of discarding the chronological text of her friend's testimony, forcing us to face the full, unblemished impact of Auschwitz time.

The thrust of Mado's existence is backwards, as if loyalty to her dead and sometimes murdered friends requires her to embrace a rupture between then and now that infiltrates and finally pollutes the purity of her aspirations toward the future. When her son is born she tries to feel happy. But memory will not allow her to. "The silky water of my joy," she says, "changed to sticky mud, sooty snow, fetid marshes. I saw again this woman — you remember this peasant woman, lying in the snow, dead, with her dead newborn frozen between her thighs. My son was also that newborn" (261–262). Thus even her present family is shrouded by the subtext of dying in the camps. The challenge of learning how to live while continuing to participate in the unnatural death of others haunts Mado as a persistent melancholy legacy from that time.

As the habit of "holding out" *then* nurtures in Mado the practice of "making do" *now*, a psychology of endurance breeds in her a new sense of who she is, of what she has become. She recalls her companions arguing in the camps that if they returned home after the war, everything would be different. But they were wrong. "Everything is the same," Mado discovers. "It is within us that nothing is the same" (263). This represents not a loss of identity but a *shift* in identity, a painfully honest confession that the self has been split not by some psychotic condition but by the twin realities that inhabit her spirit. Mado admits that to forget the durational subtext in order to return to the chronological narrative of her life would be atrocious, then adds that it would be impossible too. "People believe memories grow

vague," she ends her monologue, "are erased by time, since nothing en-
dures against the passage of time. That's the difference: time does not pass
over me, over us. It doesn't erase anything, doesn't undo it. I'm not alive. I
died in Auschwitz but no one knows it" (267).

Of course, Mado is right. No one but she and Delbo and the few dozen
other Frenchwomen who returned from their transport to Auschwitz can
expect to enter the dark inner realm where the theme of being dead while
alive enacts its paradoxical drama. Yet perhaps she is mistaken too. Her
words allow us to see feelingly, then to imagine the contours of that alien
world, and the missed destiny of death that assaults it. An alliance with
atrocity is part of the burden of modernity, though it is both simpler and less
troublesome to pretend that it is not. Atrocity narrative requires us to abandon the conviction that the gift of life is antithetical to the menace of
unnatural death. Writers like Delbo entreat us to discard this consoling
template of reality as a remnant of an ancient nostalgia rather than retaining it as a still useful blueprint for designing the future after Auschwitz.

Sometimes episodes surface in Holocaust testimonies that seem to trans-
gress our sense of the possible, to reveal a reality so beyond our imaginings
that we rush to consign them to the realm of fantasy. But anyone immersed
in this world of atrocity will be forced to concede that few powers of invention could conjure up some of the most gruesome moments of the camp
experience. From an eyewitness in the Natzweiler concentration camp
comes the following account to confirm the intricate bond linking living
and dying for the victimized in the Holocaust universe:

> On July 8, 1942, I was witness to a terrifying event that will never fade from
> my memory. In the corridor of the infirmary stood six coffins in a stack.
> They were crates hammered together of rough boards, out of which blood
> seeped through the joints. Suddenly a knocking could be heard from the
> bottom coffin. A weak voice quavered, "Open up! Open up! I am still
> alive!" The greens [deported criminals] pulled out the bottom coffin and
> opened it. A Polish prisoner with an injured head and broken legs stared
> out at us from the coffin, in which he was lying with a dead man. I wanted to
> intervene, to free him from his terrifying situation, but I was immediately
> pushed aside by one of the professional criminals. A few dull thuds, then
> the coffin was nailed shut again and sent to the crematorium.[5]

Edgar Allan Poe's literary fascination with similar imagery seems an ama-
teurish harbinger of this grisly historical version of a troika joining the
living, the dying, and the dead. It introduces into the discourse of atrocity a
fresh concept for defining consciousness after the Holocaust, the idea of a
"coffined self" to share with more vital features of identity the numbing
legacy that the unnatural death of others has bequeathed us.

The visible distance separating life from death was at times narrowed to a
fine line in the Holocaust universe; at others, it seemed to disappear en-

tirely. As the reverence for life vanishes, the customary reverence for the dead and the dying fades too. For students of this era, some space must be found for an intellectual response to reports like the following from Buchenwald, which violate our sense of reason and logic, to say nothing of humanity, but which nevertheless form part of the memory of those open to their impact:

> In my service as a mason during the building of the new crematorium, I could observe things that probably are still not known. As long as the new ovens were not yet finished, the old one was still used. Between the old and the new ovens was a wall of boards. After the first new oven was ready, the wall was moved between it and the second new oven under construction.
>
> At this time many Russian prisoners of war were murdered by shots to the base of the skull. When the murderers arrived with a truckload of victims, the bodies were delivered directly into the basement through a built-in chute. Every time the Nazis let bodies slide down into the cellar, howling and groaning arose — proof that many of the victims were not yet completely dead, since they returned to consciousness when they struck the cement floor of the cellar. Whether these still-living, unfortunate victims of the murderous beasts were then beaten to death or were sent into the ovens while still alive, I don't know.
>
> When we built the chimneys of the crematorium, I once saw three and another time two Russian soldiers standing alive, in the courtyard. They were led into the crematorium — and then I saw nothing of them again. (239–240)

To familiar tales of the living dead we must now add sinister hints of the dying living, drawn not from the annals of medical history or superstition but from an authentic record of witnessed incidents.

Straight narrative cannot begin to help us absorb the shock of this brutal transition from life to death without any clear sign of the cessation of one before the advent of the other. As the conditions of being and non-being merge and blur, we are left groping for a way to extend the range of implication that assaults us from the region of that crematorium. "For those who were in Auschwitz," Charlotte Delbo wrote in *A Useless Knowledge*, the second volume of her Auschwitz trilogy, "waiting meant racing ahead of death" (168). For those who returned from Auschwitz, she might have added, memory became a path leading to and through death; she sought to capture this twisted journey of consciousness in a concise poem that entwines two domains in a knot of intimacy that not even reading can disentangle:

> I've come back from another world
> To this world
> I had not left
> And I know not
> Which one is real
> Tell me did I really come back

7

From the other world?
As far as I'm concerned
I'm still there
Dying there
A little more each day
Dying over again
The death of those who died
and I no longer know which is the real one
this world, right here,
or the world over there
now
I no longer know
when I am dreaming
and when
I do not dream. (204)

If lines such as "dying over again / The death of those who died" express not merely a memory of the past but also an abiding presence, then we are left dwelling in a middle realm where living and dying mix and re-form, and for which few narrative strategies help us to understand how they might blend in contemporary consciousness.

Fortunately, at least one writer has made this issue the focus of his artistic career, and his extensive reflections on the theme allow us to enter the anteroom of the creative imagination as it struggles to nurture its vision with the residue of unnatural death. Born in Spain in 1924, raised and educated in France after the defeat of the Spanish republican forces, Jorge Semprun joined the French resistance movement as a teenager and in 1943 was arrested by the Gestapo. In January 1944 he was deported to the Buchenwald concentration camp near Weimar, where he remained until his liberation in April of 1945. Among his translated works, the novels *The Long Voyage* (1964) and *What a Beautiful Sunday!* (1982) and the memoir *Literature or Life* (1997) explore the fictional and non-fictional narrative possibilities of his Buchenwald experience, whose corrosive influence, as with Primo Levi, remained imprinted on Semprun's imagination long after the time of the ordeal itself.

In *Literature or Life*, originally published in 1994 as *L'écriture ou la vie* (*Writing or Life*), Semprun addresses the question of which obstacles the writer must overcome in order to evoke the reality of Holocaust atrocity. He is blunt in dismissing the common charge that the event is indescribable. "The 'ineffable' you hear so much about," he alleges, "is only an alibi. Or a sign of laziness." The problem was not with the "form of a possible account."[6] but with the *content* which, though describable, might be unbearable. How to tell what is too painful to be told, how to turn an experience, grotesque and agonizing as it may have been, into narrative? The French

8

title, *Writing or Life,* implies that whatever model Semprun devises for a narrative frame, it will sanction an alternative to rather than an expression of his existence after Buchenwald. The details of his camp experience were like unwieldy clay, stubbornly resisting efforts to mold or shape them into a form that an audience not used to such dense material might recognize and accept.

Semprun left Buchenwald still bathed in the odor and memories of the death that had consumed so many of his underground companions, to say nothing of the thousands of others, especially Jews, who had perished in other parts of the camp. Indeed, as we learn from the text, he initially planned to call his memoir *L'écriture ou la mort* (*Writing or Death*), here suggesting an equivalency rather than an opposition, but subsequently changed his mind, leaving to his readers the chore of deciphering the subtle meaning of the shift. What he had discovered was that the joys of writing could not dispel the sorrows of memory. Having learned to identify the many smells of death in Buchenwald, Semprun was left with the dilemma of luring readers committed to an aromatic life into a malodorous milieu, the domain of what he called "despairing memory." This was no easy task. One who outlived the catastrophe wrote about it with a ghost mentality, struggling to connect to the living while mired in the legacy of a locale that changed the identity of virtually all victims into effigies of future corpses.

Despairing memory is a prime source of narrative consciousness, as Semprun searches for the precise brew that will combine the sense experience of unnatural death with its verbal expression. "And suddenly," he writes, "borne on the breeze, the curious odor: sweetish, cloying, with a bitter and truly nauseating edge to it. The peculiar odor that would later prove to be from the crematory ovens" (6). The transition is swift: "The strange smell would immediately invade the reality of memory. I would be reborn there; I would die if returned to life there. I would embrace and inhale the muddy, heady odor of that estuary of death" (7). He has only to close his eyes, and in an instant he is sucked from what he calls "the shimmering opacity of life's offerings" (6) back into the maw of death at Buchenwald. There is memory as recall and memory as affliction, and Semprun nurses both until they swell into a surge that engulfs him without offering warning or refuge.

Semprun is left with two problems: finding a style to depict how the reign of death in Buchenwald has burdened him; and making this feeling accessible to his audience without shocking them into flight or disbelief. Death is a constant companion of this survivor: "I'm struck by the idea," he writes, "if one can call it an idea . . . struck by the sudden overwhelming feeling, in any case, that I have not escaped death, but passed through it. Rather: that it has passed through me. That I have, in a way, lived through it. That I have come back from it the way you return from a voyage that has transformed and— perhaps—transfigured you" (14–15). It was as if Buchenwald were surrounded by a river Styx: souls ferried across it into the realm of death left some of their lives behind, while those who violated its rule by returning in the other direction — we call them survivors — had left some of their *deaths* behind but brought back with them the memory of their own premature and partial demise.

The result in Semprun's language would be a transfigured ghost, though I think a more accurate name would be a "disfigured" one. If the impact of a journey through the otherworld of Buchenwald is to be properly characterized, then we might do well to avoid terms like *transfigured* that echo a spiritual reality far from Semprun's intentions. Indeed, Semprun seems aware of this danger when he ironically introduces a vocabulary of redemption to subvert its relevance to his ordeal: "Perhaps I have not simply survived death, but been resurrected from it. Perhaps from this moment on, I am immortal" (14). He invites his readers to distinguish between a near-death and a "post-death" experience, knowing that the only language available to them is the language of immortality that he has just used himself. The main thrust of his discourse is to sabotage the value of such words in the context of Buchenwald memory. For most of us, the idea of a post-death experience is a logical impossibility when it is beyond the pale of debate about eternal life. Semprun invites us to consider an unprecedented passage from life through death back to life, not as a voyage into a mythical underworld such as the one undertaken by Odysseus or Aeneas, or Dante's spiritual pilgrimage though Inferno, but as a human journey on earth. The ensuing paradox is not easy to absorb, to say nothing of translating it into the art of narrative. But Semprun is ready for the challenge: "On this April morning [the day of his liberation from Buchenwald], it is exciting to imagine that thenceforward, growing old will not bring me closer to death, but quite the contrary, carry me away from it" (15).

In his novels one of Semprun's greatest innovations was to break the hold of chronological time and to find a narrative technique to sustain a new disjointed relationship among past, present, and future. He struggled in his memoir to chart the near-mortal injury that death in Buchenwald had inflicted on chronology:

> the essential thing about this experience of Evil is that it will turn out to have been lived as the experience of death. . . . And I do mean 'experience'. . . . Because death is not something that we brushed up against, came close to, only just escaped, as though it were an accident we survived unscathed. We lived it. . . . Because it's not believable, it can't be shared, it's barely comprehensible — since death is, for rational thought, the only event that we can never experience individually. . . . That cannot be grasped except in the form of anguish, of foreboding or fatal longing. . . . In the future perfect tense, therefore. (188–189)

As the past continued to overtake and displace the future, society had to consider a new phenomenon, the deathlife of the self that the Holocaust had introduced into current dialogue about the possible effects of atrocity on modern consciousness. Semprun expressed more lucidly than any of his literary confederates the philosophical and artistic idea that was invading Holocaust thinking and marked the difference, as he saw it, between traditional and post-camp sensibilities. He distinguished between living life and living death, arguing that rational reflection had no category for the special encounter with reality launched by the camp ordeal. Semprun boldly redefined brotherhood as having lived the experience of death as a collective and even fraternal occasion. It took time for him to understand what this meant. He described the impasse that led him, some months after his release from Buchenwald, to suspend writing for more than a decade on the novel that would become *The Long Voyage*. He wrote of this delay: "The two things I had thought would bind me to life—writing, pleasure—were instead what estranged me from it, day after day, constantly returning me to the memory of death, forcing me back into the suffocation of memory" (108–109). Semprun's meditations on this finding provide a dramatic instance of the literary imagination at work trying to shape what I call a narrative of atrocity. "Fundamentally," he concluded, "I was nothing other than a conscious residue of all that death" (120).

As he elaborates, savoring his words as if they were items on a gourmet menu, we overhear the voice of the artist in search of an imagery to join ordinary present consciousness to extraordinary past experience: "An individual patch in the impalpable material of that shroud. A dust mote in the ashy cloud of that agony. A still-flickering light from the extinguished star of our dead years" (120). Surviving the unnatural death of others, at least *this* death of *those* others, shrinks (without effacing entirely) the life impulse. Slowly, Semprun drafted the terms for turning this insight into narrative: "I possess nothing more than my death, my experience of death, to recount my life, to express it, to carry it on. I must make life with all that death. And the best way to do this is through writing. Yet that brings me back to death, to the suffocating embrace of death. That's where I am: I can live only by assuming that death through writing, but writing literally prohibits me from living" (163). Originally, as we have heard, he called his memoir *Writing or Death*, only to discover that his presumed antonyms had become synonyms; hence the change to *Writing or Life*, stressing the hard-won reversal that had emerged from his discovery of the price one must pay for an art of atrocity.

These are strange intellectual aromas for those of us who have not breathed the toxic air of German concentration and deathcamps until it became a natural form of inhalation, leaving a residue in the lungs of memory that a return to normal living could not purge. Semprun called it a wisdom of the body, a physical knowledge that would last forever in the secular eternity where his mental intelligence dwelt. Buchenwald time was durational rather than fleeting, and throughout his career Semprun strove to fashion a literary voice for this notion. That voice, he came to believe, must be artistic, not historical, since only the art and artifice of fiction could beguile the imagination into embracing what was being said. Writing, he insisted, revived and sharpened the sorrow of memory, whose barbs were constant reminders of the interlocking truth that what he had lived through was also and at the same time what he had died through. For all their other merits, he felt, historians could not convey the ambiguity of this essential truth of the Holocaust universe with the vigor and conviction of the literary craftsman.

To have as an artistic goal "to make life with all that death" through writing is to specify the main hazard of Holocaust narrative, and like George Steiner and others Semprun is wary of the limits of language that hinder this labor. In his memoir Semprun struggled with various translations of Wittgenstein's seemingly obvious statement that *"Der Tod ist kein Ereignis des Lebens. Den Tod erlebt man nicht"* — "Death is not an event in life. Death cannot be lived" (170, 171) because he knew that Buchenwald had vandalized its accuracy. Semprun varied the translation, striving for more precise meaning. For "Death cannot be lived," he substituted the more active "One cannot live death," and later, "Death is not a lived experience." Finally, he decided that "Wittgenstein's pronouncement ought to be phrased like this: . . . *my* death is not an event in *my* life. I will not live *my* death" (171). For Semprun and his fellow survivors, death *was* an event in life, and they *had* "lived" death, the death of others, though no available explanations helped make the magnitude of that insight more credible. *"Erleben"* meant to live through an event, but there was no word to signify an event that one had died through (*"ersterben"* means to die away or become extinct). Yet Semprun knew that a Holocaust literature lacking this concept could not be totally authentic or faithful to the incidents it tried to imagine.

The imagination was the crucial faculty that had to be addressed and transformed, injected with a literary serum to enable it to add a wholly new power of representation to its capacity. Semprun's search for a narrative "I" to recreate for his readers "death experienced right up to its blinding limit" (181) took him far beyond the aspirations of Tolstoy in *The Death of Ivan Ilych.* For Tolstoy, suffering, even the extreme physical agony of the dying Ivan Ilych, could be a redemptive occasion because Tolstoy and most of his readers shared belief in the model of a compassionate Redeemer. Writing Ivan Ilych's story was an act of spiritual liberation. Contrast this with Semprun's account of the impact on him of writing his Buchenwald novel, *The Long Voyage:* "it thrust me back into death, drowning me in it. I choked in the unbreathable air of my manuscript: every line I wrote pushed my head underwater as though I were once again in the bathtub of the Gestapo's villa in Auxerre [where Semprun had been tortured to try to make him reveal the names of other underground members]. I struggled to survive. I failed in my attempt to speak of death in order to reduce it to silence: if I had continued, it would have been death, in all probability, that would have silenced me" (250). Only after he absorbed into his own consciousness the recognition that life and death were no longer a sequence but an unsettling alliance, a fusion of forces that constantly operated on each other, could he finish his novel. He pacified death's pursuit of him in memory by allowing his pursuit of death in narrative to dominate the world of his imagination. Narrative form displaced the chaos of remembering.

Watching a familiar newsreel, after the war, of bulldozers shoveling dead bodies into mass graves, Semprun intuitively grasped why such images of atrocity seemed so inadequate: "They were silent above all," he writes, "because they said nothing precise about the reality they showed, because they delivered only confused scraps of meaning" (200–201). For him, the process of witnessing was not enough. Images had to be situated "not only in a historical context but within a continuity of emotions" (201). The impulse that steered Semprun to the vocation of Holocaust writer was enshrined in controversial assertions such as the following, which are still subject to dispute among Holocaust commentators: "One would have had to treat the documentary reality, in short, like the material of fiction" (201). The revelation freed him to invent the imagined universe of *The Long Voyage,* a novel whose roots reach deep into his Buchenwald experience but which achieves its narrative form by rearranging in its narrator's mind the details of the deathlife he has survived.

Concepts like *deathlife* and *the coffined self* are not to be found in histories of the Holocaust. Tracing the course of Germany's mass murders through documentary records is an essential scholarly task for our understanding of those events, but their psychological and emotional milieus constitute equally compelling themes whose expression requires utterly different narrative strategies. The first-person narrator of Semprun's *The Long Voyage* is in a boxcar on its way to Buchenwald throughout the novel, but his journey is internal as well as external. Even as he undergoes the ordeal of the trip in the present, he remembers and "foremembers," since the experience has fragmented him into a splintered self: he is simultaneously a partisan in the French underground, a deported prisoner of the Germans, and a survivor of Buchenwald. Details of his life in past, present, and future flow through his memory like multiple currents in an unimpeded stream. Death spreads its tentacles in every direction, tainting recollections of innocent pre-war friendships because he learns later that many of his comrades have been killed, and poisoning his post-war life through his discovery that being alive after Buchenwald is not the same as having survived it intact. By recreating consciousness as an intersection of three time zones, Semprun is able to duplicate for the reader the fluid, timeless ordeal of the camp inmate who has lost his sense of life as a chronological passage from yesterday through today into tomorrow. He also converts the idea of death as a single, natural fate into a mutation that plots death as a common, unnatural doom.

Semprun's narrator begins to learn about this unnatural doom on the journey itself, which lasts for five days and four nights. He is jammed up against another deportee whom he calls "the guy from Semur" (a village in France), and during the voyage they exchange reminiscences about their earlier lives and speculations about their destination. They appear to be bonded in life, whatever the future holds for them, but as they arrive at Buchenwald death anticipates them, as the exhausted guy from Semur slumps against the narrator's shoulder and dies. Earlier the guy from Semur had complained that he felt as though his heart were dead, and when the narrator asks him what that means, he replies: "I wouldn't know how to tell you. . . . You don't feel anything in your heart, like a hole, or else like a very heavy stone."[7] It is a workable definition of the condition I call *deathlife*, although it will be some time before the narrator grasps its meaning. The act of *foremembering* gives us a glimpse into how that process will work.

The narrator has a vivid impression of the impact of deathlife on memory while dining at a friend's house after the war, when his hostess announces that she has planned a Russian dinner. This triggers a time warp in consciousness for the narrator, who explains: "and so it was that suddenly I had a piece of black bread in my hand, and mechanically I bit into it, meanwhile continuing the conversation. Then, the slightly acid taste of the black bread, the low mastication of this gritty black bread, brought back, with shocking suddenness, the marvelous moments when, at camp, we used to eat our ration of bread. . . . I was sitting there motionless, my arm raised, with my slightly acid, buttered slice of good black bread in my hand, and my heart was pounding like a triphammer" (126). His hostess asks him if anything is the matter, and his reverie continues: "Nothing was the matter. A random thought of no consequence. Obviously I couldn't tell her that I was in the throes of dying, dying of hunger, far far from them, far from the wood fire and the words they were saying" (126).

As someone who had fended off death in Buchenwald, Semprun belongs to a generation of survivors — their numbers continue to grow today — who enact in a portion of consciousness "the throes of dying" even as they move on with their lives. As unnatural dying, mass murder or some other form of atrocity spreads across the landscape of modernity, Semprun's struggle to find for it an artistic voice seems an early recognition of its complex and disconcerting force. Elie Wiesel once remarked of his father's miserable end in Buchenwald that the Germans had deprived his father not only of his life, but also of his death,[8] and this is the very paradox from which Semprun seeks to wrest some significance in his narrative. But the first step is to find a way of expressing the idea that the meaning of one's life can no longer be separated from the meaningless death of others, and to do this Semprun literally transmutes consciousness into a physical substance and plunges the reader directly into its wounded core:

In the spongy mass that sits behind my forehead, between my painful neck and burning temples, where all the throbbing pains in my body, which is breaking into a thousand pieces of sharp glass, in that spongy mass from which I would like to be able to draw with both hands (or rather with delicate tongs, once the bony plate which covers it has been lifted) the cotton-like filaments, streaked perhaps with blood, which must fill all the cavities and keep me from thinking clearly, which becloud the whole interior, what they call consciousness, into that spongy mass there works its way the idea that perhaps my death will not even manage to be something real, that is, something that belongs to someone else's life, at least one person's. Perhaps the idea of my death as something real, perhaps even that possibility will be denied me, and I cast about desperately to see who might miss me, whose life I might affect, might haunt by my absence and at that precise moment, I find no one, my life hasn't any real possibility, I wouldn't even be able to die, all I can do is efface myself, quietly eliminate myself from this existence, Hans would have to be alive, Michel would have to be alive for me to have a real death, a death somehow linked to reality, for me not to vanish completely into the stench-filled darkness of this boxcar.[9]

Hans and Michel are two of his murdered comrades, and if memory and consciousness cannot resurrect them, at least through the anguish of Semprun's art they may be made to seem less dead. This must be what Semprun had meant when he wrote in his memoir, "I possess nothing more than my death, my experience of death, to recount my life, to express it, to carry it on. I must make life with all that death" (163). To make life with all that death: it may be that the anxiety nurtured by this issue in *The Long Voyage* and in much other Holocaust testimony and narrative will prove to be nothing more than a prophetic prelude to a fundamental unrelenting challenge that is destined to burden modern consciousness well into the future.

2

ANNE FRANK REVISITED

On May 5, 1944, an anonymous teenager began to keep a diary in the Lodz ghetto. This was his first entry:

I have decided to write a diary, though it is a little too late. To recapitulate past events is quite impossible, so I'll begin with the present. This week I committed an act which best illustrates the degree of "dehumanization" to which we have been reduced. I finished my loaf of bread in three days, that is to say, on Sunday, so I had to wait till next Saturday for a new one. I was terribly hungry, I had the prospect of living only on the workshop soups, which consist of three little potato pieces and two dkg. [dekagrams, a few ounces] of flour. Monday morning I was lying quite dejectedly in my bed, and there was my darling [12-year-old] sister's half loaf of bread "present" with me. To cut a long story short: I could not resist the temptation and ate it up totally. After having done this—at present a terrible crime—I was overcome by terrible remorse of conscience and by a still greater care for what my little one would eat the next 5 days.

I felt like a miserable helpless criminal, but I was delivered from the terrible situation by the reception of a B-allotment [extra rations]. I suffer terribly, feigning that I don't know where the bread has gone and I have to tell people that it was stolen by a supposed reckless and pitiless thief. And to keep up appearance, I have to utter curses and condemnations on the imaginary thief. "I would hang him with my own hands if I come across him." And other angry phrases. Indeed, I am too nervous, too exhausted for literary exertions at the present moment. All I can say is that I shall always suffer on remembering this "noble" deed of mine. And that I shall always condemn myself for being able to become so unblushingly impudent—that I shall forevermore despise that part of "mankind" who could inflict such infernal woes on their "co"-human beings.[1]

Two days earlier, on May 3, 1944, Anne Frank, soon to turn fifteen, had entered in her diary the following:

> I've often been down in the dumps, but never desperate. I look upon our life in hiding as an interesting adventure, full of danger and romance, and every privation as an amusing addition to my diary. I've made up my mind to lead a different life from other girls, and not to become an ordinary housewife later on. What I'm experiencing here is a good beginning to an interesting life, and that's the reason—the only reason—why I have to laugh at the humorous side of the most dangerous moments.
>
> I'm young and have many hidden qualities; I'm young and strong and living through a big adventure; I'm right in the middle of it and can't spend all day complaining because it's impossible to have any fun! I'm blessed with many things: happiness, a cheerful disposition and strength. Every day I feel myself maturing, I feel liberation drawing near, I feel the beauty of nature and the goodness of the people around me. Every day I think what a fascinating and amusing adventure this is! With all that, why should I despair?[2]

Ironically, at almost exactly the same time, early in May 1944, a young teenager named Elie Wiesel arrived at a place called Auschwitz, where he witnessed babies being thrown alive into flaming pits. He did not have a chance to write about it in his diary.

On June 27, 1944, the anonymous adolescent in the Lodz ghetto wrote of the humiliation of his fellow Jews by their German oppressors:

> What kind of world is this and what kind of people are these who are able to inflict such unbelievable and impossible suffering on human beings?
>
> Our nearest ones have been murdered, some by starvation, some by deportations (modern civilian death). In a manner unheard of in history, we've been crippled physically, spiritually, emotionally—in our whole personality. We vegetate in the most horrible misery and need; we are slaves who, deprived of our own will, feel happy when we're being trodden upon, begging only that we not be trodden to death. I don't exaggerate: we are the most wretched beings the sun has ever seen—and all this is not enough for the "strong man": they continue deporting and tearing our hearts to pieces—while we'd be happy to live even as enslaved, wretched insects, as abject, creeping reptiles—only to live . . . live . . .[3]

On the same day, June 27, 1944, Anne Frank confided to her diary: "The mood has changed, everything's going enormously well. Cherbourg, Vitebsk, Zhlobin fell today. They're sure to have captured lots of men and equipment. Five German generals were killed near Cherbourg, and two taken captive. Now that they've got a harbor the British can bring whatever they want on shore. The whole Cotentin Peninsula has been captured just three weeks after the invasion! What a feat!"[4] Even as she wrote, the Germans were deporting seven thousand Jews from the Lodz ghetto to be murdered in the mobile killing vans at Chelmno. It was a feat she knew nothing of. How could she? A little more than a month later, four days before her attic hiding place was discovered, most of the remaining 68,000 Lodz Jews were shipped to Auschwitz-Birkenau, where the majority were sent directly to the gas chambers.

The contrast in mood, tone, and content between these excerpts is clear, though there are other pages from both diaries where mood, tone, and even content overlap. Like Anne, the anonymous teenager has his moments of hope, and then his very language begins to sound like hers: "I am sitting and dreaming — dreaming and floating in the clouds. I am overtaken by an indescribable longing for life, life as I conceive it, full of beautiful things, of intellectual interests, a passion for books, theater, movies, radio, oh (it is not fair to sigh) — and yet I am trapped in such a swamp."[5] But that swamp introduces a crucial difference, because in her hiding place Anne Frank was never forced to breathe its fetid vapors, and she could remain convinced that her dreams *might* become less fetid realities. The boy from the Lodz ghetto, despite his moments of hope, knew he was facing a bad ending to a terrible life. Anne Frank, despite her genuine flashes of despair, believed, as she wrote, that she was facing "a good beginning to an interesting life." One can find in her *Diary* a few attempts to acknowledge the enormity of the threat confronting Jews outside the annex, but they are based on rumor or vague details provided by BBC radio broadcasts or the Dutch friends who were helping to hide them. Because she has no specific experience of the horror, because her greatest fears, of being caught and of the occasional air raids, were only intermittent, because hunger or terror was never a steady internal presence in her mind, she was affected rather than afflicted by the circumstances outside the hidden annex. After living there for more than eighteen months, at a time when most of European Jewry had already been murdered, she wrote in February 1944: "Riches, prestige, everything can be lost. But the happiness in your own heart can only be dimmed; it will always be there, as long as you live, to make you happy again."[6]

Lines like these should remind us how shielded Anne Frank was from the worst realities of the event we call the Holocaust. She is in no way to blame for not knowing about what she could not have known about. But readers are much to blame for accepting and promoting the idea that her *Diary* is a major Holocaust text and has anything of great consequence to tell us about the atrocities that culminated in the murder of European Jewry. The happiness in her heart was genuine, not only because she was so young but also because the notion of a future was still a vivid and meaningful possibility for her. Contrast her recurrent optimistic tone with the attitude of a twelve or thirteen-year-old girl from Lvov named Janina Heshele who was sent with her mother to a prison cell to await deportation:

> Mother, who was deathly pale, lay in bed. I lay down near her and asked her "Why are you so crushed? I am still alive." She replied, "I do not care what happens to me. I have a poison tablet which will bring instant death. But what will happen to you?" She broke out in loud sobs and implored me, "Anula, save me from further anguish. Go away. I don't want you near me. I don't want to see what will happen to you." But I refused, saying, "what have I to live for? Without documents I cannot exist on my own. Mother, do you want to prolong my agonies? Isn't it better to make an end to my life once and for all? Let us die together, with me in your arms. Why live on?"[7]

When we contrast Anne Frank's words with the gloomy finality of such excerpts, we realize how relatively uncontaminated she was able to keep her imagination, in spite of her ordeal. How else can we explain the cheerfulness of a sentiment such as the following, which engages our collective desires while remaining insulated from the historical milieu in which Anne found herself: "The best remedy for those who are frightened, lonely or unhappy is to go outside, somewhere they can be alone, alone with the sky, nature and God. For then and only then can you feel that everything is as it should be and that God wants people to be happy amid nature's beauty and simplicity. As long as this exists, and this should be forever, I know that there will be solace for every sorrow, whatever the circumstances. I firmly believe that nature can bring comfort to all who suffer."[8]

Passages like these provide a clue to the universal appeal to both younger and older readers of Anne Frank's *Diary* as a classic text about the Holocaust. They seem to offer concrete support for the welcome notion that in the midst of chaos, even the chaos of mass murder, the human imagination, to say nothing of other features of the self, can remain untainted by the enormity of the crime. While the diaries of other children immersed in the slaughter record tales of innocence corrupted by circumstances imposed on them by their oppressors, Anne Frank's account of her ordeal, despite scattered moments of genuine if limited vision into the darker reality, tells a story of innocence preserved. Her irrepressible enthusiasm for life triumphs over threats to her security, furnishing a template for managing those threats that can be transferred to her readers. The vast gulf between insight and foresight that is the hallmark of her narrative is nowhere more ironically revealed than in her entry after she discovers that her precious fountain pen has been burned in the oven together with the day's garbage: "I'm left with one consolation, small though it may be: my fountain pen was cremated, just as I would like to be someday!"[9]

Instead of asking what we can learn about the Holocaust from *The Diary of a Young Girl,* perhaps it would be useful to begin by inquiring what we cannot. Readers of the *Diary* learn little about the events leading up to the Frank family's departure from Germany, and less about the situation of Jews in Holland after the German occupation. They learn nothing about Dutch collaboration, or of efforts by the Dutch underground to hide and rescue Jews. (Since Otto Frank made his own arrangements for going into hiding, he did not need to involve members of the resistance.) They hear once or twice about roundups, but learn few details about deportations, from Holland or any other country in Europe. They learn nothing about the worker's strike in Amsterdam, after which Dutch non-Jews were sent to Mauthausen, where many of them died or were killed. They hear once about Westerbork, but do not know that it is a transit camp for Auschwitz or Majdanek, places no one in the attic had ever heard of. They learn nothing about ghettos, concentration camps, labor camps, deathcamps. They learn nothing about selections, starvation, exhaustion, and disease. They hear gassing mentioned twice, but if we had to depend on these two references to enhance our understanding of the extermination of European Jewry, the tabula rasa of our mind on this subject would be left nearly blank. And we hear nothing at all, except for one mention of the Führer, about the Nazi leaders and their minions who planned, organized, and executed the event we call the Holocaust.

So what are we left with? Anne Frank was not unaware of what was happening in Europe. On March 31, 1944, she writes: "Hungary has been occupied by German troops. There are still a million Jews living there; they too are doomed." But how is a fourteen-year-old girl in hiding to translate that ominous word "doomed" into a context of atrocity that would give it shape and meaning? She had neither the knowledge, the ability, nor the desire to do so. The next sentence in her *Diary* reads: "Nothing special is happening here. Today is Mr. van Daan's birthday." The juxtaposition of the impending murder and thus temporal end of the lives of more than three hundred thousand Hungarian Jews in Auschwitz — Anne Frank's figure was much too high — with the normal passage of time in the secret annex registered through the chronology of birthdays gives us a glimpse into the diarist's habit of shifting placidly from lethal themes to adolescent matters. The entry for the next day begins, "And yet everything is still so difficult. You do know what I mean, don't you? I long so much for him to kiss me, but that kiss is taking its own sweet time."[10]

In fact, one could argue that Anne Frank's *Diary* sanctions and indeed enacts in its very text a designed *avoidance* of the very experience it is reputed to grant us some exposure to. Anne herself wrestles with the need to take utterly seriously the details of what is going on "outside" that Mr. Dussell relates shortly after his arrival in the annex. She feels guilty sleeping in a warm bed while some of her dearest friends may be dropping from exhaustion. But she has a practical primer of advice for handling this disheartening information: "It won't do us or those outside any good if we continue to be as gloomy as we are now. And what would be the point of turning the Secret Annex into a Melancholy Annex?" She is simply too young to handle the finality of atrocity; she knows it is "a disgrace to be so cheerful," but she has a solution, and it is by no means certain that it reflects an age-related disposition: "am I supposed to spend the whole day crying? No, I can't do that. This gloom will pass."[11]

Readers of the *Diary* are encouraged to embrace this philosophy, a perfectly sensible and even admirable attitude for anyone seeking to recover from "normal" adversity. But the Holocaust is not an instance of normal adversity, and by applying to it the formula of "this gloom will pass," we identify with Anne's need to keep it from invading the other parts of her life, or of her imagination. Thus her work helps us to transcend what we have not yet encountered, nonetheless leaving behind a film of conviction that we have. Instead of reading it for its real virtue, as a gifted but youthful writer's precocious story of female adolescent yearning as it unfolds in the restricted setting of the secret annex, those who regard it as a valuable Holocaust text approach it with a reverence that has led, as we all know, to the near canonization of its author. This serves neither her reputation nor the cause of historical truth. If Anne Frank was a casualty of the Holocaust, her *Diary* is a casualty of the difficulty we still have in dealing with her post-*Diary* doom. The book is a victim of one of the worst features of American culture, the effort to force us to construe the reality of an event before we have experienced it, to confirm an agenda in advance in order to discourage us from raising disturbing questions that might subvert the tranquility of our response.

The model for construing Anne Frank's *Diary* was established early by Meyer Levin in the *New York Times Book Review* on June 15, 1952. The odd and still unexplained paradox is that unlike Anne Frank, Levin had not been sheltered from the worst details of the Holocaust. He knew exactly what it had meant for European Jewry. During the last week of World War II he had seen Ohrdruf, Buchenwald, and Bergen-Belsen shortly after they had been liberated by Allied forces, and he wrote about them then and later with a precision that did not invite his readers to decipher reality according to some theoretical affirmative agenda. Reporting from Buchenwald on May 2, 1945, Levin wrote:

> All week I have been talking to Jews who survived the greatest mass murder in the history of mankind. . . . my mind, after this week, faintly reflects their minds. It is a composite image of trains running three-tracked into smoking crematoriums, of remote Polish villages whose mud ruts were filled with human bodies, of a German officer, playfully lining up a group of Jewish children until they were precisely one head behind the other and then putting a single bullet through the line [an extraordinary claim to anyone

familiar with the laws of physical resistance], of a woman holding her baby aloft over her head while savage police dogs ripped her apart, and through every image I see the brown, earnest undeniable eyes of a survivor who tells me this, and over each image is stamped the ever-recurring line, "I saw it, I saw it with my own eyes."[12]

In spite of occasional exaggerations, the eyewitness testimonies that Meyer Levin sent back to readers in America refused to gloss over atrocity for the sake of minimizing its impact. In fact, he predicted that some day a literary talent would emerge equal to the challenge of conveying the enormity of what his journalist's pen could only sketchily represent.

Given Levin's oft-expressed fear of bearing false witness, of presenting the murder of European Jewry as anything other than the overwhelming evil it was, how can we account for his enthusiastic conclusion upon reading *The Diary of a Young Girl* that "Here, at last, was 'the voice from the mass grave' for which he had long been searching"?[13] Seven years earlier, Levin had *seen* some of those mass graves, and heard the dreadful tales of those who had escaped them. Yet after less than a decade he was prepared to describe Anne Frank's *Diary* as a "classic" account of "a group of Jews waiting in fear of being taken by the Nazis." Although more than half of the *Diary* could have been written without the Holocaust ever having happened, in the sense that its "drama of puberty" (as Levin himself describes it), its sibling rivalry, conflicts with parents, adolescent romance, and awakening sexuality might have been enacted anywhere, in his *Times* review Meyer Levin invented for it a designation that has defined its reception up to the present: "Anne Frank's voice becomes the voice of six million vanished souls."[14] Before our eyes a myth is being forged, because nothing could be further from Anne Frank's intention *or* her achievement. As any aspiring writer knows, the initial task is to create a personal voice that is *different* from any other, a distinctive tone and point of view that sets the author apart from dissimilar literary efforts.

Although Anne Frank's greatest accomplishment is the honesty and fidelity with which she records her emerging personality even when her admissions might embarrass her or those around her, including her family, and although Levin acknowledges this in his review, he feels compelled to create the impression that the *Diary* ranges more widely in its interests. He cites only one other Holocaust-related work for purposes of comparison with the *Diary*, John Hersey's novel of the Warsaw ghetto, *The Wall*. Although Hersey's novel has its limitations as a fictional narrative, at least it takes us inside the ghetto to dramatize some of the conflicts that unfolded there. Yet Levin is content to argue that "Anne Frank's diary probes far deeper than 'The Wall' into the core of human relations, and succeeds better than 'The Wall' in bringing an understanding of life under threat."[15] Those familiar with the deportation of hundreds of thousands of Jews from the Warsaw ghetto to their death in Treblinka in the summer of 1942 and the courageous but catastrophic uprising the following spring, leading to the total destruction of the ghetto and the execution or deportation of its remaining inhabitants, will marvel at how much Levin had forgotten (and how easy it was for him to forget) about Holocaust atrocity when he wrote those lines.

For reasons we cannot explain today, in his review Levin decided to ignore the exceptional nature of the event whose consequences he had witnessed in 1945 and chose instead to universalize the experience by skirting the details of its horrors. In so doing, he devised a pattern for avoiding the Holocaust that remains a popular approach to the subject today. Of Anne's presumed account of "life under threat" he wrote: "And this quality brings it home to any family in the world today. Just as the Franks lived in momentary fear of the Gestapo's knock on their hidden door, so every family today lives in fear of the knock of war. Anne's diary is a great affirmative answer to the life-question of today, for she shows how ordinary people, within this ordeal, constantly hold to the greater human values."[16] This is the illusion we need to hear: that in spite of atrocities like the Holocaust, and its many smaller-scale but equally vicious successors, the "greater human values" — whatever Levin might have meant by that empty piece of rhetoric — survive intact.

Levin ends his review with language that still clings like a burr to the flesh of much Holocaust response, invoking consolation rather than confrontation as the ultimate goal of that endeavor. Although he is candid enough to admit that "Hers was perhaps one of the bodies seen in the mass grave at Bergen-Belsen," he makes an easy transition from that grim image to the claim that she goes on living through her *Diary*, the kind of sentiment that "normalizes" death by casting it into the familiar frame of any memorial ceremony. Levin's concluding words in his review replace the finality of mass murder with the immortalizing possibilities of its aftermath: "this wise and wonderful young girl brings back a poignant delight in the infinite human spirit."[17]

Poignancy may be one reaction to the fate of Anne Frank, but there are others, and if we are to do justice to her talent, we need to acknowledge them. If we really believe that the journey from mass murder can end in a celebration of the human spirit, we can arrive at that point only by ignoring Anne Frank's increasing willingness to recognize the complex nature of her ordeal, especially in the final entries in her *Diary*. She would have rejected with scorn Levin's charge that she spoke for six million perished souls. She was not a representative victim, and certainly not a representative teenager. Her feminist instincts long before the birth of the movement set her apart from the average young girl of her time. Her insistence on being treated as "Anne-in-her-own right" rather than as the typical adolescent her father thought she was confirms how much the attempt to universalize her experience violates her independent spirit. Her shrewd summary of the reasons for the collapse of her relationship with Peter surprises us with its sophistication; she herself is a little shocked by her discovery that he is shallow, in thought and aspiration. We insult her special identity by "typifying" her; but we may unintentionally insult the special identity of those five to six million other souls by accepting Meyer Levin's opinion that she in any way represents or speaks for them.

One idea Anne Frank vigorously defended was what we might call the principle of multiple selves, the belief that several Anne Franks, some more authentic than others, inhabited the same body and the same mind. Without knowing how to elaborate on it, she defined the problem of facing the Holocaust that still haunts us today: "we're forced to think up a solution, though most of the time our solutions crumble when faced with the facts. It's difficult in times like these: ideals, dreams and cherished hopes rise within us, only to be crushed by grim reality."[18] The acuteness of this observation can be lost on those who continue to insist that the triumph of the spirit may redeem the problem of the defeat of the body in gas chambers and crematoria. The grim reality Anne Frank mentions surfaces occasionally in her comments, but not often enough to inspire her to examine how her notion of multiple private selves would function in the public sphere. That would be a post-Holocaust challenge, but she did not live long enough to meet it. In the meantime, she meditated on the split between her exuberant, cheerful, and joyful self and her deeper, finer, and more serious self. Her *Diary* ended before she was driven to reconsider how Westerbork, Auschwitz, Bergen-Belsen, typhus, and starvation might have affected her theory of the divided self. Hence readers are left with the illusion that even after the Holocaust the two versions might easily be reconciled.

Anne Frank's *Diary* finishes with her wishing "to find a way to become what I'd like to be and what I could be if . . . if only there were no other people in the world." Unfortunately, there were many other people in the world, among them those who were determined to destroy her. Intermittently fearful as she was of those people, she could not begin to imagine how their efforts would sabotage her desire to become what she'd like to be. Nor can her *Diary* give the slightest hint of what her fate was to become. If we teach it without rectifying that omission, we abuse it, but I have never seen any edition of the text, at least in English, that tries to incorporate into it a vivid and accurate portrayal, beyond the mere facts, of events subsequent to the last entry. We need this for many reasons, not the least of which is the frequency with which the *Diary* continues to be read with blinkered eyes, perpetuating the myth that it remains a major source of information about the murder of European Jewry. When the "definitive" edition of the text was published in a new translation in 1995, the reviewer on the front page of *The New York Times Book Review* did not hesitate to call it "the single most compelling personal account of the Holocaust,"[19] as if Primo Levi and Elie Wiesel, to name only two, were amateur dabblers in comparison to the author of the *Diary*. This kind of mindless overspeak in regard to the *Diary* is among the severest abuses of its value. As early as 1946 one of its first "discoverers" wrote in a Dutch review that it embodied "all the hideousness of fascism, more so than all the evidence at Nuremberg put together."[20] Anyone familiar with the atrocity film excerpts shown at the Nuremberg trials, to say nothing of the evidence presented there, must marvel at such extravagant and foolish claims. Thus there is a long and "respectable" — though maybe we should begin to call it disreputable — tradition of misjudging the content of the volume, and one has to work through the thick armor of that misjudgment in order to arrive at a fair estimate of the work's real merit.

I myself once wrote in a review of the "definitive" edition of the *Diary*: "if Anne Frank could return from among the murdered, she would be appalled at the misuse to which her journal entries had been put. Above all, her journey via Westerbork and Auschwitz to Bergen-Belsen, where she died miserably of typhus and malnutrition, would have led her to regret writing the single, sentimental line by which she is most remembered, even by admirers who have never read the *Diary*" but only seen the play based on it.[21] I mean the line about people being really good at heart. It seems obvious to me that the idealism of such a gifted writer would have suffered a wrenching jolt had she survived. But little can be taken for granted when the romantic imagination applies its maudlin energy to the fate of this girl. Alvin H. Rosenfeld has pointed out the ease with which "her death is either glossed over or given a hopeful, even beatific character. According to one popular version of her end," he continues, "Anne Frank went to her death with 'a profound smile . . . of happiness and faith'; according to another, 'she died, peacefully, feeling that nothing bad was happening to her.' "[22]

Thanks to the research of Willy Lindwer, the culture of disregard prompting mirages like the ones I have just cited can be discredited. One woman who was with Anne in Auschwitz describes the conditions there: "We didn't always talk of sticking together. We were set against each other and the closest relatives would begrudge each other a few potato peels. That wasn't meanness. That was hunger or nakedness. You became dehumanized in spite of yourself."[23] This was a milieu unfamiliar to the Anne of the *Diary*, and though it need not have dehumanized *her*, it certainly would have led her to modify the privileged view of human relations that the crowded but civilized climate in the secret annex had inspired. Two of the women Lindwer interviewed provide eyewitness accounts of Anne Frank's final days, and they should be imprinted on the minds of all who read or teach the *Diary*. The purpose is not to inflict pain, but to highlight one of the most unsettling truths of the event we call the Holocaust: how for Anne Frank and almost all of her fellow Jews the ultimate shape of the catastrophe eluded the prophetic instincts of the human imagination. These descriptions clarify the limits of foresight in her *Diary*, and invite us to ponder what her attitude might have been had she written her own memoir, her *Night*, her *Survival in Auschwitz*:

At a certain moment in the final days, Anne stood in front of me, wrapped in a blanket. She didn't have any more tears. Oh, we hadn't had tears for a long time. And she told me that she had such a horror of the lice and fleas in her clothes and that she had thrown all of her clothes away. It was the middle of winter and she was wrapped in one blanket. I gathered up everything I could find to give her, so that she was dressed again. . . .

Terrible things happened. Two days later I went to look for the girls. Both of them were dead![24]

The other account is more detailed:

The Frank girls were so emaciated. They looked terrible. They had little squabbles, caused by their illness, because it was clear that they had typhus. You could tell even if you had never had anything to . . . do with that before. Typhus was the hallmark of Bergen-Belsen. They had those hollowed-out faces, skin over bone. They were terribly cold. They had the least desirable places in the barracks, below, near the door, which was constantly opened and closed. You heard them constantly screaming, "Close the door, close the door," and the voices became weaker every day.

You could really see both of them dying, as well as others. But what was so sad, of course, was that those children were still so young. I always found it so horrible that as children, they had never really lived. They were indeed the youngest among us. The rest of us were all a bit older.

They showed the recognizable symptoms of typhus—that gradual wasting away, a sort of apathy, with occasional revivals, until they became so sick that there wasn't any hope. And their end came. I don't know which one was carried out earlier, Anne or Margot. Suddenly I didn't see them anymore, so I had to assume that they had died. . . . The dead were always carried outside, laid down in front of the barracks . . . At the time, I assumed that the bodies of the Frank girls had also been put down in front of the barracks. And then the heaps would be cleared away. A huge hole would be dug, and they were thrown into it. That I'm sure of. That must have been their fate, because that's what happened with other people. I don't have a single reason for assuming that it was any different for them than for the other women with us who died at the same time.[25]

The journey from "Anne-in-her-own-right" to an undifferentiated corpse in a mass grave at Bergen-Belsen marked a defeat for everything Anne Frank had hoped for and believed in. If we return now to some of her earlier convictions, both written within six months of her arrest, they leave a sour taste in our throat and draw a curtain of dismay over our imagination: "As long as [nature] exists, and that should be forever, I know that there will be solace for every sorrow, whatever the circumstances. I firmly believe that nature can bring comfort to all that suffer," or "Every day I feel myself maturing, I feel liberation drawing near, I feel the beauty of nature and the goodness of the people around me."[26] This is in no way a censure of her talent or her personality, but a commentary on the culture of human disregard that extended to the sinister intentions of Nazi Germany, a "culture" that few of the potential victims could imagine. Anne Frank confirmed an impulse we still share when she protested that it was utterly impossible for her to build her life on "a foundation of chaos, suffering and death." But the history of the Holocaust tells how the Germans were busily assembling that foundation for the very people who could not bring themselves to believe in it. Those people might conjecture the worst, but this did not include the unthinkable. Having encountered it, who among them could repeat what Anne Frank had earlier written, "I have to laugh at the humorous side of the most dangerous moments"? Like most of them, she had been raised in a culture of mutual *regard,* not disregard, and she had to believe that even in the direst conditions, that bedrock of humane behavior would endure. She was utterly mistaken, but there is no hint of this in her *Diary* entries, even in her gloomiest moments. The *Diary* is one of the best examples we have of the failure of the imagination of disaster, a failure not to be blamed on its author but on the unprecedented cruelty of the Nazi regime, a cruelty that Western civilization was unable and unwilling to anticipate.

This kind of failure was recently ratified by the appearance in English of the diaries of Viktor Klemperer, a converted Jew from Dresden who was married to a Christian woman and thus was never deported. He kept a detailed account of his experiences in Germany throughout the war. The first volume ends on December 31, 1941, by which time the deathcamp at Chelmno was already in operation. Klemperer writes of the deportation to Lodz of the Jewish population, including members of his own family, from Berlin, Frankfurt, and other large German cities. We know, or should, that soon after their arrival most of these German Jews were sent to Chelmno, where they would be gassed in mobile killing vans on the way to the burial site. But Klemperer had no inkling of their fate; rather, he worried about how his ailing sister would manage in the cramped and alien environment of a foreign ghetto. The irony of his shortsightedness is a powerful antidote to some of his benign concerns, but only if we bring to the reading of his diary an intimate acquaintance with the circumstances that he was unable to imagine.

And the same must be said of Anne Frank's *Diary of a Young Girl.* The irony of her innocence is a compelling feature of the text, but only if we relentlessly measure what she did know against what she didn't. And in order to do that, we need to have an audience both wary and aware, wary of the excessive claims that have been made for her work and aware of the great gaps about the destruction of European Jewry that qualify her response. Indeed, after we acknowledge how much she didn't know, we are forced to wonder why her work has been canonized for so long. As a narrative of adolescence only peripherally concerned with the Holocaust it may have served a purpose, but perhaps it is time to abandon it and to turn to more adult fare, like the stories of Ida Fink or the novel by Carl Friedman called *Nightfather.* These texts are not suffused with terror and dread, nor do they drown us in unbearable chronicles of atrocity. They are accessible to younger readers, but they do not depend on the irony of exclusion for their impact. They contain sufficient evidence in their unfolding narratives to signal the presence of the unthinkable and its impact on the spirits of their youthful protagonists.

In one of her stories, no more than four pages long, Ida Fink describes a group of young Jewish girls about Anne Frank's age on a work detail in a forest clearing a few kilometers from the Polish shtetl where they live. On this particular day their work has been suspended while an *aktion* is taking place in the village. Because they are close to the railroad tracks, they are listening for the approaching train that will carry off members of their families to their doom. They are outdoors rather than in hiding, so the nature that Anne Frank longed for is very much present to their imagination — but with what a difference:

> We lay on the grass, not saying a word, as if our voices could have drowned out the thundering of the train, which would pass near the edge of the forest, not far from where we were working. Only one girl was crying. . . . It was silent in the forest. There were no birds, but the smell of the trees and flowers was magnificent. We couldn't hear anything. There was nothing to hear. The silence was horrifying because we knew that there was shooting going on and people screaming and crying, that it was a slaughterhouse out there. But here there were bluebells, hazelwood, daisies, and other flowers, very pretty. Very colorful. That was what was so horrifying — just as horrifying as waiting for the thundering of the train, as horrifying as wondering whom they had taken.[27]

Such a passage helps us to understand the limitations of using Anne Frank's *Diary* as an entrée to the Holocaust experience. Her *Diary* does not invite us to consider whether, had she lived, she might have written afterward, "I feel the beauty of nature and the [*evil*] of the people around me." Instead, it encourages us to believe that she could have rescued her innocence and *joie de vivre* even after her journey into the blackness of darkness. Of course we can only speculate about the impact of that voyage on the sequel she would surely have written had she survived Bergen-Belsen. But we get a glimpse of the new feelings that it might have inspired from the words of one of the women who saw her die there: "Assimilating these experiences is very difficult. Actually, I never have. . . . If I had been able to assimilate it all, then it wouldn't be so difficult. We have learned to live with it and we have perhaps been able to put a little distance between what happened and the present. But it was such an unreal and such a catastrophic time in my life, that there is no question of its assimilation. A tiny movement, a small noise, or the smell of burned food — and I'm right back, where I was. You can talk about it, but no one can ever relieve you of it."[28] In the absence of a sequel, we are left with the unfinished saga of Anne Frank's life and mind. In spite of her fears, the controlling premise of her *Diary* is that she will avoid deportation and whatever might lie beyond it. The nostalgia of preservation that fills its pages and comforts those who read it long after the event verifies a principle that seems to exert greater and greater force in our encounters with the Holocaust: that many of us seek and find the Holocaust we need. This is the real if unintended legacy of Anne Frank, and it bears with it an enduring danger: by embracing the need she fulfills, we may fail to identify and thus neglect the truths she did not know.

3

LIFE IS NOT BEAUTIFUL

Today we continue to marvel at movie masterpieces like *Les Enfants du Paradis* and *Citizen Kane* years after their initial appearances. Their artistry transcends their box office appeal; their place in filmdom's hall of fame is secure. Ten years from now, who will be able to say the same about Roberto Benigni's *Life Is Beautiful* (1998), which was received with such a furor of enthusiasm in entertainment circles despite the efforts of a handful of discerning film critics to help the public distinguish between serious cinema and tasteless — some might even say offensive — farce? Although Benigni has described the two halves of *Life Is Beautiful* as a shift from comedy to tragedy, the buffoonery that rules the first part continues through much of the second, up to the moment of Guido's apparent execution. The inner and outer anguish we associate with tragedy remains locked in Benigni's imagination, a frustrated desire, if it really was one, that never escapes to the screen.

From beginning to end, *Life Is Beautiful* unfolds a series of comic routines, though the settings in the later episodes are more somber than those of the earlier ones. The film's allure is based on a willing suspension of disbelief: that in Benigni's version of a deathcamp milieu it really was possible for a victim to preserve enough physical and spiritual mastery to "outwit" single-handedly the murderous intentions of the Germans. Benigni seems unconcerned that by infusing the gloom of his Holocaust scenario with the comic ingenuity of his character he allows Guido's antics to profane the solemn impact of the surroundings. The ironic barbs of Lear's fool that intensify the king's misery play no role in *Life Is Beautiful*. The spirit of comedy is misused in the film to deflect our attention from the atrocity of mass murder (not to be dignified with the designation "tragedy" to begin with). And because death, especially brutal death, is anathema to the spirit of comedy, no one is seen dying in the film. Death is reduced to something heard, the sound of a pistol shot around the corner. The audience is spared the experience, witnessing instead the survival of the child, and thus the triumph of the father's will. The reassuring message of the film is that in the encounter between volition and mortality in its most ruthless form, human resolve is capable of defeating its enemy. The illusion is a comfort to a generation still perplexed by the randomness of Holocaust violence.

Benigni has thus shaped a legend of survival to counter the darker truth of how the Holocaust experience threatened and eroded the reigning image in Western civilization of an inviolable self. Defenders of the film have exploited its supposed evolution into "fable" to refute the charge that it violates historical truth. But a single term such as "fable" cannot banish from memory the associations that a narrative set in fascist Italy rife with antisemitism would rouse. This is especially true after Jews from the town are deported to a deathcamp. Locales like Auschwitz were not metaphors, but killing sites in German-occupied Poland. Art Spiegelman spoke out forcibly on this issue in an interview on Christopher Lydon's former program *The Connection*.[1] He disclosed a curious piece of little-known information: "Benigni claimed to have been inspired to do this film because of *Maus* and I was asked to do the film's posters. . . . I'd like to erase his memory of having seen my book, and it's because he'd misinterpreted what I'd done *as* a fable." Spiegelman is characteristically candid in his disdain for the film: "Auschwitz becomes a metaphor for a big bummer. . . . and the movie becomes 'Man, you really can survive this big bummer as long as you've got a good attitude and can keep your sense of humor.' " He objects to Benigni's taking history and turning it into a metaphor of a father's love for his son, knowing from his research and his personal experience that in the presence of such atrocity metaphors fell apart, and "couldn't hold the story." The oft-heard disclaimer that *Life Is Beautiful* isn't about Auschwitz and the Holocaust at all, but about a father's determination to protect his son in an "extreme situation," represents a typical avoidance of the grim plight of the pair after their deportation. Although Benigni seems utterly indifferent to the fact, choosing an extermination camp as an example of an "extreme situation" not only universalizes the historical distinctness of the place but also limits the options available to a character like Guido who wishes to control the chances for survival. Readers of Spiegelman's *Maus* volumes will recall the fate of his younger brother, who is sent to "safety" by his parents, only to meet an unpredictable end almost too dreadful to imagine. Spiegelman's misgivings about Guido's whimsical ingenuity in saving his son reveal a deeper understanding of the fragility of family life during this time of terror. There may be a role for ingenuity in the saga of solitary survival, but it was balked more often than it succeeded, and it was never far from a feeling of desperate fear.

If we tease out some of the implications behind Benigni's approach to experience in *Life Is Beautiful,* we may gain better insight into his comedic response to the threat of extermination. The film begins with an auto careening down a hilly road out of control: the brakes have failed. The episode ends safely, but its symbolic hint establishes a motif for the entire film. Gaining and maintaining charge of a situation is the first step toward reaching a happy conclusion. A sense of humor, a ready wit, a verbal gift for turning potential trouble into personal triumph all invest one with the power to maneuver reality, almost like laughing oneself back to health from a severe illness. Through the nostalgia of a manufactured memory, Benigni restores to the imagination the one factor most missing in the concentration- and death-camp environment: the freedom to choose. In a single stroke he invents the chimera that there was little substantial difference between how one elected to exist inside and outside the camp. Just as the suitor in the first half of the film was able to cause obstacles almost magically to fall away in his pursuit of another man's fiancée, so the father in the camp will use the same talents to preserve his son. If it were true that unwavering parental love could have insured the survival of one's child, even at the price of one's own life, then thousands of Jewish martyrs would have been honored after the war by their spared children. History, of course, tells a darker story. The ease with which Benigni was able to displace it with and gain acceptance for his frivolous fairy-tale version is a sad commentary not only on his limited appreciation of post-Holocaust reality but also on the acute need of his audiences to embrace the untruth of his "fable."

Benigni's devotion to an atmosphere of hilarity in the midst of peripheral threats reminds us of a classic predecessor to his opus, Chaplin's *The Great Dictator,* to which it owes a certain debt. In true satirical fashion, Chaplin's thrusts against the posturing of Mussolini and especially Hitler were designed to ridicule pretension and unblinker the eyes of their enthusiastic admirers. Chaplin may have underestimated the cruel ambitions of the two dictators, of which by 1940 there was evidence enough, but at least he did not set his comedy in a context of mass murder. In fact, Chaplin is reported to have said after the war that had he known in 1940 about the impending extermination of the Jews, he would have abandoned his project. The first part of *Life Is Beautiful* resembles the spirit of *The Great Dictator* in its ability to puncture the presumptions of totalitarian regimes with jeers of derision.

The scene in which Guido impersonates a fascist bureaucrat before a class of schoolchildren is carried off with Chaplinesque panache. The school principal informs the pupils that the visitor from the ministry of education "will demonstrate that our race is a superior race — the best of all." In a facetious impersonation, Guido parodies the theory, though his performance betrays not the slightest consciousness of the sinister implications of its later use as a motive for murder.

Benigni seems committed to suppressing the imagination of disaster, lest it hinder or foil his comic intentions. Even when he can no longer avoid the obvious presence of racial scorn, he converts the ominous moment into another occasion for comic relief. When Guido's son asks his father why a shop has a sign in its window reading "No entrance for dogs or Jews," the film arrives at a crucial structural crossroad: do we begin a rite of initiation, the cinematic equivalent of a *Bildungsroman*, or pursue instead a casual humorous denial of implicit danger? At this precise turn the film chooses its destiny as a modern fairy tale (the ancient ones were far more subtle) built on the naïve belief that it is both possible and desirable to preserve childhood innocence at all costs, as if life were nothing more than an enchanted forest through which the young wander protected by adult talismans energized by the force of the comic spirit. Guido changes his son's earnest question into a joke, dismissing its grave forecast of the future with a witty rejoinder about his personal aversion to Visigoths and spiders.

An earlier episode provides the philosophical foundation for this attitude. As they retire on their first night in the city, Guido's cousin furnishes him with the principle that will serve Guido equally well in winning a mate and saving his son: "Schopenhauer says that with will power you can do anything." It is a reductive version of the American spirit of self-reliance: "I am what I want to be." Emerson's "Trust thyself: every heart vibrates to that iron string" echoes in the wings. It is no wonder that Hollywood greeted *Life Is Beautiful* with such unrestrained glee. As Guido drifts into sleep, his mind plays with variants of the formula for success: "It's a matter of thought. It's serious, and it takes time. . . . It's deep. You have to think it." Schopenhauer's idea sinks into his unconscious, to emerge later at critical instants to come to his aid. It would have us embrace the resultant "commedia seriosa" as a kind of thoughtful laughter, replenishing the drained spirit in time of need, but for the reflective viewer it emerges instead as a form of humor disguised as farce. Farce is a diluted form of comedy, excluding the realm of bitter mirth that, if it were present, might have made *Life Is Beautiful* a more compelling film. But who can take seriously the issues that Benigni's protagonist refuses to take seriously himself? Although Guido is detained by the Gestapo, then rounded up with his son and deported to a deathcamp, he persists in enacting the ludic quality of the experience. Another decisive fulcrum in the action arrives as the two are being transported by truck to the station where cattle cars await them. "Where are we going?" Joshua asks his father. We have reached a critical point, a junction of the imagination, a *quo vadis* of modern rather than classical inquiry: is paternal love best expressed by ignoring this ritual query, one that through a truthful answer might prepare the pair for the uncertainty that lies ahead; or by lies and evasion that preserve the carnival atmosphere of their "adventure," thus shielding childhood innocence even at the frontiers of pain?

Benigni is willing to accept the view that nothing human is alien to comedy, but recoils at its corollary that everything inhuman is. The Holocaust moves beyond tragedy toward a vision of atrocity that is still searching for fit forms of artistic expression. But there is no room for a gas chamber in Benigni's kingdom of humor; he pushes it beyond the boundaries of his narrative of survival, giving us the briefest glimpse of its domain, where good manners prevail over fear and confusion as the dominant gesture. A certain stark necessity drives the fate of the tragic figure, and the doomed victim of the deathcamp as well, though the German "plot" is more central to the unfolding of destiny in the camps than is Jewish character. But plot is more incidental to comedy, which depends on the wit and energy of its creatures to shape their future. We have already seen how in the realm of normal life the highest form of suffering for Guido is the thwarting of his will. The film goes astray, at least for this viewer, when he resolves to transfer his understanding of Schopenhauer to the region of abnormal death by pretending that this region differs only superficially from the existence he has left behind. He retains his role as a Lord of Misrule, and this is nowhere more evident than in the scene that Benigni himself considered the comic pinnacle of the film — Guido's *faux* translation of German instructions to the new arrivals in the camp barrack.

One of the major challenges to Holocaust literature has been the quest for a language to express the ostensibly inexpressible. This has been less formidable than some critics have claimed, as writers like Charlotte Delbo and Paul Celan have shown. Benigni, however, reverses the process by having Guido in his improvisation literally repress the expressible, mocking the power of language to bear the burden of injurious truth. For the message that he suppresses, that he does not even make an effort to understand, is that swift execution is the penalty for any violation of the camp's strict rules. Is this episode funny in the movie theater because the members of Benigni's audience have been trained to react to it not by Holocaust history but by *Hogan's Heroes*? The SS in the film stand by stupidly during Guido's performance, unsuspecting, as if they are only awaiting the entrance of Colonel Klink to complete the farce. Earlier in the film, in the period of "normalcy," Guido, his wife, and son are about to set forth on the family bicycle when Joshua exclaims, "I've lost my tank!" "Don't worry," his father replies, "we'll find it." His "translation" in the barrack about a contest with a real tank as the prize signifies his belief that the way to avert a sense of approaching catastrophe is to behave as if the motives and actions of pre-camp life were transferable to the death-camp milieu. Guido pursues this delusion not only for his son, but for himself as well.

Is there an authentic man behind this face of tomfoolery, this façade of verbal gesticulation? *Life Is Beautiful* offers no convincing evidence that there is. If Guido had been torn between the desire to protect his son and his own realization of the near impossibility of doing so, then we might have been presented with an anguished clown, a revelation that behind the mask of the comic spirit hovered the terror of losing control. But there is no sign of this conflicted self. Instead, Guido appears in an odd reversal of roles as a shallow version of Goethe's Mephistopheles in *Faust*, a pale parody of "the spirit that endlessly denies." In *If This Is a Man* (*Survival in Auschwitz*) Primo Levi reports that one more day of carrying around heavy metal pipes would have led to his collapse from physical exhaustion. Luckily, he is relieved of this labor. Guido is trapped in a similar situation, dragging around anvils too heavy for him to bear; but when a fellow prisoner tells him he will be killed if he puts one down, the will to endure magically restores his resolve. He returns to the barrack barely able to walk but talks himself out of his fatigue by regaling Joshua with tales of the joyful games he has been playing all day: "We laughed like crazy today! I died laughing! Boy, did I have fun." Goethe's cordial devil is driven to negation by a cynical vision of human frailty and the pleasure he takes in exploiting it. Guido's denials to his son, however, force him to refute his own reality too, with an ease that virtually eliminates peril and makes him an imposter before the menace that surrounds them. It is hard to explain why this "dis-education" of Joshua, which turns both father and child into refugees from truth, should have had such universal appeal.

Although we are supposed to celebrate Guido's constancy in keeping up the pretense, there are a few occasions when the son innocently prods his father toward a higher level of comprehension and a more sincere basis for their relationship. I doubt if these are intentional on Benigni's part, but they offer the disenchanted viewer some clues about directions a more honest film might have taken. Although it was rare, there were instances when a parent was able to save a child from death, more often in labor camps than in deathcamps. But testimony confirms that such strategies always depended on apprising the child of the dangers that threatened to engulf it. The "cheerful" clown cannot accept this compromise because it would undermine his belief in the power of the controlling will. When a frightened Joshua tells Guido that the other children say, "They make buttons and soap out of us," the father can refute this piece of camp fantasy with one of his familiar routines. He faces a stiffer challenge when the boy next announces, "They burn us all in the oven." Guido's nervous patter during his comic disclaimer never betrays a deeply troubled demeanor, as if Benigni knew that putting the soul of his comic protagonist at risk would sabotage the buoyant intentions of the film. Perhaps he believed that his superficial concession to a "tragic" atmosphere was enough to dignify the impulses to amuse. But like

Guido, Benigni is caught up in a spirit of denial, and he may never know how close he came to achieving a genuine triumph of cinematic art.

It is hard enough for the tragic figure to acknowledge what can be learned from the sweeping power of evil. King Lear's wrenching admission, "I am a very foolish fond old man / Fourscore and upwards," strips him of his inflated self-esteem and exposes his human frailty. It enrolls him in the community of poor naked wretches who have been abused by the moral and physical tempest that has been threatening to consume him too. But even though the clown's motley in *Life Is Beautiful* has been traded for the striped vestments of the camp prisoner, Guido only wears a disguise. He seems immune to any trial of his comic façade, equal almost to the very end to the cruel intentions of the Germans. Without jeopardy he finds ways of communicating with his wife in the woman's section and securing extra food for his son (at a meal where he joins German officials' children, who — incredibly — have been playing "hide-and-go-seek" on the grounds of a killing site!). For the comic spirit, adversity is not a teacher but a challenge to ingenuity. We are expected to overlook the absurd detail that official visitors are allowed to bring their wives and children to dinner inside a deathcamp in the first place. But when Guido leaves this social occasion where he has been waiting on tables (his job *before* deportation too), his weary son asleep in his arms, he momentarily loses his way in the fog that has cloaked the locale of the barracks. He stumbles on a sight that could have dissolved his comic defenses and recruited him into the fellowship of those "poor naked wretches" who embodied the ultimate destiny of the Jews — who at this point even remembers that Guido and his son are Jewish? — in a place like Auschwitz.

Looming through the mist, dim to Guido's view as to ours, is an obscure vision of horror, a hill of death, the essence of German evil, a mountain of bodies and bones more terrifying than anything Dante sees in his rendezvous with sin in the morally ordered circles of the Inferno. Guido stares in dazed amazement at this gruesome testimony to the chaos inherent in the universe of extermination. It is as if the film itself has suddenly blundered into a more compelling Holocaust, only to discover that it cannot contend with what it has found: that way madness lies, and a mad clown would subvert the offices of Benigni's comic intentions. Cinematic art, with its insistence on the visual, rarely has a role for the immutable terrors of the deathcamp, a view many consider too fearful to behold. The idea that such atrocity is beyond human comprehension supports the myth of mystification that still clings to some accounts of German ruthlessness, and Benigni is not prepared to dispute it. Guido retreats from the spectral bleakness before him, a mixture of awe, fear, and confusion in his eyes. To pursue its shrouded meaning would require a compromise with the triumphant human spirit that Guido is unable and Benigni unwilling to embrace. At this point the film fails the test of its own authenticity; nothing, not even truth, can be allowed to contaminate the masquerade that lies at the heart of its comic enterprise.

The agile clown has no amulet in his bag of tricks to vanquish the power of this hill of corpses. Guido simply backs off. If we allow the dreadful spectacle to enter our consciousness now it may taint the future with the poison of remembrance. Joshua conveniently sleeps through the episode, sparing his invincible innocence. As for his father, there is no evidence of epiphany in his subsequent behavior. Events determine his action, as the Germans begin to evacuate the camp and the father finds a secure place for his son to hide until the liberators arrive — though to us the hiding place seems a perfectly obvious one. Any hint of an intuitive metamorphosis disappears when Guido improbably exerts the magic force of his will to divert an SS man and his dog as they are on the verge of noticing the hidden boy. From a distance, his hands literally wave them away, as if they were puppets controlled by invisible strings extending from his fingers.

At this point, manipulation subverts discovery and revelation, two qualities that might have elevated *Life Is Beautiful* to a higher order of achievement. Like the German atrocities in the deathcamps, comedy is built on improbable possibilities — though for most students of the Holocaust these atrocities show little potential for humorous use. In Benigni's view, such possibilities are the pulsing heart of the film, and they succeed only if we allow a layer of amnesia to insulate our minds from the pain and squalor that might have diverted us from this chronicle of survival. Just as Dora's red suit amidst the gray garments of the other female arrivals at the camp had been a tribute to a similar scene in Steven Spielberg's *Schindler's List,* so the American tank roaring around the corner of a barrack, signaling the arrival of the liberators, evokes a contrary moment from the end of his *Saving Private Ryan.* Hollywood is the home of uplifting endings, and Benigni is eager to feel welcome there. Subsequent Oscar recognitions proved how shrewdly apt his imitations were. Did Benigni know or care that American troops never liberated a deathcamp? This gesture toward the United States as the culture where hope prevails and evil never wins is inherent in both title and content of *Life Is Beautiful.*

There is a level at which one wishes that Benigni had been capable of consciously designing a parody of serious cinema to infiltrate his film's ending, but there is no evidence that he intended such an effect. Are we to be gripped by comic delight when Joshua "wins" his tank, sitting atop the giant mechanical war machine like a triumphant conqueror, heedless of his father's disappearance and exhibiting not the slightest distress from his recent ordeal? Ancient comedy may have found certain of its origins in ritual sacrifices to the gods of winter and infertility, dramatic pleas for the resurrection of a new and fruitful season. It represented a victory of the life spirit over temporary subjugation to suffering and death. But suffering and death were not temporary during the Holocaust, and pagan motives play no role as mother and son are reunited in *Life Is Beautiful,* exclaiming to each other "We've won!" They can rejoice because they are spared the image of the defeated and helpless clown, disguised to the end — this time as a woman — pinioned to a wall by the glare of a German searchlight. Its beam signals the source of evil that has consumed his fellow Jews and now will destroy him, but he is merely blinded by its brightness.

Sentiment replaces illumination, and a squinting Guido will die without any insight into the nature of German cruelty or the limits of the comic spirit in the milieu of atrocity. His wife and son will survive with a similar innocence. Joshua's final reprise as a child echoes his father's earlier language, not lamenting the frailty but celebrating the strength of the comic shield: "A thousand points to laugh like crazy about. We came in first. . . . We won!" As columns of surviving prisoners shuffle by mother and son to the blare of inappropriate military music, who is asked to recall the thousands of reasons for weeping instead of laughter? The ending of *Life Is Beautiful* might have been bathed by cascades of intersecting ironies, but Benigni aborts this potential by shifting our attention to a hypothetical narrative of forfeiture and salvation. He returns us to the voice of the adult son with which he began, excluding from our consciousness the peripheral victims of the larger disaster: "This is my story. This is the sacrifice my father made. This was his gift to me." In other words, "He died that I might live" — an odd note of Christian piety in a story involving the murder and survival of Jews. The abuse of language here joins the misuse of comedy, though by this time the audience has grown so used to deceit and denial that it probably does not notice. In fact there has been no sacrifice; the fates of both father and son have been shaped only by improbable possibilities. Guido has not chosen or even accepted death in order to save his son; the Germans have simply shot him and left his body, we assume, as if it were a pile of discarded refuse. The voiceover in the present invites us to believe what the film's latent evidence has shown us to be false, but this has been the strategy from the beginning.

According to Benigni's vision in this film, Nazism and fascism merely challenge the ingenuity of the human will; if the hero can find a horse, no matter if it be a "Jewish" horse, he will carry off the "principessa" in triumph. We may salvage some humor from such bizarre knightly exploits when they are undertaken on a social occasion still surrounded by the superficial trappings of civility. But the ludicrous is miscast when it enters the stage of the deathcamp; comedy can only thrive there by denying that death has primacy over life. By making the will a miraculous antidote to the threat of annihilation, Benigni inverts that hierarchy and restores a more amenable balance between hope and despair for those unable to tolerate the random disorder at the heart of the Holocaust experience. He does so by reducing history to a vague framework for a drama of family devotion, making the killing of many an incidental detail when compared to the deliverance of one. It is as if Benigni would have us feel, to our great relief, that the saving of a single life can really redeem the whole world. Millions of murdered have taught us to believe otherwise.

38

One of the most difficult facts to accept about the Holocaust is that it has raised the stakes of artistic — including cinematic — representation of the event by forcing us to ask not only whether it is true to life, but also whether it is true to death. It is easy to imagine why a comic artist like Benigni refused to embrace this maxim. By sacrificing inhumanity to wit, he bestows on art the formidable and some might argue unethical responsibility of modifying history for the sake of entertainment. After all, comedy cannot outlive its failure to amuse. And since in a place like Auschwitz to survive was to outwit death, this must be the thrust of Benigni's film. Few would dispute that the urge to remain alive, and to a lesser extent to sustain others, was a powerful impulse for prisoners in the camps. This helps to account for the relatively low number of suicides that occurred there. But an authentic representation would have to show this struggle in its proper context: fear, hunger, exhaustion, disease, depression, and despair. Such tension, however, does not comport well with the comic spirit, so Benigni is forced to discard it. For Guido the challenge of keeping his son alive is more like finding the solution to a riddle — one of the recurrent motifs in the film. Once again we encounter the world of normalcy reaching into the realm of the abnormal and wrenching its twisted features back into a familiar visage. The game of life, Guido is convinced, is not so different from the puzzle of death, if you know how to finesse the rules. Sudden turns and abrupt ruptures in the rhythm of experience do not sit comfortably on the shoulders of the comic artist, who depends on popular perceptions to capture the sympathy of his audience. But when this becomes the guiding principle for a film using the deportation and murder of the Jews as its background, we are forced to conclude that what has been sacrificed in *Life Is Beautiful* is not the father, but the truth.

Does Holocaust art have an obligation to historical accuracy no matter which venue it chooses for its form and content? One way of resolving this issue in regard to *Life Is Beautiful* is to argue, as so many do, that the film is not "really" about the Holocaust at all, but only about a father's love for his son and his efforts to protect him in an "extreme situation." But this view does not bear scrutiny, since it is evident that the danger threatening Joshua is death in the gas chamber. He initially avoids this peril by refusing to take a shower, another echo of a normal pre-camp scene in the film, when he similarly refused to take a bath. He simply runs away from the SS, who are leading the other boys to their death. How he managed to do this the film does not address, nor does it disclose how he is able to wander around the camp undetected until he finds the factory where his father is working. Although he has been in the camp long enough to have learned what is going on there, Guido unaccountably insists that the boy join the others to take his shower. Joshua continues to refuse, thus for the moment saving his life *in spite of* his father, and hides by kneeling unnoticed near the corner of an extending wall. The premises behind this sequence include the utter incompetence of the SS and the historical naïveté or ignorance of the audience. This is a classic example of how "ought" replaces "is" in some Holocaust discourse, since it ought to have been possible to conceive of ways, whether through a stubborn will or some other kind of determined resistance, to avoid extermination in the gas chamber. Few among Benigni's viewers, and even fewer among his Hollywood admirers, were willing to admit that the frantic search in art for a maneuver to outwit the enemy might be related to a desperate quest for a ruse to deceive oneself.

Misrepresenting the Holocaust is more than a pastime; it serves masters other than history, including the deep psychological need to develop a worldview capable of numbing the horrors of annihilation, especially those that arose from the vicinity of the gas chamber. As we have seen, one explanation for the misleading role that the history of the Holocaust plays in the development of Benigni's story is that its details were simply too troublesome to be allowed to intervene seriously in the unfolding of his comic narrative. But the history of Italian cinema was not, and arguably was far more influential on the genesis of Benigni's ideas. In addition to being a response to the Holocaust, *Life Is Beautiful* is a reaction to thematic material in the scenario of two of its best-known precursors, Vittorio De Sica's *The Bicycle Thief* (1948)[2] and Lina Wertmuller's *Seven Beauties* (1976). Each in its way had more to do with shaping the pattern and content of its successor than the murder of European Jewry. Italian audiences of a certain age would recognize instantly Benigni's debt to these predecessors. I would go so far as to suggest that *Life Is Beautiful* represents a conscious attempt to contest the cinematic assumptions that informed these bleak films. It seeks to restore to Benigni's Italian audiences—though there is no reason for restricting our discussion to them—a gratifying sense of how film can fabricate from the raw ingredients of an unpromising history the durable illusion of a hopeful future.

In the first half of *Life Is Beautiful*, the bicycle is a principal means of travel for Guido. A metamorphosis occurs as the family is about to set forth on its last journey together on this vehicle before deportation when Joshua complains that he has lost his tank. "Hold the bicycle, I'll get it," Guido tells his wife, and suddenly we witness the planting in the father's imagination the seed of a new icon of salvational transportation. It will sprout and flourish in the camp, but it will remain a toy, a private joke, a decoy to conceal the truth. At the end of the film it will be the emblem of a fake journey, a hypothetical voyage through evil that Joshua has never understood or even had to experience internally. It is as if the father had announced from beyond the grave that "I restore you to the childhood innocence you never lost and purge you of the transgressions you never committed and the grief you never knew. Welcome home intact from the deathcamp!" Once more the spirit of parody might have rescued the script from the absurdity of this impossible probability, but it seems clear that Benigni was serious about the fervent affirmation of his conclusion.

In De Sica's 1948 film, the bicycle is not a playful vehicle hunting for a substitute but is essential to a family's survival. Although the father in this story is only struggling against the social and economic chaos of post-war Italy and not the threat of extermination, the dreary monochrome setting of *The Bicycle Thief* resembles the conditions of Holocaust oppression more than the technicolor camouflage of *Life Is Beautiful.* Exploitation has replaced teamwork in the fight to stay alive. Whereas Benigni delights in paying tribute to Hollywood's penchant for romantic fantasy, De Sica ironically contrasts it with the cheerless atmosphere of the post-war milieu by having a protagonist whose job is to hang posters of Rita Hayworth on the shabby walls of urban structures. Without Schopenhauer for support, the will is defenseless against the assaults of an unprincipled community of the indigent, reduced to various forms of scavenging to gain an economic foothold in a disintegrating society. But once his hard-won bicycle is stolen and he sets out with his son in search of it, the father's conflict moves beyond mere financial need and must face the challenge of retaining parental respect and regaining his dignity as a man.

Here Benigni's magical self-help formulae are of little use. Instead of easily recovering the stolen means of transport or of finding a "tank" equivalent to deflect his son's disappointment, the father meets humiliation and failure at every turn. One can almost hear Benigni's imagination churning with plans to modify this half-century-old version of a father's desperate efforts to sustain a bond of mutual regard with his son. Perhaps post-war consciousness could appreciate an account of personal shame and lost honor, but modern audiences in a prosperous culture need more sanguine fare. As the son beholds his father's inability to reclaim lost pride in work, in self, in family, he initiates a bitter education in the frailty of private will and the limits of paternal love as external circumstances conspire to usurp their strength. The odyssey of father and son looking for the lost bicycle is an exercise in futility. Together with the boy, we witness the painful spectacle of the sabotaging of the myth of paternal competence. *Life Is Beautiful* seeks to undo that pain by mending the damage that *The Bicycle Thief* inflicted on the myth.

Thematically De Sica's post-war film has nothing to do with the impact of the Holocaust. But its dénouement, in which a decent man is driven to a shameful act in the presence of his child by the need to recover if not personal dignity then at least a minimal level of subsistence, resembles far more than *Life Is Beautiful* some of the most agonizing family moments from the universe of ghettos and camps. In a short story called "Crazy," Holocaust author and survivor Ida Fink records the anguish of a father who observes from a distance the roundup and deportation by the SS of his three small daughters but is too terrified to intervene. "Papa! Papa, come to us," the two youngest called out, he recollects in his first-person account, but he remained squatting out-of-sight between two buildings, paralyzed by fear. Years later he is still searching for some medicine to cure his nightmares of remembrance, in which he shouts, "I'm coming! I'm coming" long after his murdered children can hear him.[3]

The relentless torment of this situation was of course unthinkable to Benigni's Guido, who to the last moment of his life stubbornly refuses to internalize the grim implications of his ordeal. Indeed, a situation parallel to the one portrayed by Fink in her story occurs in *Life Is Beautiful*, but the analogy is shattered by the feel-good philosophy of the film. For just as in Fink's tale, Guido is hiding at a distance when some SS men and their dog — trained, we should note, to sniff out and attack strangers — approach the spot where Joshua is concealed. Surely reason, history, and artistic honesty require the boy to be discovered, at which point the father would be forced to decide whether to endanger his own life by interceding. How would he greet the revelation that paternal love is impotent in the presence of German cruelty? This would have dramatized the corrosive dilemma of choice in the deathcamps and compelled Guido to acknowledge that his antics were constrained by a barrier of perilous consequences. Instead, he drives off the danger through the sorcery of willful gesture and happily but implausibly insures the security of the paternal blessing. The mindless quality of the exploit confirms the general tenor of a film not to be esteemed for its ethical or intellectual depth.

A much more challenging moment of moral uncertainty occurs near the end of *The Bicycle Thief*, when the son must assimilate a deed that he is loath to identify with his admired parent. The boy watches as his father in a sudden fit of despair yields to temptation and momentarily joins the ranks of the very bicycle thieves who have undone him: he steals a bicycle. The effect on his son's emotional and psychological education will be prolonged beyond the film's conclusion. We are left to brood on what human beings may be reduced to when adverse events exceed the capacity of the individual to control them. Father and son join hands at the end not in reconciliation and mutual regard but in a distressing confession of humiliation and shame, still bound by the traditional family tie but united too by an afflicted memory that fluctuates ambiguously between disenchantment and love. We have already learned, however, that in Benigni's charmed world there is no room for afflicted memory or disenchantment. His answer to De Sica is to sidestep loss and assuage pain by imposing on his narrative a teleology of triumph. No one in the film, with the ironic exception of an SS doctor, is asked to pay a moral price for the horrors in which he or she has been immersed. Guido is victimized by atrocity, as Joshua survives it, without meaningful consequences. And for the demanding viewer, a life or death without serious consequences must be judged inconsequential.

Lina Wertmuller had the courage to undertake in *Seven Beauties* what Benigni later refused even to consider, testing against deathcamp brutalities the romantic illusions of a Hollywood-driven culture. Like Benigni, she is casual about some of the details of Holocaust history. Mass executions did not occur on German soil, nor was an extermination camp ever located there. And certainly no female commandant ever ruled such a place. Nonetheless, Wertmuller is determined to make the impact of atrocity on individual moral vision the context for her film, beginning it with documentary clips of a posturing Hitler or Mussolini alternating with violent episodes of land combat or aerial ruin. However comical these dictators may appear in rhetorical guise, the results of the doctrines they espouse are catastrophic. Thus even before the film begins, the viewer is prepared for a rupture in consciousness, a discrepancy between expectation and reality, that lay at the heart of the Holocaust experience. Before our eyes, the comic spirit withers in the domain of barbarous death.

In *Life Is Beautiful,* verbal felicity is an armor against harm, the very reverse of *Seven Beauties,* where the principle of language as refuge is sacrificed to the superior power of ruthless force. Only after comparing the two films do we realize how absent physical savagery is from Benigni's story, his SS men remaining anonymous robots rather than agents of slaughter. Indeed, the most sympathetic figure in the camp episodes is the SS doctor on the verge of losing his sanity because his composure is so shaken by the job of selecting candidates for the gas chamber. Wertmuller, on the other hand, refuses to pretend. However exaggerated and ludicrous are Pasqualino's efforts to seduce the camp commandant, the director never lets us forget — never lets *him* forget — that his doomed maneuver is nothing more than a frantic but futile scheme to foil the fate that awaits him. His quest for respect in Naples seems trivial now that he has crossed defenseless into this alien realm swarming with corpses.

Like Guido, Pasqualino turns first to the shallow values that he has inherited from his "normal" life, drawing on his mother's trite advice that there is a way to stir the heart of every woman, even the monstrous female commandant of a deathcamp. But instead of lauding the virtue of this view, Wertmuller unmasks the pathos of the male ego once it has lost the freedom and vigor to exploit its female victims. Just as Guido has always lived by his wit, so Pasqualino thrives through his eyes, which constantly survey the scene before them in an effort to control what they behold. They seem in turn shrewd, suspicious, appealing, remorseless, duped, and finally defiled by the visual memory of what they have witnessed. In the contest between knowing and seeing, Guido's ominous surroundings in a romance of danger only strengthen his ingenuity, whereas in his house of death Pasqualino slowly succumbs to a depleted vision, finally becoming a reluctant instrument of the barbarism that tears his bravado to shreds. For Benigni, a fertile and resourceful imagination is the supreme requisite for survival, no matter what the milieu. But Pasqualino quickly learns that when habitual response encounters the unpredictable, especially in the form of pitiless contempt, the latter will prevail. He asks the question that Guido feels not the slightest need to face: "How did the world get to be like this?"

Like Guido, Pasqualino resolves to live, initially retreating to familiar strategies to survive, then realizing that in the absence of control he must learn to adapt. The price of that adaptation is the core disclosure of *Seven Beauties*, though its import unfolds slowly and is not wholly exposed until the very end. As with students of the Holocaust, the process begins with a visual education, the urgency of seeing "how it was," that through the osmosis of insight gradually engages with more complex moral issues. Such "learning" demands its own payment in intellectual distress, and perhaps one reason for the popular success of *Life Is Beautiful* is that it relieves its audience so painlessly of this exacting task. In a sense, Benigni "historicizes" the Holocaust by adopting a chronological structure for his film, allowing for a temporal transition from past to present without disrupting the psychological assumptions of his protagonist. Nothing is more reassuring than the guarantee of continuity when events conspire to jeopardize its dominion. By contrast, the constant shift between past and present that threads through Wertmuller's film dramatizes a breach in the transition from order to chaos that pure chronology falsifies. Benigni seems determined to restore integrity to the unsettling spectacle of the dismembered self—literally *and* figuratively, as it turns out—that surfaces in *Seven Beauties*, whose alternating structure replicates the tension between apparent stability and genuine collapse that characterizes the era which gave it birth.

Just as "past time" before the Holocaust could not anticipate the atrocities that lay ahead, so "future time" after the Holocaust cannot entirely escape the atrocities that lie behind. During their ordeal in the camps both Guido and Pasqualino depend on memory of an earlier time, of the kind of conduct that insured success in pre-war society, to guide them in their new and singular surroundings. For Guido this means pursuing a strategy of deceit and self-deceit, a firm denial of the change in family status that has come with deportation. Pasqualino begins by following a similar path, echoing hollow formulas like "I'm a man of honor; I won't be a clown," without recognizing the irony of his unwitting revelation. Before he can approach the intricate question of how to survive "with honor" in a German deathcamp, he must gain access to the nature of the beast that threatens. Then he must realize how the flux of language can conspire to lead him to unforeseen behavior: "Nothing could be worse than here," he confides to a fellow prisoner. "I'll do anything to get out. I'll do anything to live." For Benigni's Guido this simply means manipulating events like an artful conjurer. But Pasqualino is allowed to learn that "anything" in a deathcamp does not mean the same as it did in the pre-war world. This process of education destroys both the "man of honor" and the "clown," leaving a pathetic shell who must now clothe himself with the knowledge that life and death are no longer opposites but conspirators in a debasing and vicious ritual of moral compromise.

Although Wertmuller chooses a moment of melodrama to illustrate her

LIFE IS NOT BEAUTIFUL

idea, it seems necessary in order to underscore one of the most agonizing but quintessential truths of the deathcamp experience for those who endured it: no one's survival could be detached from the death of someone else. It was a code of complicity (utterly alien to Benigni's Guido) that originated with the German murderers, who bore full responsibility for its implementation. Nonetheless, victims could be made instruments of that policy. Prisoner doctors accompanied by SS were sometimes forced to select for death from among the "patients" in the crude infirmaries under their supervision those most ill, in order to spare the lives of those more likely to get well and return to work. It was always a choice between bad or worse, not to be graced with the ethical dignity of authentic moral practice. Thus when Pasqualino is ordered by the malicious camp commandant to pick six men for "elimination" or to face the execution of all the men in his barrack, he must internalize a diabolic accounting system under which a few are granted a fleeting reprieve as "reward" for the murder of others. It is the penultimate defining moment of *Seven Beauties* and its chaotic world, where human and inhuman shed their original semantic distinctions, fusing into a single paradoxical decision to authorize death in order to stay alive. It has no parallel in Benigni's *Life Is Beautiful*. There the hints of atrocity are muted: although Guido's uncle is sent to the gas chamber, Guido himself is never required to reflect on this grim fact, almost as if Benigni were determined not to trouble his consciousness — or ours — with the bleak implications of this appalling event.

Pasqualino's encounter with brutal death, on the other hand, leaves us and his fellow prisoners floundering in a moral void. By eliminating the common options of "living well" and "dying well" and providing no satisfactory substitutes, Wertmuller plunges us into the abyss of a civilization gone awry. The most humane of Pasqualino's associates, an anarchist inmate, can no longer tolerate a world in which human beings are forced by fear for their own lives to act as indirect executioners. Exclaiming "Man in disorder!" — the ruling principle of the world of destruction we call the Holocaust — he leaps into a pool of manure, but whether he dies by drowning or from the shots of the pursuing SS men is left to our imagination. His last words are not a cry of defiance but of despair; his "final resting place" deprives his gesture of the solace of martyrdom. The protest he initiates among the frantic prisoners leads to the climactic moment in the film, when Pasqualino must enter the universe of Holocaust death as an agent instead of an observer to discover that the definition of choice has changed from an option between bad or good to one between bad or worse.

Following the death of the anarchist, Pasqualino's closest companion in the camp reaches the limits of his endurance and cries out in exhausted protest against the barbarity of his oppressors. German guards seize him and are about to shoot him when an SS officer, in a gesture of pure German malice, pulls out his pistol, offers it to Pasqualino, and orders him to execute the kneeling offender. It is an ultimate moment of moral decision, a test of the newly achieved vision that exposure to atrocity has granted him. Unlike Guido in *Life Is Beautiful,* he acknowledges and meets the challenge through the silent expressive refusal of his eyes. But Wertmuller knows that the deathcamp was not a site for uncontaminated heroic gesture, since failure to comply could lead to the death of Pasaqualino and the other members of his work detail. It is a classic example of what I elsewhere have called choiceless choice, an act with no beneficial outcome. When his friend pleads with him to shoot so that the Germans will not do it instead, Pasqualino pulls the trigger, and as the film segues back to Naples and its liberation by American troops (much like the ending of *Life Is Beautiful*), it is clear that for Pasqualino there is to be no escape from his complicity in the dehumanized world that he has outlived.

He is a voyager who has endured a modern version of the Inferno shorn of its sacred trappings, not a Dante en route to Paradise but a petty hoodlum who has been so afflicted by what he has seen that his eyes have assumed a permanent expression of weary grief. He returns to his mother's apartment where we see on a bureau a framed photo of the earlier Pasqualino, its self-satisfied visage and slicked-down hair reminders of the shallow comic façade that once dominated his personality. The death of the former self is complete. But the old corruption still surrounds him: his sisters have taken up with American soldiers and the pretty young girl he once met now earns her living as a prostitute. The universe of atrocity has passed them by; "normal" social forces have stirred their moral decay. "You're alive!" Pasqualino's mother happily exclaims, and enjoins him to forget the past. "Yes, I'm alive," he mutters, but the look on his face contradicts his admission, and counsels the viewer to consider that his survival may have been not a triumph but a defeat. In the background with derisive crescendos a gravelly voice sings with ironic insistence the same refrain we had heard earlier from the still-innocent adolescent. It means something like "Keep on living, keep on going," but it now echoes a final mocking commentary on Pasqualino's alienation from a milieu that has failed the test of perception.

It is also a moment that could have given birth to the screenplay for *Life Is Beautiful,* whose title and subsequent scenario seem a sharp rebuke to the bleak conclusion of Wertmuller's film. Pasqualino's pretentious façade of honor and respect in the first half of *Seven Beauties* parallels Guido's comic antics in the initial sequences of *Life Is Beautiful.* Both protagonists are then exposed to a vision of atrocity that threatens the assumptions driving their earlier existence. But here the similarity ends, and one may discern Benigni's calculated effort to redirect his audience's imagination into more positive terrain. For that audience the terrible deaths of the Holocaust inhabit the fringes of consciousness, occurring off-stage. In the end, mother and child are reunited and survive, while the savior-father vanishes from the scene. Unfortunately, the Holocaust was accompanied by no such miracles.

The muted (and oddly inappropriate) Christian theology of this moment may help to explain Benigni's insensitive behavior when he accepted the Oscar for best film at the Academy Awards. He dedicated his prize to the memory of those who died so that we today might proclaim that life is beautiful. Such sentiments may flourish on a Hollywood rostrum, but they say little about the anguish of parents and children trapped by the ruthless brutality of the Holocaust domain. In that realm, death and life flowed easily into each other, erasing the usual breach between them. But the comic vision has small space for the irony of hope, whose vista is shrouded by the deadly memories that attend any prospects for a better future.

FRAGMENTS OF MEMORY:
A MYTH OF PAST TIME

Since the reinvention of the self is a notable theme to readers of imaginative literature, it is a wonder why so few of them were able to recognize Binjamin Wilkomirski's "memoir" *Fragments* as an example of the genre. Students of American culture have long been familiar with the odyssey of James Gatz from the backwaters of the Midwest to a mansion on Long Island, and with his metamorphosis along the way into the glamorous figure of Jay Gatsby. On another continent in a later era, a Christian boy named Bruno Grosjean, soon to become Bruno Doesseker, undertook a different kind of fictional pilgrimage, from the snow-capped peaks of Switzerland to the bleak Silesian plains, backward rather than forward in time, changed his name to Binjamin Wilkomirski, and emerged with a new persona as a Jewish child born in Riga, Latvia, who had survived the Majdanek extermination

48

camp. Subsequently (though not in his original text), he claimed that he had outlived Auschwitz-Birkenau, too, as well as some medical experiments by doctors in that infamous locale.

The difference between *The Great Gatsby* and *Fragments* is that Fitzgerald assumed he was writing a novel from the start. Wilkomirski, on the contrary, offered his work to publishers and the public as a memoir, a painfully reconstructed version not of the American dream but of a European nightmare. Whereas Gatsby discards his mediocre past in order to redraw himself as a romantic personality, Wilkomirski rejects an equally inglorious origin as the child of an unwed mother for a far more dramatic and violent tale of a childhood spent as a Jewish victim of the Holocaust. His account, now definitively exposed as a fabrication,[1] was received in America and abroad, especially in academic circles, with instant critical acclaim, some reviewers writing with a tone of reverence usually reserved for the ordeal of saintly martyrs.[2]

There have been other Holocaust hoaxes before this one, but none as charged with emotional intensity for the author and his audience. For example, in 1983 the scholarly world was stunned by the news that many hitherto unknown volumes of Hitler's diaries had been unearthed in Germany. No less an authority than the British historian H. R. Trevor-Roper initially vouched for their authenticity. The voices of skeptics were drowned by the enthusiasm of profit-hungry publishers or overshadowed by a frantic media quest for sensational issues, which quickly obscured some rather obvious reasons for doubting the "retrieved" material. Although the West German weekly magazine *Stern* (one of whose reporters claimed credit for the find, though it later turned out that he had conspired with a not-too-clever forger to deceive his bosses and the public) declared that experts had verified the Führer's handwriting, no one seems to have thought at first of testing the age of the paper and the ink. Once this was done and the fraud was exposed, little was left to discuss except the uncritical haste of those who greeted the chicanery with such widespread and wide-eyed approval.

This remains a fascinating matter, not irrelevant to the case of Binjamin Wilkomirski's pseudo-memoir *Fragments*. The appetite for new insights into the ordeal of European Jewry and the motives of those who murdered them seems insatiable, but this alone cannot explain the impact of the book and the author on its relatively narrow circle of educated admirers. Contrary to what many readers believe, the volume was never a great literary success.[3] Translated into nine languages, during its first four years (1995–1999) before the burgeoning scandal killed most sales, it sold fewer than 70,000 copies *worldwide*. The English-language editions did the best (about 33,000 copies), while only 13,000 purchasers bought the original German text. One can conclude from these comparatively meager figures that the general public showed little interest in *Fragments,* and probably never even heard of the dispute it spawned. The Holocaust launched a culture of remembrance among those who outlived it as a personal ordeal and those who embraced it as part of their history, but their numbers have never been large despite recent arguments that most American Jews derive their sense of Jewishness through association with that event.[4] There is simply no statistical evidence that such Jews, or non-Jews for that matter, know anything but the most elementary details about the catastrophe. A desire to learn more may indeed account for whatever limited appeal *Fragments* achieved, as it surely does for the popular success of *Schindler's List*, a film with some powerful moments but no substitute for the patient and prolonged study that a complex episode such as the Holocaust requires. But this does not help us to understand why knowledgeable members of both academic and survivor communities initially lionized Wilkomirski and celebrated his work.

This issue continues to puzzle me because from my first reading I assumed that *Fragments* was a fictional narrative. Even the brief afterword by Wilkomirski, included at his German publisher's insistence, seemed part of the invention, a reluctant but determined effort to strengthen the illusion of truth that novelists as far back as Hawthorne (in America; Defoe is an earlier English precedent) had used to convince their audiences that their subject was real rather than imagined experience. In a preface to *The Scarlet Letter*, Hawthorne maintained that he had found an old manuscript in an attic, a trace of history from Puritan times that he was simply preserving for posterity. Of course, in the 1850s few readers were fooled by this common ruse. Why then were virtually all readers and reviewers convinced that *Fragments* was a genuine memoir and not a work of the imagination? Perhaps they could not be expected to note the historical inaccuracies that made scholars like Raul Hilberg dubious from the start. But they should have been informed enough to question why the Germans would allow a small child to remain unsupervised in a children's barrack in Majdanek; or why they would then send him to another camp, presumably Auschwitz (though, as mentioned earlier, only identified by Wilkomirski after publication), where once more he would not be gassed on arrival but allowed to live. Most perplexing of all, why did readers and reviewers not consider the evidence in the text that they were faced with a contrived narrative, where certain scenes and images prepare for subsequent ones, composed by a writer with considerable descriptive talent and a keen eye for drafting grotesque details of the horrors of the Holocaust?

Before we turn to this textual evidence, I should mention another reason why I believed that *Fragments* was an invented story and not a memoir. We will probably never know what kind of internal ferment drove Wilkomirski to offer as his own experience the painful imagined journey of a very young child during the Nazi era, but the decision is not without literary precedent. During my initial reading of *Fragments* I kept having the uncomfortable feeling that I was wandering through familiar terrain. The theme of a young boy separated from his parents, plunged into repeated atrocities, losing his voice and after the ordeal ending up in an orphanage was not a unique refrain, and only a few moments of reflection led me to realize where I had heard that literary chord before: in Jerzy Kosinski's novel *The Painted Bird* (with whose German translation, as we now know, Wilkomirski had long been acquainted). Although *The Painted Bird* appeared as fiction, one of Kosinski's biographers reports that until the last moment his editors were divided about whether to issue the book as a novel or a memoir.[5] Kosinski had been telling friends for years that many of the episodes that ended up in the novel were autobiographical, and when I interviewed him for a television documentary in 1968, he told me that what happened to him during the war was *worse* than what happened to the boy in the novel. This was untrue, since during the war Kosinski had been in semi-hiding with his parents in several small Polish villages under an assumed name (the real family name was Lewinkopf). Moreover, Kosinski had told Elie Wiesel, who reviewed *The Painted Bird* for the *New York Times,* that he was not Jewish, another lie. Throughout his life Kosinski wove tales about his past and his identity in a pattern that sheds considerable light on the subsequent behavior of the man who calls himself Binjamin Wilkomirski. Kosinski once told me that he never read reviews of *The Painted Bird;* in a few days a thick envelope arrived from him marked "special handling" containing dozens of reviews of the novel in several languages. He once called to cancel a talk he was to give at my college because (he said) he had had a mild heart attack and his doctor had warned him not to travel. After a week his companion (later his wife) phoned to say that he was coming to Cambridge to give a lecture at Harvard Law School and wondered whether my wife and I could join them for dinner. When I inquired about his health, she said it was fine — certainly no hint of a heart attack. Apparently both he and Wilkomirski subscribed to the belief that every existence could be a fabrication invented by its own author. Kosinski's biographer asks of him, and we might well apply the question to Wilkomirski: "Did Kosinski know the truth and consciously embellish it, or had he lost the ability to distinguish between the real and the products of his imagination? Or is there some intermediate state? . . . A thorough pursuit of the answer must include a careful examination of the concept of truth."[6] And, one might add, the concept of fiction.

The similarities between *The Painted Bird* and *Fragments* cannot be accidental; I would go so far as to argue that the latter could not have been written had the former not existed first. Images of graphic physical excess abound in both texts, forming a unifying structural principle, along with episodes designed to rouse in the reader a combination of horror and disgust that simultaneously attracts and repels, what we might call the fascination of revulsion, a kind of fantasy-dread that one could tentatively identify as Holocaust gothic. Maybe Kosinski's publisher finally agreed that the improbabilities of fiction could justify such strategies better than the actualities of history; clearly, Wilkomirski's did not. I have found that after many readings the powerful initial impact slowly fades as the contrived violence of both narratives causes us to realize how thin is the substance of the human drama, how dependent it is for its impact on the strictly external shock of brutal gesture.

But the links between the careers of Kosinski and Wilkomirski extend beyond the boundaries of their written chronicles. In an attempt to shape reader response to his novel after its first appearance, Kosinski continued to alter the text in subsequent printings. The first hardback edition of *The Painted Bird* in 1965 contained an epilogue that briefly traced the journey of its young protagonist from eastern Europe to America, where the child would escape his nightmare memories in a landscape of possibility alien to his constricted past. Kosinski told me that his publishers asked for the epilogue to relieve the persistent gloom that dominated the work (though others have argued that the epilogue was his own idea). What is certain is that he simply dropped it from later editions. But he added other embellishments. In 1976, a second hardback edition appeared "with an introduction by the author" located at the front of the book though it was mischievously titled "Afterward." Here, with disarming candor (which others might label effrontery or guile), Kosinski blamed early reviewers for launching the question of whether the novel was a thinly disguised version of autobiographical narrative. Although for a long time he had been dropping hints about his painful trial during the Holocaust, he now announced that "Well-intentioned writers, critics, and readers sought facts to back up their claims that the novel was autobiographical. . . . Facts about my life, I felt, should not be used to test the book's authenticity."[7] One can imagine (without any evidence) Wilkomirski noticing these lines and finding in them a germ for the design of *Fragments:* if writers, readers, and critics were so eager to encounter a Holocaust account of childhood survival that was bluntly frank in its descriptions of the horrors that shaped (or distorted) a young boy's memories, he would avoid the confusion that Kosinski faced (and in part generated) by insisting on the fidelity of his report from the beginning. But he would make himself a little younger than Kosinksi's six-year-old protagonist, thus creating the safeguard of assigning to the haze of young age the vagueness of much of his reconstructed ordeal.

Indeed, Wilkomirski might have acquired much more inspiration from Kosinski's model. Kosinski believed that the success of his work required keeping not only his book but also its author constantly in the public eye. He did this in part by continuing to weave tales about his childhood to win the reader's compassion, knowing how easily such a strategy would cloud reason and paralyze the critical mind. In his "Afterward," he tells how during the war his parents were forced "almost daily to seek new hiding places, their existence became one of fear, flight, and hunger." But according to Kosinski's biographer, the Lewinkopfs changed their residence less then a half dozen times during the Nazi occupation, and lived fairly comfortably among their Christian neighbors; Mrs. Lewinkopf even kept a maid. Some of their acquaintances knew they were Jewish, others merely suspected it: but no one betrayed them. Kosinski further speaks of his parents being "constantly tortured by the possibility that their decision to send me away had been wrong," even though he had remained with them throughout the war. And finally, he mentions "their anguish as they saw young children being herded into the trains bound for the ovens," though there were virtually no Jews left in the areas where they lived.[8] Kosinski was an avowed believer in the power of prose not only to shape truth but literally to forge it, to create a probability out of mere potential and through the persuasive potency of language to transform it into lived experience. This has always been one impetus for narrative art; but Kosinski was convinced that it would work for history too. Was he putting to effective use his early training in communist-dominated Poland?

Although the personalities of the two writers were very different, Kosinski possessing a voluble and aggressive manner while Wilkomirski (at least when I met him, but other reports sustain this portrait) appearing reserved and even shy, they shared the wish to gain a status in society that would counter the anonymity of their childhood. By changing Jerzy Lewinkopf into Jurek Kosinski in order to stay alive, Kosinski was forced to practice a concealed identity, and this emerged as a need to manipulate his environment in his adult years. The impulse to control that was thwarted in his early life, leading to the creation of the boy-victim of *The Painted Bird*, became in later years and later fiction a motif for his existence. The theme of technological ingenuity that turns up in some of his novels is a metaphor for entrapping others and turning them into victims that reflect reversals of his disempowered and humiliating youth.

Much the same might be said of the boy born out of wedlock and surrendered by an ailing mother first to foster care and then to adoption, following a similar shift in identity from Bruno Grosjean to Bruno Doesseker to Binjamin Wilkomirski. But unlike Kosinski, who was determined to fashion a stronger self-image without dismissing his heritage, Wilkomirski was not driven by a desire to restore his lost self but to purge himself of undesirable identities while discarding an unheroic legacy of rejection and replacing it with a saga of suffering and misery that would quickly rouse empathy in the reader. It is worth noting that the boy in *The Painted Bird* is never identified as Jewish, while Wilkomirski adopts a Jewish persona from the start. Now that we know all the details of the process leading to this transformation, there is too much evidence of the appropriation of a history that was *not* his own and the adaptation of a history that *was* to the requirements of fictional narrative to allow us to ask any more, as many did, whether he really believed the biography that he came to invent for himself.

Those still reluctant to condemn *Fragments* as a conscious fraud and censure Wilkomirski's continued manipulations of the truth following its publication might be more easily persuaded by studying the guiltless ease with which Kosinski surrounded the genesis of *The Painted Bird* with a wall of distortions long after its original appearance. When the revised paperback version of the second edition of *The Painted Bird* came out in 1978, thirteen years after its initial issuance, it contained at the end a brief unsigned biographical essay simply called "On Kosinski," though following Norman Mailer it might more accurately have been titled "Advertisement for Myself." Although it is written in the third person, one is justified in suspecting that the author himself contributed to its text. It is a brazen attempt to solidify the myth that *The Painted Bird* is autobiographical, and that Kosinski was a surviving victim of wartime atrocities. Writing of Kosinski's childhood during the war, the alleged anonymous author uses language that more closely describes the ordeal of the novel's protagonist: "Abandoned, suspected of being a Jew or a gypsy, he fled alone from village to village in Nazi-occupied eastern Europe. . . . At the age of nine, in a traumatic confrontation with a hostile peasant crowd he lost the power of speech, and was unable to talk for over five years."[9] Not a word of this is true, nor are the following details about his family or the manner of his departure from Poland to the United States. Rather, we are witnesses to the ease with which someone who has learned the unlimited extent of public gullibility can metamorphose a synopsis of fiction into the summary of a life. For complex psychological reasons, stories of catastrophe, and particularly of the Holocaust, sometimes seem to temporarily paralyze the critical intelligence. Shrewd tacticians like Kosinski and Wilkomirski, the one aggressively, the other with consummate modesty, know how to take advantage of this situation.

Far more than Kosinski, who was after all a professional writer always thinking about his next novel, Wilkomirski carried his campaign for acceptance well beyond the pages of his book. He embraced adult strangers whom he recognized as fellow residents of a Krakow orphanage that (as was later revealed) hadn't opened until after (by his own account) he had left Poland for Switzerland. One of those adults was a woman who claimed to remember her "Binjy" from the orphanage, though subsequently she was unmasked as a total fraud who had been born in America and never been outside the United States. Wilkomirski's campaign to accumulate solid evidence to support his admittedly vague recollections in *Fragments* took on the features of a steamroller effect, with an especially strong impact in America. The United States Holocaust Memorial Museum sponsored a national speaking tour for Wilkomirski. He was interviewed at length (in English) by the head of the section for survivor testimony there, as he was at even greater length (this time in his native German) at Steven Spielberg's Shoah Foundation in Los Angeles, but neither interviewer, though ostensibly trained in the activity and presumably well-informed about the history of the Holocaust, seems to have doubted his integrity or suspected the authenticity of his narrative. The confidence man has long flourished in our culture of fakery, though his success normally has depended on the greed of his audience. In the case of Kosinski and Wilkomirski, a different yearning was at work, an intuitive awe-filled regard for so-called heroic suffering that finds little opportunity for expression in a nation so immune to the darker promptings of the human spirit. In the case of *Fragments,* sentimental response to details of childhood pain smothered the critical intelligence. The attitude of reverential silence that still greets public presentations of survivor testimony in this country does not discredit the teller or the tale, but it reveals how unprepared modern audiences remain to find a niche in consciousness for the horrific substance of such narratives. In the absence of such internal locales, fake stories like Wilkomirski's, awash in feeling, are able to flourish and gain a sympathetic ear.

The response of genuine Holocaust survivors to *Fragments* and the publicity that surrounded it raises problems of another sort. Oddly, Wilkomirski gained considerable support from the very people he turned out to have been impersonating. When the scandal over *Fragments* broke, I received several messages from Holocaust survivors asking me to intervene on Wilkomirski's behalf. One example will suffice. A woman wrote from France in October 1998, three years after *Fragments* was published and two months after the original article questioning its truthfulness had appeared:

> I would be very grateful if you could write something about the controversies related to Wilkomirsky's [*sic*] book which were prompted by some revisionist's writings in Germany and Switzerland, and are acquiring wider legitimacy even among Jewish scholars. . . . Since I belong to the group of youngest survivors, this controversy is of the utmost importance to some of us. We need your wise intervention to stop this harmfull [*sic*] discussion. In my case, I had two false identities and was never registered under my parents' name . . . It took many years and some luck to establish my true identity. Not all the members of our group are capable to do so for many reasons which are beyond their control as you may easily imagine.

The fear that one rotten fruit might ruin an otherwise healthy crop, that the effect of a single lie is to corrupt truth everywhere persists with special durability in the field of Holocaust testimony. Although I sympathize with this apprehension, I do not subscribe to it, and since I thought Wilkomirski's tale suspect from the start, I could not act on this particular request.

One of the unfortunate results of the Holocaust is that numerous child survivors are still haunted by uncertainty about their past. Some were raised in Christian families and only told later in life that their Jewish parents had been killed during the Holocaust. Others were not told by survivor parents pretending to be Christian after the war that they had been born as Jews. Thus Wilkomirski's narrative seemed to confirm the vague memories of child survivors like my correspondent, who feared that any suspicions about Wilkomirski's honesty might threaten their own fragile identities. This may help to account for the support Wilkomirski has received from various members of the survivor community, one of whom, as cited earlier, claimed that Wilkomirski must have been in the same Krakow orphanage where he had stayed after the war. The most bizarre consequence of *Fragments* to date occurred when an elderly man in Israel contacted Wilkomirski to say that he thought he recognized in the child narrator his own son, long believed to have been a victim of the Holocaust. Wilkomirski flew to Israel, and observers recorded an emotional reunion between the two. Subsequent DNA tests established that they could not have been related. Wilkomirski used this "discouraging" episode for a time as an excuse for refusing future DNA testing, the results of which might have proved far more valuable in establishing his true identity after his birth father and his mother's brother had been located.

In his "defense," one can concede that Wilkomirski never insisted on the unimpeachable accuracy of his memory. Most of *Fragments* is told from the point of view of a very young child, ranging in age from three to six, depending on which date of birth one accepts. Wilkomirski seems to remember the violent murder of his father and the wretched death of his mother from starvation and disease, but has only a dim sense of his siblings. Although the adult author recording the boy's experience has a graphic memory, the child himself has a very indistinct one, based on a limited grasp of what is happening around him. This is one of the beguiling attractions of the narrative: it unfolds in brief episodes that omit far more than they include, making the reader an active participant in reconstructing the tale. The technique allows the boy's mind to develop with an imperfect awareness of the threats in his environment; as a result, the reader responds to the mounting terrors of the text with far greater intensity than the boy. Audience revulsion at the unfolding events, and sympathy for their victim, displace the self-pity and fear that we would ordinarily expect from a reflective character. Wilkomirski pretends that he is simply too young to process the horror and violence that engulf him. By merely reporting the grim details without interpreting them, intellectually or stylistically, the author imposes the obligation of emotional response on his readers. Those who accepted the memoir as authentic may have been swept up in a drama of substitute parental protective custody, a surge of fervent rapport with the hapless orphan that exceeded a much earlier parallel response to the ordeal of Anne Frank. Of course, hers was genuine, and though many readers remain oblivious to the particulars of her miserable end, they at least know that they are dealing with a Jewish victim who did not survive.

The near-universal praise that greeted Wilkomirski and *Fragments* underlines the deep and continuing need in contemporary society to find ways of paying homage to the catastrophe we call the Holocaust. Whether this represents a surplus of compensating compassion that earlier generations were unable or unwilling to express, or a more general empathy for children all around us who continue to be victimized by atrocities, it is difficult to say.

Although there were ample historical and textual clues to rouse suspicion, reviewers and readers and prize juries (as well as Wilkomirski's publishers and agent) paid them scant attention, preferring to leave unexamined the possibility that their initial enthusiasm may have been nurtured by at least partially questionable motives. Wilkomirski's abashed Swiss agent finally hired a historian to do an "objective" analysis of the whole case, and the volume resulting from his inquiry established beyond question the fictional status of *Fragments*.

But in addition to the fruitful inquiries of the professional historian, the critical investigations of a skeptical literary analyst might and should have furnished even earlier evidence for the possible bogus authenticity of the text and the naïve not to say deceitful intentions of its author. The platitude that virtually introduces the story— " 'He who remembers nothing gambles away his future' a wise man once said"—is embarrassing in its pseudo-gravity, a clumsy variation on George Santayana's often-cited statement, today transformed into an equally solemn cliché in Holocaust discourse, that those who cannot remember the past are condemned to repeat it. The formulaic truism that follows Wilkomirski's initial remark—"If you don't remember where you came from, you will never be able to know where you are going."[10] is typical of the earnest tone in a work that substitutes style for substance and camouflages the absence of serious reflection or insight. It is no match for the crisp aphorisms that introduce the comedy of *Pride and Prejudice* or the tragedy of *Anna Karenina*. Wilkomirski's efforts to justify his explorations of a horrible past by framing it in the language of a jejune philosophical wisdom should have roused suspicions from the start.

But there are other reasons for doubting the integrity of the text. By placing the center of consciousness in the mind of a young child, Wilkomirski injects a deliberate vagueness into his story, in which fragmented episodic visions of an oppressive past become the narrative's structural principle. Veiled by lapses in temporal continuity, the boy's memory "sees" everything with only partial clarity. Here is a literature with an uncertainty principle of its own, but whatever its artistic advantages—which might have been considerable if *Fragments* had been offered as fiction—it provides the author of a supposed memoir with an excuse for limited accountability. A good example is Wilkomirski's sketchy representation of his departure from Riga, the alleged city of his birth. The language is tentative and conjectural, providing a built-in protection against possible later charges—which eventually emerged—of inaccuracies: "It must have been Riga"; "My brothers maybe"; "maybe my father" (5, 6). The reader may never realize that in this hazy universe an author is free to invent what he pleases: indecision justifies imprecision as a narrative device. A tone of "automatic writing" often intrudes, a kind of oracular language that hangs over the story like a counterfeit cloud: "I see a tiny room, darkened, the only window hung with bits of cloth" (7). The unrestricted possibilities of this method abound, which must be why I initially read *Frag-*

ments as a novel without worrying about questions of authenticity. But when history replaces the imagination as the primary context of a literary work, one is obliged to read with a warier eye. It is possible that many admirers were seduced by the emotional impact expected of fiction into overlooking the historical and psychological improbabilities that thread through the tale.

A book like *Fragments*, if it is to be convincing, must observe carefully the distinction between the child consciousness that experiences events and the adult narrator who retrieves them for the reader. Wilkomirski created problems for himself when he included the years 1938–1945 in the subtitle of the original German edition of his memoir. This fixed span enabled an observant reader to estimate the age of the child as he progressed through his various ordeals. Subsequently realizing that such precise information might compromise his otherwise vague recollections, Wilkomirski omitted the dates from the English translation. But this created additional dilemmas. Lacking specific details about age, the reader is forced to guess: a child too young would remember virtually nothing, while the innocence and incomprehension that dominate consciousness in the narrative would be unpersuasive in a child beyond a certain age.

For example, if he had really been born in 1938, the boy would have been little more than three when the Germans occupied Riga in the summer of 1941, and little more than four when he was sent to Lublin-Majdanek in 1942 (he mentions freezing in the barracks there, and it could not have been the winter of 1943 because by then Majdanek was no longer used as a death camp). How old would a child have to be in order to recall that the destination of the family's journey from Riga to Poland had "something to do with Lemberg [Lvov]" (9)? Or to be able to reflect, as the child-narrator does when viewing a peaceful scene during their flight, that "This isn't real peace. There's something wrong—it's only their peace!" (9). The text is crowded with moments like these where the adult author intrudes on the consciousness of his younger self, violating the consistency of point of view and leaving the reader to wonder at, and in unguarded instants perhaps to admire, the sudden maturity of the victimized protagonist. But the vagueness of certain scenarios and the contradictory specificity of others introduces an unintended note of travesty to the issue of authorial reliability, as Wilkomirski wrestles with the problem of maintaining reader sympathy for his early ordeal.

Wilkomirski tells us that because of his photographic memory he retains visual snapshots of episodes from the past. That assertion is legitimate enough. Sounds and physical sensations contribute to his reconstructive powers, and that too is in harmony with the nature of childhood recall. But he never satisfactorily explains the matter of language or communication, and because of this he creates insoluble difficulties for himself in the text. He admits that his native tongue must have been Yiddish, but he seems to have forgotten it soon after his painful adventure begins, though he never explains why. But in a scene in the camp when a woman guard comes to bring him to his dying mother (an episode that demands close study), the two have a long conversation. The guard obviously speaks German, but what language does Wilkomirski speak, and how do they understand each other so easily? We never learn. Fiction allows a certain suspension of disbelief, but a memoir demands an explanation. Later on, Wilkomirski appears to realize that dialogue is a crucial issue in the text. An older boy named Jankl befriends him in the barracks at Majdanek and alerts him to the dangers that threaten survival. "Jankl didn't say much," we are told. "He knew I didn't understand much of his strange dialect anyway. So most of the time he taught me silently, just by the way he moved his hands" (73). This remark is clearly designed to answer objections such as the one I have raised. Lacking language, Wilkomirski manages to communicate with his companion through gestures. The only problem is that just two pages earlier Jankl and Wilkomirski had conducted a lengthy verbal exchange about two infants who had been thrust into the barracks one evening and were found dead the next morning. A fluent discussion occurs between them about the meaning of the episode, neither participant signaling or hesitating in order to make himself understood. Only the contrived emotional intensity of some of these moments could cause the reader to overlook such obvious internal paradoxes in the text. How the author, his editors, and reviewers failed to notice them remains a mystery. Are we to conclude that the sanctity of the Holocaust as a subject, especially where children are concerned, disarms the critical faculties?

In at least one instance, a consciously planted detail betrays the spontaneity of recall that supposedly governs the unfolding narrative. One freezing night in the barracks in Majdanek the door opens and two "bundles" are thrust in and dumped on the floor near the entrance. Instantly the narrator provides us with some oddly incongruent details, given the nature of the situation: "They were tiny babies, they had their first teeth, but they couldn't talk yet" (70). I remember wondering the first time I read this why "teeth" were worth mentioning and how anyone could spot such tiny excrescences from the distance of a bunk in a dimly lit or totally dark barracks. But it quickly becomes clear that the teeth are vital to explain one of the most grisly if outlandish moments in the text. The next morning the boy discovers that the flesh has disappeared from the infants' blackened frostbitten fingers, leaving only the bare bones, "little white sticks that looked broken, each pointing in a different direction." Uniformly unenlightened, he relies on the reticent Jankl, whose "dialect" we are about to learn he cannot understand, to explain with lucid assurance and physiological expertise what has happened: "Frozen fingers don't hurt. Sometime in the night they chewed their fingers to the bone—but they're dead now" (71). It doesn't take an epiphany to perceive that without "first teeth" none of this self-cannibalizing could have transpired. One wonders at how easily such an inept piece of narrative foreshadowing, swathed in horror, could anesthetize the faculty of critical judgment and suspend one's reasonable sense of what is physically possible.

Jerzy Kosinski had been fond of using gross imagery, what we might call metaphors of disgust, to draw his readers into the world of atrocity, and Wilkomirski imitates this strategy. In the imagined world of fiction such devices may flourish, but in the literal universe of the Holocaust memoir some stricter limitations apply. The novelist may stretch history in ways that Wilkomirski may not, although in *Fragments* he seeks to exploit the advantages of both genres. He prepares us for a scatological episode by noting that in the beginning the so-called children's barrack in Majdanek was disorganized and without supervision, with no one responsible for keeping things clean. To anyone familiar with the Germans' worry about uncleanliness in the camps — not for the prisoners' sake but for their own, since they were in constant fear of disease and epidemics spreading to their own ranks — this observation is inconceivable. But the absence of control is necessary for Wilkomirski to conjure up the squalid atmosphere in which the children must live, degraded by their own filth. "When we weren't allowed for long periods to go outdoors, we had no choice but to relieve ourselves in the long passageway between the two-tiered racks of bunks. Nobody cared, nobody cleaned up, until the shit was ankle deep" (58). Although the children are already virtually suffocated by the odor of the ordure, Wilkomirski is still not satisfied with this immense quantity of excreta: "Once I had to get down from my bunk, and sank up to my calves in shit" (59). It might take a large herd of cows weeks to supply this quantity of dung, but a further detail unobtrusively sabotages the imaginative impact of this monumental human mess. When "new" barrack rules are instituted and a bucket is provided for toilet functions, the children are enjoined from using it once it is full. The results were especially torturous, we are told, "because lots of us had diarrhea" (61). This physical fact casts a dark cloud of suspicion over the prior insistence that one could clamber down from a bunk and sink up to one's calves in shit. Certainly not if it were liquid! Such textual lapses of memory may glide by unnoticed in early readings, absorbed as we are by the perpetual haze of anguish that surrounds the beleaguered narrator. But further leisurely scrutiny raises questions of credibility that the text simply fails to resolve.

Principal among these is the issue of the child's mother. Until the boy arrives in Majdanek, we hear nothing of her. We are present at the violent "maybe" death of his father, but the mother is not mentioned. In the woods of Poland the child is in hiding only with his brothers, but they disappear and he is sent to the camp alone. How did the mother get there, how does she know that her son is there too, how does the woman guard who brings them together know that they are related? Since prisoners in the camps had numbers not names, engraved on their forearms or attached to their garments, how would the guard know the boy's name? Even more perplexing, however, is *why* she would care to know it. The notion of camp guards identifying Jewish prisoners by name and treating them with compassion, however briefly, is beyond absurdity. Coincidence conspires with the ahistorical in this episode to breed an irrepressible skepticism that undermines narrative conviction. Even from the child's limited, not to say dimwitted point of view, the scenario in this incident contradicts other textual evidence. The guard initially summons the boy by asking, "Is there a Binjamin here?" (47). The boy instantly recognizes his name. Yet later, during the evacuation from another camp, when a strange woman appears to recognize him and calls out his name, he has no idea whom she is addressing. We are asked to believe that in a little more than twelve months he has forgotten his identity. We are also expected to accept, as the encounter with his "mother" unfolds and she gives him a piece of bread hidden beneath a filthy straw mattress, that in the four or five years of his life, to say nothing of his stay in Majdanek, he has never seen this food before. "What is this?" he asks, and the guard replies, "That's bread" (50). Mother and child fail to address or even recognize each other. The bread is so stale that it must be "softened" in water before it can be eaten and probably contains more sawdust than flour, yet — most preposterous of all — after swallowing it the boy speaks of "the indescribably delicious smell of bread on my fingers as I held them to my nose again and again" (51).

It is not the bread of affliction; there are few religious echoes in *Fragments*. But it doesn't take long for us to realize that the murdered father, the vanished mother, and the orphaned child are the stuff of myth, not history, drawing inspiration from literary rather than literal sources. The boy's career is a picaresque adventure devoted to the theme of abandonment and only remotely related to recognizable details of the Holocaust. He emerges from the mists of time, from an uncertain place, stripped of rather than immersed in the history of his origins. The concept of cumulative experience never exists for him. Presumably during his stay at the orphanage in Krakow after the war he had learned that food in normal quantities was once more available, yet when he later arrives at another orphanage in Switzerland he unaccountably retrogresses, behaving as if he were still in Majdanek, stuffing his mouth with cheese rinds as if the interval in Krakow had never occurred. His responses seem driven by Wilkomirski's whim at a particular moment rather than by fidelity to temporal sequence, more to prevent loss of sympathy for his protagonist/self who remains mired in the memory-space of atrocity with a kind of infantile persistence. "Why am I always the only one who doesn't understand?" (107) may be an accurate refrain for much of the narrative, but it carries the force of statement rather than insight, lacking as it does any persuasive argument for the boy's continuous state of ignorance. His immunity to external change empowers his immunity to internal growth, and although his mistrust of people may be justified, his mistrust of everything else long after his ordeal has ended often seems less dramatic than farcical. If the dating in the original edition of *Fragments* were correct, Wilkomirski would have been nearly eight years old when he entered the home of his foster parents, but he still reacts as if he were a naïve child of four or five. He is terrified by the shelves containing fruit in the food cellar because he is convinced that they are disguised bunks for a future camp barrack, and sees the coal stove as "a huge black monster" that he stares at in "deathly fear" as a smaller version of a crematorium oven (125). We are not faced by a fictionalized form of paranoia, but a life literally governed by imagery of atrocity, as if all the items of normality were nothing more than a disguised threat: "The camp's still there, they just hid it. They'll bring it out if I don't obey them" (125).

Toward the end of *Fragments* we have reentered the world of time; the text has more and more difficulty sustaining the illusion that nothing has changed and that mentally the boy still inhabits the universe of the camps. Even Wilkomirski concedes that he "may" have reached the age of ten or twelve. This means that several years have passed since the end of the war. During most of that interlude he has been living in Switzerland, yet during the entire period, he tells us, he has never seen the snow-covered Alps. Visual innocence thus conveniently accompanies his stagnant intellectual growth. We are supposed to believe that he has never seen skis either, which he calls "wooden boards," nor does he know what a ski lift is. Wilkomirski's description of the ski trip he took with his class is a poor parody of Hans Castorp's near-fatal mythologized snow excursion in *The Magic Mountain*. Here memory not nature is filled with menace, and the effort to graft one on the other is awkward and transparent. The engine that drives the ski lift becomes a "death machine," and the voyage to the peak nothing more than a journey to a grave inside the mountain. The boy and his girl companion, who suddenly appears as another child survivor, feel a motiveless terror, their mock death encounter unsupported by any graphic description or interior monologue but only by the most superficial dialogue like "We'll go together" or "It's caught up with us" (142). Stylistically and psychologically, it is one of the least compelling episodes in the narrative, as if Wilkomirski had tired of his own deceptions and decided to plod along with his weakened power of invention. The anonymous girl soon vanishes from the story, leaving behind no witnesses to verify the encounter.

Only a tendency to honor the testimony of every professed survivor, no matter how extravagant his or her claims, could have allowed *Fragments* to gain the enthusiastic support that it did. When we combine this with a host of careless readers — we will never know how many of Wilkomirski's followers were responding to his notoriety and not to his text at all — not versed in the details of the deathcamp experience, we find a vulnerable audience whose readiness to be fooled must have surprised even the author. There is no doubt that the origins of *Fragments* lie in the "traumatic childhood memories" that Wilkomirski mentions in his Afterword, but we now know that those memories have nothing to do with the Holocaust. The impulse to create a more sympathetic image of his orphaned self than the true story of illegitimacy and abandonment is pardonable, though the invention — and subsequent exploitation — of a Holocaust past is not. We cannot expect to hear from Wilkomirski an honest version of the motives and process that led to the creation of his mock documentary narrative. But other sources could contribute valuable insights into this cautionary tale of deception too quickly embraced. An embarrassed silence continues to inhibit the voices of those initially misled, and one would hope that eventually some among them will break through that barrier, not in order to construe a needless apologetics but to engage in a frank self-scrutiny that might enlighten future audiences about the ongoing dangers of fraudulent Holocaust accounts.

5

WOUNDED FAMILIES IN
HOLOCAUST DISCOURSE

Anyone familiar with the stories of Jewish children during the Holocaust understands that it is inaccurate to describe their trying to stay alive inside or outside the ghettos and camps as a collective experience. Normally childhood proceeds in an uninterrupted rhythm from infancy through youth to the vestibule of maturity. Theirs did not. The Germans assaulted Jewish identity before they attacked Jewish life, so that many children were forced to practice public concealment even when they were not literally in hiding. Those trying to pass as Christians with forged papers were under a constant strain to deny their true selves, to pretend to be who they were not: slowly an external charade became a pressing internal performance. Anne Frank could comfortably affirm her Jewishness to her diary, but those existing under a camouflaged identity had to develop daily strategies to prevent a disclosure that might imperil their lives. All dwelt in fear of discovery, though the intensity of that fear was governed by the differing circumstances of each particular child.

The archetypal account of a hidden child remains Anne Frank's *Diary of a Young Girl,* but readers who restrict their interest in the subject to that familiar work gain little insight into the complex and disruptive quality of the ordeal as it was experienced by others. Because Anne did not survive her hiding, her story remains unfinished, a narrative without sequel that omits the episodes following her capture. Even what remains of her story is atypical, because very few hidden children had the "luxury" of living in concealment with an intact family, as she did. Generations of students project their image of seclusion from Anne's chronicle, and as a result gain scarcely a glimpse of the ceaseless tension that eroded the security and contaminated the innocence of tens of thousands of other threatened children.

We can reconstruct the distress of these thousands a voice at a time, weaving a tapestry of erratic patterns that only confirm the scarcely shareable privacy of the event. "I grew up without images of my home town," says Mira B., "no streets, no parks, only the interiors of apartments and hiding places." She was born in 1938 and when she was five her parents threw her over a wall of the Bendzin ghetto, where by pre-arrangement the sister of a former family servant picked her up and took her home. Her mother said she would come for her soon; instead, her mother was deported to Auschwitz. "But the days passed and my mother didn't come," Mira remembers. "She had promised me. I felt abandoned." Her Polish rescuer dyed Mira's hair red and passed her off as a relative from the country. But as so often happened with Jewish children taken in by Christian families, Mira's potential salvation proved to be a mixed blessing. Within a year, the woman died of a sudden illness, and the five-year-old Mira was left with the woman's husband, a Polish nationalist who himself was in hiding from the Nazis. He taught her to read and write, but he was a strict disciplinarian, and when she faltered in her learning, he whipped her. (He also whipped his own children, often more severely.) "Buried beneath my childhood memories," Mira later recalled, "was a dark sense that I myself was to blame for what happened to me after I was rescued." The legacy of guilt did not easily dissipate even when normal family life was restored. Mira was more fortunate than most: both of her parents survived and returned to reclaim her. But she is not alone in reporting confusion rather than joy as a strong component of her reunion with her mother: "She looked very different. But it was clearly my mother. And yet for years after the war I had this fantasy that I was adopted, that my parents weren't my real parents."[1] When norms of being are radically disrupted, as they were for children during the Holocaust, they are not so quickly retrieved.

Indeed, as soon as we scrutinize the idea of *the* hidden child, it explodes into fragments, never to be repaired. There is no more an archetypal hidden child than there is a survivor syndrome. Those hidden "externally" like Nechama Tec, whose appearance and knowledge of Polish enabled her to circulate openly while her Yiddish-speaking parents were forced to remain indoors in the house of the Christian family hiding them faced crises different from those encountered by children hidden "internally," cut off from contact with others and daily fearing discovery. The only way to illuminate the hardship is to listen to as many viewpoints as possible while recognizing that few models may emerge to justify legitimate generalizations.

For some of those in "external" hiding, the first problem was the immediate split in one's sense of self. It was unsafe to be who you really were, and even more dangerous to forget who you were supposed to be. Nechama Tec describes the psychological impact of the dilemma: "Our daily existence was tied to two closely connected requirements: giving up our Jewish identity and silence. Giving up our identity meant playing a part, becoming someone else. The better we played the role, the safer we were. Sometimes we were so caught up in the new part that we actually forgot who we really were. Though helpful, this temporary forgetfulness was emotionally costly. For many of us, giving up our true identity created an emotional void and made us feel anxious, worried that we would never recapture our past. We also felt ashamed for giving up what had been cherished by our parents, those we loved."[2] At a time when most children were seeking to strengthen their egos, Tec and others like her were forced to shun that development. The consequences were often bizarre, as Tec describes in her memoir of the period, *Dry Tears* (1984), where she tells of having to ignore her Polish friends' antisemitic comments without flinching in order to maintain her Christian persona.

We can only speculate about what this must have done to the personality of an adolescent like Tec. "An extra layer of secretiveness," she relates, "combined with a fear of discovery, became part of my being. All my life revolved around hiding: hiding thoughts, hiding feelings, hiding my activities, hiding information. Sometimes I felt like a sort of fearful automaton, always on the alert, always dreading that something fatal might be revealed."[3] The gradual displacement of self that resulted is difficult to imagine. "A slow transformation was taking place in me," Tec writes. "It was as if in certain circumstances I lost track of who I really was and began to see myself as a Pole. I became a double person, one private and one public. When I was away from my family I became so engrossed in my public self that I did not have to act the part; I actually felt like the person I was supposed to be" (144). The ensuing guilt and embarrassment made her feel like a traitor: "It was as if, as I gave up my old self, I was giving up my family as well" (145). The question of divided loyalties is an exasperating issue that continues to bedevil interpreters of the Holocaust experience. Unlike Mira B., Nechama Tec was not physically separated from her parents during the war, so that part of the time she could reinforce the family bond and confirm her status as the offspring of a stable domestic unit. But at other moments she became the family breadwinner, even engaging in illegal black market activities, reversing her role by risking her freedom and turning into a kind of custodian for her parents.

The Tec family survived intact, but this does not mean that they faced an undamaged future. Nechama's abnormal childhood is a paradigm for the uncertainty that continued to disturb survivors after the war. Reclaiming one of his factories upon returning to Lublin, her father aroused the hostility of a dissident Polish underground group, and only through the help of a double agent were the police able to foil an assassination scheme at the last moment. The Tecs abandoned hope of resuming a regular existence and chose to emigrate. Exile from home thus followed exile from childhood, and in her adult scholarly works Nechama Tec returns to the site of her early ordeal to explore the forms of rescue and resistance that enabled her family to survive at the price of her normal adolescence.

Intact families, of course, were the exception rather than the rule. Although like Nechama Tec, Yehuda Nir speaks of missing his youth in his memoir, *The Lost Childhood,* his experience was in most ways the exact opposite of hers. In July 1941, a few weeks after the Germans occupied Lvov, the eleven-year-old Nir watched a column of men, including his father, being marched out of town. His father gave him a faint smile; Nir waved back, but couldn't catch his eye. He never saw his father again. Years later he learned that the men had been taken to a forest outside Lvov and shot. But during the preceding interval he always expected his father to return. "My father never died," he says, repeating a sentiment often expressed by survivors; "he just faded away, was carried off into nowhere. It was as if he were dead and alive at the same time. Even after the war, in 1945, when we found out that he had definitely been killed on the day of his arrest in July 1941, we continued to search for him through the Red Cross."[4] Although a fragment of the family unit remained — Nir still had his older sister and his mother — they could not resume normal life. Traditional roles disappeared; age and experience ceased to matter as what Nir termed the brutal game of survival displaced the familiar routines that had governed their existence before the war.

The notion of being alive and dead at the same time, especially as it affects the imagination of a child, is a complex but widely cited idea that emerges from Holocaust testimonies, though it has never been sufficiently studied. In a terse short story entitled "The Key Game," Ida Fink — who as a teenager survived the war moving from hiding place to hiding place with her sister in Poland — condenses the issue into a painful dramatic moment of family role reversal that explodes the notion of mutual support usually associated with the situation she depicts. The "brutal game of survival" isolates family members from each other and makes of the child in the narrative a helpless victim even before the Germans have assigned him that role. Because the Jewish father in this family appears to be at greatest risk and his three-year-old son less vulnerable, the child and his mother play a game named "searching for the key" while the father scrambles into a tiny prepared hiding place in the bathroom. The mother mimics the sound of a doorbell announcing the arrival of the Germans while the child pretends to look for the key that his mother, away at work, will have put somewhere, all the while calling out to the Germans theoretically waiting on the other side of the door that he will find the key "in a minute." Meanwhile, the father disappears into his very real hiding place. After a few moments he reappears, complaining that he needs more time, that his son — three years old, we remember — must spend more time "looking" for the key. Terror for his own safety has displaced his paternal instinct, though his wife, reminding him of that role, urges him to say something, and he mechanically intones "you did a good job, little one, a good job."[5]

The mother, more sensitive to the child's requirements, recollects her role, though her tender words of reassurance are filled with a wrenching irony rarely available to the authors of autobiographical memoirs about similar situations: " 'That's right,' the woman said, 'you're really doing a wonderful job, darling — and you're not little at all. You act just like a grown-up, don't you?' " The fictional milieu allows Fink to shift from character to character, uniting innocence and fear in a sinister alliance that ultimately confuses the meaning of each. Asked what he would say if someone were *really* to ring the doorbell, the child engages in the following exchange:

> "Mama's at work."
> "And Papa?"
> He was silent.
> "And Papa?" the man screamed in terror.
> The child turned pale.
> "And Papa?" the man repeated more calmly.
> "He's dead," the child answered and threw himself at his father, who was standing right beside him, blinking his eyes in that funny way, but who was already long dead to the people who would really ring the bell.[6]

When the Nazis violated traditional family hierarchies among their own citizens by inviting members of the Hitler youth to report any disloyal sentiments they might overhear in household conversations, they redefined the bond linking children to their parents. They substituted a covenant between the citizen and the state for the earlier domestic intimacy, offering a form of psychological security that members of the organization could share with each other. For their Jewish victims, however, the Germans provided no such new external support. The child in Fink's story — obedient, bewildered, terrified, and betrayed — leaves us, like himself, searching for a non-existent key, the solution to the enigma of how the self should behave when threatened by extinction. The very effort to preserve identity by staying alive, or helping to keep someone else alive, simultaneously erodes identity, leaving a painful legacy to be unraveled when and if normal family relations return. Childhood is not the time for children to be custodians of their parents.

Many witnesses who were children during the Nazi era speak in their testimonies of their dilemma without offering any evidence that it has ever been resolved. Rachel G. was born in Brussels in 1934. In 1941, after the

Germans had occupied Belgium, she was taken by a priest to a convent, where she was hidden along with several other Jewish girls. On her seventh birthday, her father paid her a secret visit there; she never saw him again. Her name was changed, and during the war she was moved from convent to convent, finally being sent to a childless Catholic family living near the French border. They raised her as their own daughter, and she stayed with them until the liberation. Meanwhile, she learned that her parents had been deported to Auschwitz. Interviewed as an adult, Rachel G. speaks of the dual heritage from her childhood. She remembers both a loss and a transfer of security. Shifting loyalties at an impressionable age, she gradually "forgot" her real family and established emotional ties with whoever was protecting her at a particular time. Between the ages of seven and eleven, as the memory of her parents grew dim, she adapted to the life of a Jewish girl pretending to be a Catholic.

What emerges gradually from this testimony is the story of *two* childhoods, the one Rachel G. was born to but lost, and the one she experienced with adults other than her parents. On one hand, she is pained by having to describe the childhood she *had* rather than the one she missed. The absence of the latter leaves a lacuna in her sense of self. But when she is asked how she feels about being Jewish as an adult in 1981, since she was raised as a Catholic, she replies that every time she sees a priest or a nun, she wants to kiss them. After the war, the couple who had been taking care of her wished to adopt her, but Belgian law required a ten-month waiting period, to insure that neither of her parents had returned from the camps. She was sent back to her original convent and attended school there as a Catholic. Just before the waiting period was up, a nun entered the classroom one morning and looked at her. "I knew my mother was outside," says Rachel G.

But instead of describing a joyful reunion, she speaks of her resentment toward her mother for having abandoned her. "I didn't want to go to my mother," she says. "I was too angry at her." For the moment, she recalls, she was hostile, even though her mother had been in Auschwitz for three years. Her father did not return. She admits that it took her a long time to realize that her parents' decision to send her into hiding is what saved her life. Yet she speaks more fondly of the nuns than of her mother and the dual parental experience remains locked in her memory, leading to a heritage of divided allegiance that she cannot escape. She has raised her children to be Jewish, but they are confused by her confusion, since she speaks so enthusiastically about her childhood among the priests and the nuns.[7]

Even more disconcerting is the narrative of Menachem S. Born in 1938, he remembers moving to the Krakow ghetto in 1942 when he was four, then to the Plaszow labor camp the following year. In 1943, when he was five, his parents bribed a guard to allow the little boy to leave, tied a scarf around his neck, and pinned on his jacket an address, which turned out to be a brothel. He realized years later that the choice was a shrewd one, since his parents hoped that among the many women there one might be willing to care for him. His mother gave him her high school ID card, "just in case you need to recognize me when we come," and they promised to return for him after the war. He then offers a harrowing tale of how he drifted around as an "adult" rather than a child between his fifth and seventh years among street gangs of orphaned or abandoned children, staying in the brothel at night until things got "hot" and he was taken in by a family in an outlying village. His parents survived as Schindler Jews, and in the summer of 1945 they came back to Krakow to seek him out. But when he sees them they are so emaciated that they are unrecognizable. His father, more than six feet tall, weighs 88 pounds and his teeth are hanging loosely from his gums. They are utter strangers, and for a long time, he says, he addressed them as Mr. and Mrs. S. He makes no mention of joy, relief, pleasure, or satisfaction at finding the family unit intact. For five years he was unable to manage a transition back to normal reality. Instead, when he tried to become their child again, his pain intensified, and his life disintegrated into a constantly recurring cycle of disabling nightmares.

The coda to his testimony is filled with a rueful amusement. When his first child was born, he went on a buying spree, spending hundreds of dollars on toys, many of which, like electric trains and a bicycle, were inappropriate for a newborn infant. Perplexed at first by his behavior, he only slowly realized after his wife's prompting that he was buying the toys for himself, in commemoration of the buried youth that he never experienced. But it took him twenty-five years to speak about this to his children, because he feared transferring to them the anxieties that continued to plague him. Wounded memory operates like a parasite on the consciousness of some adult survivors long after they have passed beyond adolescence; it ambushed Menachem S. repeatedly after his liberation, culminating in a return to the traumatic time of his deprived childhood at the very moment when he became a father himself.[8]

The temptation to romanticize the experience of hiding or passing and to idealize the rescuers is very strong, especially among those who are reluctant to face the boredom and the terror, to say nothing of the shattered identity that afflicted the youthful victims. It is a view bearing little resemblance to the truth. Anne Frank inadvertently contributed to the myth when she wrote in her diary, "I look upon our life in hiding as an interesting adventure, full of danger and romance." It is unlikely, had she survived, that she would have confirmed this sentiment after Westerbork, Auschwitz, and Bergen-Belsen. Edith H., a Dutch contemporary of Anne's, spent three years in hiding in Holland, partly alone, partly with her mother, and partly with both her parents. All survived, together with a sister who was in hiding elsewhere. Yet she complains bitterly in her testimony, "I didn't have any life from thirteen to [nearly] seventeen," mourning her lost childhood, a time she can never recover.[9]

Marcel Proust's internal pursuit of the traces of lost time is based on a remembered chronology, not its abnormal disruption. The difference between the two is neatly captured by the testimony of Ely M., another Dutch Jewish girl who between the ages of ten and thirteen hid in various Christian homes, separated from her family. "You hear so often," she says, "that people start a new life and so on and how wonderful everything is. I personally . . . my feeling is that the after-affects are very hard for a child. When you come out of the war you don't want to be with your mother because you're estranged from your mother — for me it was [that way]."[10] Contrast this with the nostalgic pleasure with which the initial narrator of Proust's *Remembrance of Things Past* summons up the memory of his mother's leaving her party downstairs to come up to give him a goodnight kiss. The absence of such memories in the consciousness of so many child survivors leaves a void that the passage of time cannot replace. Philosopher Charles Taylor argues that the "full definition of someone's identity . . . usually involves not only his stand on moral and spiritual matters, but also some reference to a defining community."[11] But Ely M.'s "defining community" is a dead community, or more precisely, an exterminated one. In addition, during her years of hiding any stand she might have taken on moral and spiritual values were secondary to the more urgent need of keeping herself alive, a process that forestalled any meaningful expression of those values. We will never understand the concept of "wounded families" until we appreciate the feeling of estrangement that Ely M. speaks of, an estrangement not only from her mother, but also from her own youthful self.

This sense of alienation appears with great intensity in the testimony of Zezette L., born in Belgium in 1929 and hence only ten years old at the outbreak of the war. She begins by saying, "looking back on my family, and fully cognizant of the fact that you idealize what you don't have any more, we had a very good family." But the notion of a good family disintegrates in a single night after her parents receive a notice to report for "resettlement" and decide instead that they must go into hiding. There were no rules, however, for how "a good family" should behave under such circumstances. Zezette L.'s parents placed her in a Catholic convent under an assumed name and told her to forget them and to act like the other Catholic girls. They sent her brother to hide with some Trappist monks. But during the Easter vacation in 1943, the old family feeling reasserted itself, with disastrous consequences. Human responses are often fatal in an inhuman milieu such as the one that reigned during the Nazi era, but decent people were loath to embrace this principle at the time, and many students of the period today continue to resist its unsettling impact. Simply put, Zezette and her parents missed each other, and since the convent was closed for the holiday they resolved to take a chance and have her come to their hiding place. And to celebrate the reunion, since it was Easter Sunday, they thought it might be safe to go on an excursion into the country. Zezette L. never knew if they

71

were followed or deliberately betrayed, but while returning to the hiding place they were arrested by the Gestapo and sent to the transit camp of Malines. Whether they were reckless or brave remains a debatable issue, but in any event their yearning for normality proved to be their undoing. A few days later, they were deported to Auschwitz. Zezette L. was barely fourteen years old.

Upon arrival, Zezette joined those selected for work in the camp while her mother was sent to the left. The daughter's solemn comment is that she hopes her mother didn't know where she was going. She saw her father twice in the camp, but they didn't dare speak; soon after, he vanished among the mass of anonymous dead. We are now left to imagine how a fourteen-year-old orphan might experience the daily ordeal of Auschwitz. An odd dialogue ensues between interviewer and witness, the former needing to put a hopeful twist on the experience and the latter determined not to falsify her account. Asked what she did in Auschwitz, she replies, "I was dehumanized." Asked if she ever sang songs in Auschwitz, as some child survivors report, she stares with disbelief at the question. She has *no* good memories. Her most vivid one is of standing at roll call, endlessly, in the freezing cold, ill-clad, often barefoot. Asked if she had any friends, she responds that she was alone and could never understand people remembering their "friends" at Auschwitz. Maybe older people had them, she says, but not younger ones like her. "You had no one to rely on?" "No." "You had no one to relate to?" "No." "Did you have a sense of being entirely alone?" "Yes." And then she adds, "Strangely enough, I still do." Reluctant to accept the dismal vision that Zezette L. depicts, the well-intentioned interviewer persists: "Some people say that the only way to survive Auschwitz was if you had someone." Reply: "I had no one."

What Zezette L.'s testimony demonstrates is the futility of searching for an exemplary version of the adolescent experience in a place like Auschwitz. We must respond to a series of solo performances rather than a musical ensemble or chorus, prizing each "aria" separately and noting nuances of difference rather than similar or overlapping tones. There is little to celebrate about a tainted childhood, even though it need not necessarily lead to a poisoned future. Zezette L. is saddened and even embittered, but she is not disabled by her memories. When she reached the age at which her mother died, she returned to Auschwitz to say *Yizkor* for her parents, the memorial prayer for the dead. "One can talk about it in a positive way," she concludes, "if, if, if, if . . ." — but she never finishes her sentence, as the whole negative burden of her testimony intervenes to silence her latent thought, or wish. She makes a conscious statement about wanting to live for the future, but when she describes her ruined childhood, she does not say "I live with it," but "It lives with me." Her verbal assertion about living for the future stumbles against her dismal account of the past, and her consciousness of this tension is a vivid sign of her desire to restore continuity to her life. She has had the number on her left forearm erased not as a gesture of rejection, which is impossible in any case, but to cast off the public identity of Auschwitz survivor decreed by her oppressors and to choose her own useful role in the present. She balances the dignity of her current mode of being against the memory of a dehumanized adolescence. How well she manages internally is a private matter whose misgivings remain hostage to reminiscence and time.[12]

The issue of transmitting the effects of wounded childhood from one generation to the next is difficult to assess. Neither the Fortunoff Video Archive for Holocaust Testimonies at Yale University nor Steven Spielberg's Shoah Foundation has taken detailed testimony from children of survivors. There is no large archive of such accounts comparable to the thousands that are available from the parents. Perhaps the most powerful statement about this potentially burdensome legacy appears in Carl Friedman's brief novel *Nightfather*, whose survivor protagonist cannot suppress the need to recount his camp experiences to his wife and three young children. He does this relentlessly, changing the most benign occasions into analogues of his horrendous past. His memories of the camp surge uncontrollably from inexhaustible depths to wash over his children's lives and leave a touch of pollution in their wake. When the children ask their mother what is wrong with Papa, she replies succinctly "He has camp." Unfortunately, the "illness" is contagious, like the recurrent tuberculosis he brought back with him. The only cures are silence and love, but the former eludes him and the latter, which he genuinely feels, is contaminated by the narrative impulse that, fifteen years after the war, he still cannot suppress.

Friedman's narrator is one of the victims of this impulse, the middle child of unstated age but surely less than ten who tells her family's story with a mixture of innocence and dismay. She captures the confusion of any child trying to make sense of the anecdotes that survivor parents brought back with them after their release. Her father's influence is infectious in ways that reflect the spread of disease rather than enthusiasm; because the naïve children never really understand this, however, the reader is left to feel and interpret the devastating impact of family interaction. The young narrator is shrewd enough to realize, as she says, that "Max, Simon, and I are different from ordinary children," but she has no audience to help her digest the significance of her father's camp legacy. An episode in school illustrates the hermetic dilemma that engulfs her:

> "A man flying through the air!" The teacher smiles, as she bends over my drawing.
> "He isn't flying," I tell her, "he's hanging. See, he's dead, his tongue is blue. And these prisoners have to look at him as a punishment. My father is there, too. Here, he's the one with the big ears."
> "That's nice," says the teacher.
> "It's not," I say. "They're starving and now they have to wait a long time for their soup."
> But she's already moved on to the next desk.[13]

73

Overheard memories pursue the children throughout their daily adventures. On a drive into the country, the father suddenly stops the car by a ditch backed by a grove of trees:

> "Great woods," he says. We nod. He clicks his tongue. "Great woods to escape into. So thick and so deep. They'd never find you there, not the ghost of a chance."
>
> He gets out. We stay where we are and watch him jump across the ditch. The woods swallow him up.
>
> "What's he up to?" Simon wonders nervously.
>
> "The usual," I say, "just a little escaping." Simon winds down the window. "I can't hear a thing. Only birds."
>
> "You can't hear escaping," I whisper. "Escaping has to be done very quietly, otherwise it doesn't work."
>
> "And what about us?" he says.
>
> I start sucking my thumb. What does Simon know about such things? (26)

Unlike most memoirs, fiction gains its effects through omission as well as inclusion. In *Nightfather* we are obliged to brood on an anxiety of influence that has nothing to do with the literary tensions that Harold Bloom wrote of. The narrator suffers from a different stress, an insecurity resulting from the net of reminiscence that her father inadvertently casts over *her* when contending with his own unpacified past.

The narrators' siblings are also caught in the father's web of remembering. "Tell us a story," the younger brother Simon asks his father, a legitimate request from the world of normal childhood. Instead, he is barraged by a series of barbarous anecdotes about camp life until Simon grumbles with disappointment "That isn't a story. . . . That really happened." But there is no escape into the imagination from the Holocaust; its reality ruthlessly pursues its survivors, and indeed all future generations, with a pitiless intensity that Friedman captures in her narrative:

> "Do you want a story then? Okay, have it your way!" says my father. "Little Red Riding Hood is walking with her basket through the woods. Suddenly a vicious dog jumps out of the *Hundezwinger* [dog kennels]. 'Hello, Little Red Riding Hood, where are you going?' 'I'm going to see my grandmother,' says Little Red Riding Hood. 'She's in the hospital with typhus.' "
>
> "No," says Simon, "that's not how it goes." (33–34)

But for the children of this father, that *is* how it goes. His past penetrates their thinking and taints their games. The narrator buries her toys in a garden so that when the SS come for *them* they will not take the toys too. One day the narrator finds her brother Max sitting on a chair in the kitchen, his socks on the floor and his bare feet in the refrigerator. His reply to a request for an explanation is: "I want to know what they feel like when they freeze" (114). "I want to be one of them," he adds. "And you can only be one of them if you're half-starved or if you've had typhus. Being gassed a bit helps, too. Anyway, you have to have suffered damage in some way" (115). This is the same son who earlier had broken under the strain of his father's dogged reminiscences and exploded at him, "Just don't keep coming to me with stories about that stupid camp of yours. It served you right!" (83)

The tension between the need to fuse the horrors of their father's Holocaust past with the rhythms of their daily lives and to repel that past in order to make way for the future remains an insoluble dilemma for the children in Carl Friedman's vignettes. All Holocaust victims were sentenced to die, but many of those lucky enough to survive found themselves sentenced to live, a prospect that few were prepared to face with unruffled poise. The anguish of the heirs to atrocity in Friedman's *Nightfather* resides less in the words of her child characters than in what remains unsaid. The art of her fiction complements and complicates the more straightforward statements that energize the memoirs and testimonies that we have examined. As the forms of representation of the experience of children during and after the Holocaust grow more imaginative, greater demands are made on the interpretive faculty. Finally, a total collaboration is required between audience and artist if the implications of a work are to be reclaimed from the silence that surrounds it.

This is acutely true of a story like Isaiah Spiegel's "Bread," where the author's controlling irony adds a dimension usually missing from testimonies or memoirs. Even the decrepit hovel where the Glikke family lives seems to grieve beneath its sagging roof. A few Chekhovian details, like the glimpse of "black, shiny military boots" in the street below, remind us that the setting is not an impoverished shtetl but a Jewish ghetto in German-occupied Poland. The room in which the mother, father, and two small children spend their days and nights has a tiny chamber adjacent to it, with a triangular opening cut out of the wall facing the street just outside the ghetto; the prior Christian owner used it as a roost for his homing pigeons. Occasionally a pigeon, driven by instinct, wanders into the space, free — as the trapped Jews are not — to visit and depart from its ancient domicile. Because life here is as sparse as the language that describes it, the family members are forced to parody their former roles. The father prays and studies Torah all day wrapped in his *tallis* and *tfillin*, the mother is still the breadwinner, and the children, confined to the apartment, play games at imagining a more ample life. But because they are all slowly starving to death, we know that something is amiss: their efforts bring few tangible results. The tension between the habit-driven behavior of the characters and the slowly unfolding misery of their lives creates a mis-en-scène that the reader enters in medias res, without context or explanation. The impact of the action, such as it is, requires us to adapt to a basic principle infusing much Holocaust literature: the illusion of real life in the text is invariably burdened by a specific historical reality that both inspires and limits the experience it seeks to imagine. Spiegel, who survived the Lodz ghetto and Auschwitz, expects from his audience sufficient knowledge to allow them to reconstruct the motives and exploits in his painful tale.

The family in "Bread" is atomized, not as we would anticipate by internal conflict, but by external circumstance. Although the children are not literally hidden, they might as well be, since the uncertain security of their surroundings makes the streets of the ghetto unsafe for them. Hunger hangs over their lives like a sinking shroud, eroding the spiritual fare that would have nourished them in earlier times. Now, the Sabbath candelabras lie forgotten on a rubbish heap in a corner of the room. The dreary and unrelieved misery of each hour redefines individual roles as physical need usurps customs of kinship and traditions of parental responsibility. With a few brushstrokes Spiegel sketches a world where one can be old and young, caring and selfish, mired in wretched reality and floating on the wings of illusion simultaneously. Of the twelve-year-old Avremele and his little sister he says: "The few ghetto months have completely transformed the children. They are no longer children, but ancients, on whose faces sit the ravages of heavy years."[14] The condensed style of the fiction focuses the readers' attention on the dual nature of Holocaust childhood as more diffuse testimonies and memoirs cannot.

On one hand, Avremele and his sister are "terrified and lost," frightened of their father as he stands motionless next to the wall praying, "stony, frosty, a dead man" (252). On the other, when the mother leaves to search for food and the father presumably to join some fellow Jews in communal study, they sneak into the tiny chamber and are changed into anxious youngsters playing a desperate game of make believe. They peer out of crevices in the wall, he at a bakery below, located just outside the wire fence of the ghetto, and she at an adjacent shop with a "pure white cheese" (254) in its display window. The moment is like a painting within a painting as illusion temporarily displaces fact by allowing the imagination to escape from its limiting frontiers. But Spiegel's ironic control of the locale divides perception into two fields of vision, the one without and the one within. Both have substantive content, but neither is accessible to the other. In the absence of options, one may pretend that they are, but readers responsive to the "real" reality of the story, its Holocaust center, feel only the pain of deception when the narrative ostensibly defends the power of illusion and indeed, in a kind of parable, the value of the artistic imagination itself: "Through the crevices the eye can escape into a free, uncaged world. Just a single leap over the fence and you are free. You can go wherever you want: to the courtyard, from the courtyard to the open fields, from the fields to the forest, further and further. The childish eyes float out of the little chamber" (255). Such celebration of romantic yearning may have force in a normal setting, but in the environs of a Jewish ghetto under German rule it mocks with bitter irony any notion of visionary liberation or physical escape.

In "Bread," art loses its struggle with history as vision submits to the control of literal experience. As Polish customers slowly procure the rolls and loaves in the bakery, its window empties of its tempting provender. The episode records the imagination present at its own gradual demise, depleted of content as the bare shelves come to match the barren anguish of the family's starving days. The children finally fall asleep; the memory of what they saw cannot satisfy their empty stomachs. Fatal hunger is a subject that needs no literary embellishment. The central horror and pathos of the tale expands this theme, as one day the father, unable to resist an uncontrollable urge, eats the portion of his children's bread that the mother is saving for the next meal. When she discovers his misdemeanor, she sentences him to a redefinition that even his overwhelming sense of shame cannot reduce: "A father, eh? A fa—ther, is it? *Murderer!*" (253). And what are we to call a ravenous parent who steals food from his famished children? The language of familiar moral discourse fails us here, but the thesaurus of German atrocity or Jewish anguish offers no substitute. In facing the dilemma of judgmental silence and the absence of legitimate vocabulary, the reader is required to conspire with the author to enter a universe of collapsed values where faith brings no solace and moral chaos reigns. Adrift in a landscape without signposts, what can one do but grieve at this dismal loss of moral direction?

There is no closure for such a narrative, certainly no avenue to restored unity. When the father is rounded up in the ghetto streets and vanishes one day, the mother is distraught as any wife might be but is left with meager chances for mourning. Spiegel ends but does not conclude his story with a bizarre ritual that cannibalizes the father's death when mother and children "joyfully eat to their hearts' content" the whole loaf of bread that would have belonged to him. Is it payment for his shame? A ceremony of absolution? That night the family remnant sleep peacefully, and the son dreams of the father "praying over a large thick book" (256). It is tempting to think in terms of reconciliation, but our consciousness of the story's momentum leads us to believe that hunger has been appeased only as a brief reprieve. The next day it will resume its cruel regime, and misery will return. The climactic irony of the story is that the failure of art to find a final form for a reality that cannot be contained is also its supreme triumph. Spiegel's understated tale of a family driven beyond the limits of human endurance by its very existence also affirms the limits of art to translate Holocaust experience into aesthetic expression.

Artistic expression nonetheless makes available to the imagination a dimension of Holocaust atrocity that few other kinds of writing can achieve. The most extreme type of wounded childhood is one that ceases to exist: the murdered child is the ultimate challenge to a parent *or* writer seeking a language for verbal dirge. We end our survey of the evolution of this problem by comparing two ways of expressing atrocity-induced domestic grief, one a naked and unconfined emotional outburst of an inconsolable father and the other a disciplined poetic response that through metaphor and imagery finds a way of creating for one unnatural death in the Holocaust a fitting natural domain that invites our migration to its imaginative universe. One requires some context to appreciate its impact; the other, like most poetry, creates its own.

Early in September 1942, Chaim Rumkowski, the Elder of the Jews in the Lodz ghetto, announced that the Germans had demanded for "resettlement" 20,000 residents, to be chosen from the ill, the elderly, and all children under ten years of age. Although no one said so, almost all inhabitants suspected the fatal results of such selections. Some rushed to the Office of Statistics, hoping to change their children's birthdates, but the cagey Rumkowski had closed the premises. Other parents tried to hide their children so they would not be caught in the roundup. One father, while seeking a safe haven for his older daughter, hid his younger one in a big laundry basket, hoping she would not be noticed. But she began to cry, was discovered, and was taken away. The impact of wounded childhood was then transferred to the parent, who decided to give spontaneous witness to his sense of bereavement on the back of some soup kitchen records that were found and published as "A Father's Lament" after the war. In a chaotic outpouring of grief, guilt, confusion, and despair, his words register one extreme of response to the fate of victimized children during the Holocaust:

> Yesterday I lost Mookha, my sweet little daughter. I lost her through my own fault, cowardice, stupidity and passivity. I gave her up defenseless. I deserted her, I left the 5-year-old child, did not save her, and I could have done it so easily. I killed her myself because I didn't have the least bit of courage. I have blood on my hands, the guilt is mine because I did nothing to rescue her. . . . I am broken, I feel guilty, I am a murderer and I must atone, because I won't find peace. I killed my child with my own hands, I killed Mookha, I am a killer, because how can it be that a father deserts his own child and runs away? How can he run away and not save his own child? God, if you are watching, please punish me. In what name Did Mookha lose her life? Why did she have to perish?

The anonymous author, who presumably did not survive (one is inclined to add with some hesitation "mercifully") then switches from Yiddish to Hebrew and intones a version of *Yizkor*, the prayer for the dead: "O Merciful One, keep her soul forever alive under thy protective wings. As the Lord is her heritage, may she rest in peace, and let us say Amen."[15] And who can fail to echo his wish?

Yet a careful scrutiny of the father's language reveals how helpless he is to evoke his distress without summoning up a familiar vocabulary that by now an informed reader should recognize as irrelevant to his situation: courage, stupidity, passivity, save, guilt, atone, punish. They all assume a freedom of action, a sequence of act and consequence that was simply impossible beneath the net of Nazi atrocity, fed by the same illusions that Isaiah Spiegel punctured in his dreary account of ghetto life. The prayer at the end is more a desperate entreaty than an assured plea, since the work of the German murderers continues in spite of it, and no Divine Power intervenes to block their bloody task. Of course none of this diminishes the legitimacy of the father's grief, though his idiom may thrust it back into a framework more conventional than its overpowering impact deserves. A certain tension remains between the horrific nature of the event and the anguished speech that expresses it.

But it is muted, as emotion spills over the margins of restraint and drowns any chance for a controlled elegiac tone. We end our critique of family ordeals during the Holocaust with a Yiddish poem by the renowned poet Abraham Sutzkever, who through the discipline of his art finds fresh resources of language stripped of sentiment and redemptive hopes. Sutzkever's wife gave birth to their first child in the Vilna ghetto. The Germans took the infant and poisoned it. "For My Child" is a summoning back to memory of the murdered son and a requiem that rejects the consoling ritual so prominent at the end of "A Father's Lament":

> Was it from some hunger
> or from greater love —
> but your mother is a witness to this:
> I wanted to swallow you, my child,
> when I felt your tiny body losing its heat
> in my fingers
> as though I were pressing
> a warm glass of tea,
> feeling its passage to cold.
>
> You're no stranger, no guest,
> for on this earth one does not give birth to aliens.
> You reproduce yourself like a ring
> and the rings fit into chains.
>
> My child,
> what else may I call you but: love.
> Even without the word that is who you are,
> you — seed of my every dream,
> hidden third one,
> who came from the world's corner
> with the wonder of an unseen storm,
> you who brought, rushed two together
> to create you and rejoice: —
>
> Why have you darkened creation
> with the shutting of your tiny eyes
> and left me begging outside

in the snow swept world
to which you have returned?

No cradle gave you pleasure
whose rocking
conceals in itself the pulse of the stars.
Let the sun crumble like glass
since you never beheld its light.
That drop of poison extinguished your faith —
you thought
it was warm sweet milk.

I wanted to swallow you, my child,
to feel the taste
of my anticipated future.
Perhaps in my blood
you will blossom as before.

But I am not worthy to be your grave.
So I bequeath you
to the summoning snow,
the snow — my first respite,
and you will sink
like a splinter of dusk
into its quiet depths
and bear greetings from me
to the frozen grasslands ahead —

Vilna Ghetto January 18, 1943[16]
(trans. by Seymour Mayne)

Searching for a less than natural metaphor to evoke an unnatural event, Sutzkever chooses a bold cannibalistic image to convey the father's hunger for reunion with his slaughtered child. Perhaps no other way existed to purge usual responses from the urgency of a devouring love. The strategy also supports the violent conjunction between birth and death that is the subject of the poem. The merger of being with non-being that threatened all victims in the ghettos and camps left a legacy for survivors of finding a way of entering the deathworld of family members less fortunate than they, and this is precisely the challenge before the poet in this poem. The metaphor of "swallowing" suggests a fusion of identities that will not only allow the child to gain a foothold in the world of the living, but the father to share with the child its universe of death, "to feel the taste / of my anticipated future." Here even time and eternity seem to unite, rejecting the chronology that usually separates the two. But the need for convergence is only a longing and a goal, as the poet is left "begging outside / in the snow swept world" to which the newborn infant has returned.

80

Once again art signals its limited success through ultimate failure as it strives to express what is physically impossible, a "deathlife" that might allow the blood of the dead to flow in the body of the living. A "darkened creation" resists the poet's efforts to reverse its rules, and in the end he must accept the painful divergence of death that bequeaths his child "to the frozen grasslands ahead." There, as a messenger from and to the living, it will await the consummation of its father's fate. But for the reader, the tensions in the poem between poison and sweet milk, or a crumbling sun and the summoning snow grant a kind of rebirth through art to the murder victim, since at every reading the child returns from "the frozen grasslands" to engage the imagination once again in this narrative of a terrible loss. It may be a tainted immortality, but Holocaust art can promise little more. In the paradox of such aching beauty, the family ordeal during those years of anguish achieves its purest form of expression.

6

MEMORY AND JUSTICE AFTER
THE HOLOCAUST AND APARTHEID

Holocaust survivors do not need to search for memory; memory searches for them, and there is no escape from its clutches. As for justice . . .

In the summer of 1964, I sat in a courtroom in Munich, Germany at the trial of SS General Karl Wolff, Chief of Heinrich Himmler's personal staff and liaison to Hitler's headquarters. With his mild demeanor and conservative business suit, Wolff bore no resemblance to a man charged with capital crimes against humanity. As the commanding officer of all SS forces in Italy in April 1945, he had gained much credit with the Allies by meeting secretly in Switzerland with Allen Dulles, head of the OSS, and agreeing to surrender his troops about a week before the official end of hostilities. Fifteen years passed before a state investigator turned up incriminating evidence that led to his arrest, interrogation, and indictment. One of the charges against Wolff was that he had requisitioned trains to carry Jews from the Warsaw ghetto to their death in Treblinka. On this particular day of the trial, a young prosecuting attorney asked Wolff if he had ever been in the Warsaw ghetto. Wolff said he had not. The prosecutor then produced evidence to prove that Wolff was lying. When the chairman of the court, whom we would call the judge, asked the witness what he had to say to that, Wolff replied, "*Herr Vorsitzende, ich bin ein alter Mann* [Mr. Chairman, I'm an old man]. I can't remember everything." The chairman leaned forward and responded, "Herr Zeugnis [Mr. Witness], if *I* had been in the Warsaw ghetto, I would never have forgotten it!"

This brief dialogue between memory and justice surprised me at the time, because I was still a naïve entrant into the field of Holocaust studies. Today as a confirmed cynic in certain Holocaust matters I would have expected Wolff to lie, as Albert Speer lied at Nuremberg, as Viktor Brack lied at the Doctor's Trial, as ex-Grand Admiral Karl Doenitz lied after his release from prison when he swore on his word of honor to historian Saul Friedlander in a personal interview that he knew nothing about the extermination of Jews. The pursuit of justice in a court of law when the issue is war crimes provokes lying as much as and perhaps even more than it elicits truth.

Two days after leaving Munich, I found myself at another trial, this time in Frankfurt, at the so-called "Proceedings against Robert Karl Ludwig Mulka and Others," in which twenty-two Auschwitz guards and functionaries were charged with various forms of complicity in murder. Because of the unexpected public interest, the site of the trial had been moved from the Palace of Justice to a large dance hall above a local restaurant. There I watched the antics of defendants mocking witnesses, heard the audible snickering of former officials such as Oswald Kaduk and Wilhelm Boger, who seemed to regard the judicial system as a circus performance, and was astonished when the state's attorney ordered the detention of a *witness,* a former SS Hauptscharführer in Auschwitz who was *not* on trial, on suspicion of having given false testimony. From the point of view of the criminals, it was clear that there was no strong bond joining memory to truth.

The uncertainty of memory, however, does not cripple the need for seeking justice. In spite of the behavior of the accused, survivor testimony repeatedly shocked and humbled the court and the audience, opening up the question of how or whether the quest for justice could possibly appease the authors of these narratives of loss. On one of the days I attended, an elderly Haifa businessman told of his arrest and deportation to Auschwitz in June 1944 together with his family. He was the sole survivor. As he reported, his wife, his two children, his mother, his sister and her two children, his brother, his mother-in-law, and his sister-in-law were killed. His testimony, as transcribed by a journalist who was present, leaves us wondering whether the effort to link memory to justice is nothing more than an illusion fostered by our own wish to believe that we can somehow compensate for the anguish in his words:

> The witness is overcome by memories. He has gathered from reading the papers, he says with great emotion, "that these gentlemen [the accused] did not know what was happening in Auschwitz." They, the prisoners, even the children, knew it after only two days there. Then he reaches into his coat, takes a small picture out of his wallet, holds it out to the judges with a stiff arm, and says tearfully:

"Children scratched their arms and with their own blood would write on the barracks walls, as did my nephew, this child here, who wrote: 'Andreas Rapaport—lived sixteen years.' "

The boy had called out to him: "Uncle, I know that I have to die. Tell my mother that I thought of her up to the very last."

"This little boy, he knew that he had to die after two days. He did not know that his mother had already been gassed."

The witness named Glück [meaning "happiness" or "good fortune" in German] sits there, shriveled and exhausted. He sits at the table in tears, in his hand the picture of his nephew Andreas Rapaport.

Slowly Judge Hofmeyer continues to turn the wheel of the trial.[1]

It may be a wheel of justice for some, including the embarrassed members of this German audience who shift uncomfortably in their seats, but one has the sense that the crushed witness has just been racked on a wheel of pain. This is the moment most vividly etched on my memory, and I remember feeling as I looked around the courtroom that perhaps the wrong person was in the witness stand.

At the time, the Auschwitz trial was the longest judicial event in German history—it lasted nineteen months and spread over three calendar years. By the end, the cases of two of the twenty-two accused had been separated because of ill health and the court acquitted three, not because they were found innocent but (as Chairman Hofmeyer carefully announced) because of the lack of sufficient evidence to convict them. Other sentences ranged from time served in detention while awaiting trial, to life imprisonment at hard labor.

Before the announcement of the verdicts and sentencing, the defendants were allowed to make closing statements. Bernd Naumann, the journalist, sums up the tenor of their words: "They try to convey the impression that despite everything they are upright men. . . . The men speaking here—most of them—consider themselves innocent, almost as innocent as the victims of Auschwitz. Like those victims, they see themselves the pawns of a relentless fate. They checked their consciences with their superiors and it would seem that they never needed them again, never requested their return. Not to this day." Naumann's wry irony seems not far from the mark when we examine some of these statements. Robert Mulka, former adjutant to the Auschwitz camp commandant, declares, "I put my personal fate and that of my unhappy family confidently into the hands of the court, convinced that you will weigh and take into consideration all the circumstances which at the time brought me into my conflict situation. Thus all that is left to me is the expectation and plea for a just decision." Mulka is found guilty "of complicity in the murder of 750 persons each on at least 4 separate occasions" and is sentenced to 14 years at hard labor. Former Gestapo member Wilhelm Boger of the Political Department in Auschwitz says "During the reign of National Socialism I knew only one mode of conduct: to carry out the order of superiors without reservation. I did not ask to be stationed in Auschwitz. Today I realize that the idea I believed in spelled disaster and was wrong. It has been said here that I conducted rigorous interrogations as ordered. But what I saw at the time was not Auschwitz as a terrible extermination site of European Jewry but the fight against the Polish resistance movement and Bolshevism." Boger is found guilty "of murder on at least 144 separate occasions, of complicity in the murder of at least 1,000 persons, and of complicity in the joint murder of at least 10 persons" and is sentenced to life and an additional five years at hard labor. And as a last example, former camp Gestapo member Klaus Dylewski insists, contrary to the evidence of several eyewitnesses, "I was not on the new ramp in Birkenau, nor have I ever set foot in the Auschwitz crematory. I wish to state quite emphatically that I did not shoot a single person in the yard of Block 11." Dylewski is found guilty "of complicity in joint murder on at least 32 separate occasions, 2 involving the murder of at least 750 persons." He is sentenced to a total of five years at hard labor.[2]

As Dostoevsky knew, Western-style justice was not designed to explore matters of conscience or the psychology of violent crime. In *Crime and Punishment,* Raskolnikov confesses to murder without ceasing to believe in his right to have committed it. In *The Brothers Karamazov,* a jury convicts the innocent Dmitri of the murder of his father, while those culpable of joint complicity in the old man's death are neither charged nor tried. Ironically, the court refuses to believe Ivan's last-minute confession. But Dostoevsky is writing fiction and is very careful in these novels to make the murder victims more loathsome than their killers. He sidesteps the issue of the victims' anguish because paying too much attention to that would injure his efforts to parody the law and its quest for justice. He realized that questions of remorse, confession, repentance, penance, reconciliation, and what some people call "healing" were matters for an extra-legal venue, since it is in the judicial interest of most criminals, especially murderers, to deny guilt. For Dostoevsky, crime was an illness of the soul. The victims were already dead, and none of them was named Lazarus. The task of society, and specifically of the Church, was to raise from the realm of death the moribund spirit of the transgressor, who after acknowledging his misdeeds would rehabilitate through suffering his stained soul and rejoin the human community.

But how much of this was in the mind of Mr. Glück as he sat in the witness box in Frankfurt and unraveled his despair? Imagine the unlikely scenario of Wilhelm Boger rising from among the accused and apologizing to Mr. Glück for having destroyed his entire family. Would this be a self-serving gesture or a sign of genuine remorse? How does one measure the difference? And even if one could, whose needs does such an apology serve? Would this be a voluntary admission, or a response to his perilous situation? Might some on the edge of the catastrophe be inspired to conclude that except for adverse circumstances the criminal was indeed "almost as innocent" as his victims? Why would it have taken nineteen years to arrive at this moment of spiritual insight? I doubt whether Mr. Glück considered any of this as he gazed at the accused, several of whom as I recall appeared more amused than contrite at his testimony.

The kinds of questions raised by Dostoevsky, the ones rejuvenated in some circles seeking closure today, can only flourish in an atmosphere that under-rates or skirts the dilemma of the victims, both dead and alive. Whatever the merits or limitations of the endeavor in South Africa during the 1990s to establish a healing paradigm (for "political" crimes) of admission and rec-onciliation, I do not believe it sheds any light on the problem of memory and justice after the Holocaust. To my mind, there would be a kind of impiety in imposing on the murder of European Jewry an ancient vocabu-lary of the Christian dispensation, as if pouring old words onto new blood could change the eternally unpardonable nature of the transgression. Yet this was precisely the goal of the Truth and Reconciliation Commission (TRC), if not to change the crime (since the dead cannot be restored) then the attitudes of its surviving victims and agents. While the trials at and after Nuremberg were conducted in a secular setting following principles of judi-cial procedure (some of them uniquely developed for the specific crimes being tried there), the hearings in various South African cities were inspired by church doctrine. Observers have agreed that the presence of former Archbishop Desmond Tutu cast an aura of Christian piety over the proceed-ings, allowing the facts of history to be viewed through the prism of religious belief.

Although pragmatic realism in the political arena was often cited as the reason for the less than stringent proceedings, the articles of faith defend-ing this approach sound neither pragmatic nor realistic. The notion that the forgiveness of sins makes a person whole has doctrinal rather than practical evidence to support it. When the dialogue on the issue is grounded in a "prejudiced" vocabulary whose premises prejudge the outcome, then the results will be determined not by what we hope to know, but by what we know to hope. Bishop Tutu's conviction that we must turn our backs on the awful past of apartheid because life is for living ignores one of the graver revelations for students of Holocaust survivor testimonies: that after such catastrophes, life is also for dying, that, as we shall see, many rebirths are accompanied by a "redeath" that lingers in memory and consciousness long after the scarring event.[3] Why this should be different for those who en-dured apartheid no one has taken the trouble to explain. Neither Bishop Tutu nor the members of the TRC offer any evidence that the impact of wounded memory is subject to choice, that suppressing it is like turning off a switch and sending it into oblivion. Familiarity with Holocaust testimonies certainly would have taught them otherwise. One of the limitations of the TRC hearings is their habit of generating dogmatic conclusions as if they were empirically established truths.

For example, Bishop Tutu's assertion that "you can only be humane in a humane society" may be an inspiring ideal, but it sidesteps the simple fact that most societies, including under apartheid, are driven by a constant tension between forces of power and forces of compassion, and that the presence of the one does not necessarily diminish the zeal of the other. The hope of eliminating that tension by replacing punishment with forgiveness and thereby placating what many consider a morally justifiable hatred of evil seems nothing more than the dream of an inflexible optimist. It may or may not be true, as Bishop Tutu continues, that "If you live with hatred and revenge in your heart, you dehumanize not only yourself, but your community,"[4] but as he presents it this is only an abstract idea, not an accurate description of the psychological condition of those who have lived through atrocity, whether committed against themselves or against family members. Holocaust survivors may continue to despise those who betrayed, brutalized, or murdered their kin, but anyone who hears their testimony (or knows them personally) will instantly recognize that such feelings, while (understandably) affecting their outlook, have not succeeded in poisoning their lives.

Although opposing views emerged from the TRC hearings, they are only slowly becoming substance for a searching dialogue. More important than a reconciliation between criminals and victims is the need for some kind of resolution between Bishop Tutu's theoretical position on the destructive consequences of hatred and the testimony of a "colored" witness whose daughter died under apartheid: "I have not been able, despite extensive therapy and counseling, to shed the anger, rage, guilt, feelings of revenge and helpless desperation at the system that allows murderers to escape punishment." It would be small consolation to this father to hear from Bishop Tutu that "However diabolical the act, it did not turn the perpetrator into a demon."[5] This sentiment, certainly legitimate in most instances, appears in a work called *No Future without Forgiveness,* but it begs the question of how to build a society based on a principle — the "latent" humanity of the criminal — that may fail its own test as often as it succeeds.

The premise behind the Nuremberg and subsequent war crimes trials was the idea that the accused were guilty of monstrous deeds (which may indeed have been committed by normal men) that differentiated them from their accusers and the rest of the international community. Unlike the judges at the later trial of Adolf Eichmann in Jerusalem, the judges at Nuremberg were less concerned with a quest for truth than in establishing a framework for justice. The Christian doctrine that Bishop Tutu espoused in South Africa would have found few sympathetic ears there: "We had to distinguish between the sinner and the sin, to hate and condemn the sin while being filled with compassion for the sinner." Condemning mass murder while pitying the mass murderers would have reduced the Nuremberg trials to a travesty. Why then did this not happen in the various locales of the TRC inquiry? One reason lies in the willingness of victims and their families to allow themselves, at least in the public forum of the TRC proceedings, to be driven by a program carefully crafted to shape the quality of their presentation. One commentator reported: "Commissioners never missed an opportunity to praise witnesses who did not express any desire for revenge. . . . The hearings were structured in such a way that any expression for revenge would seem out of place. Virtues of forgiveness and reconciliation were so loudly and roundly applauded that emotions of revenge, hatred and bitterness were rendered unacceptable, an ugly intrusion on a peaceful, healing process."[6] We are left wondering whose truth the full disclosure of victims was supposed to serve. Maintaining the dignity of the witness is not always the best test of the value of his or her testimony.

Many years ago I heard American writer Katherine Anne Porter declare, in response to a radio interviewer's question about her feelings toward German war criminals, that we had a moral obligation to hate both evildoers and their evil. At the time it seemed a harsh and even pitiless judgment, but today I understand much better the origins of her sentiment. Against the current opinion of the TRC that forgiveness cleanses the self while hatred consumes it, Porter would have argued the opposite. Her attitude inspires us to ask why the measure of the humanity of those guilty of atrocities such as apartheid should be their responses — full disclosure, whether or not accompanied by apology — *after* their acts of violence rather than their failure or refusal to curtail them *before* they were committed. The greatest danger of using the TRC as a model for reconciliation after atrocity is that it tempts us not to face evil but to overlook it, to minimize its reflection of chaos and to redefine it as a kind of transitory damage. Lacking in the discourse about reconciliation is any systematic challenge to Bishop Tutu's charge that one consumed by rage, even at a terrible wrong, is somehow reduced in his humanity. Such language sanctifies without exploring its own premise; few Holocaust survivors are "consumed" by their hatred of German crimes and criminals under the Nazis, and even fewer express it in a manner that we might call "rage." Moreover, that hatred does not "reduce" them, and indeed may be said to offer an avenue of release, since it acknowledges the inhumanity of their oppressors, thereby restoring a sense of their own humanity.

The use of imprecise language to define personal or institutional response to atrocity has caused other confusions. Just as there are venial and grave sins, so too there are minor and major misdemeanors, and labels like *retributive* and *restorative* justice do not help to clarify the distinctions among them. Nor does equating justice itself with a form of vengeance; such verbal agility simplifies complex issues by easing naming into a form of definition. Although the text of Martha Minow's *Between Vengeance and Forgiveness: Facing History after Genocide and Mass Violence* offers a balanced discussion of its theme by addressing multiple and differing points of view, the polarity in its title supports an inference that could easily mislead the potential reader. Similarly, the TRC may have been less careful in observing such distinctions in its public pronouncements than in its actions, since it has in fact been chary about granting amnesty and willing to see those guilty of the severest transgressions sent to prison. Although its compassionate intentions have been celebrated, one observer has found that "the vast majority of victims and their families opposed the amnesty of their perpetrators, and the vast majority of perpetrators offered little remorse, regret or apology"[7] It is far too soon to examine the long-range impact of restorative justice, of which forgiveness is a central part, on the memory of atrocity. But this statistic makes clear that the TRC's stress on forgiveness over punitive justice, whatever its origins, may not be an expression of the popular or the victims' majority will.

Much is to be learned about the motives and hopes of the TRC from a particular volume that tries to pierce the façade of one of apartheid's principal murderers by searching for the humanity hidden behind his mask of evil. The premises inspiring Pumla Gobodo-Madikizela's attempt are once more implicit in her title: *A Human Being Died that Night: A South African Story of Forgiveness*. The author, a black South African clinical psychologist, served with Desmond Tutu on the TRC's Human Rights Violations Committee, hearing explicit and painful testimony from numerous victims and members of their families. Thus she was intimately acquainted with the kinds of crimes that the subject of her study, Eugene De Kock, was guilty of. De Kock, know as "Prime Evil" by many South Africans, was the chief of the apartheid government's secret security unit and thus the deviser of and a participant in various schemes to silence (that is, to kill) its enemies. He was serving two life sentences when Gobodo-Madikizela visited him in prison in Pretoria. Her express intention was to learn—indeed, to teach herself, since at one level the deepest thrust of the volume is autobiographical—how we can "transcend hate if the goal is to transform human relationships in a society with a past marked by violent conflict between groups."[8] How better to test this challenge than by interviewing one of the leading killers of the apartheid regime? This was not an unprecedented mission, since Gitta Sereny had visited Franz Stangl, the commandant first of the Sobibor and later of the Treblinka deathcamp, several times in prison (where he too was serving a life sentence). Her book, *Into that Darkness* (which Gobodo-Madikizela mentions in a footnote), records the results of those encounters, though her project was to understand rather than to achieve reconciliation with her subject. Stangl minimized some of his actions and denied others, though unlike de Kock he could not sullenly grumble that he was a scapegoat for his superiors. Even though it is unlikely that any of the defendants executed at Nuremberg had ever killed anyone, several were nonetheless convicted of crimes against humanity and hanged. The most Stangl could say in his own defense is that he was an instrument and not an agent of criminal activity.

De Kock says much the same thing, but adds the complaint that those who authorized his deeds — and today argue that they knew nothing about them — are allowed to return to society uncharged. Since it is utterly impossible to imagine trying SS camp guards and members of the German mobile killing units in the Soviet Union for capital offenses after the war while allowing Goering and other Nazi leaders to go free for the sake of social and political unity, we are left to ask why it was so easy to do this in South Africa, especially in the absence of expressions of remorse, without causing a national uprising or at least a public outcry.

One answer is the image of the self inaugurated by the members of the TRC and adopted by Gobodo-Madikizela in her study. "If showing compassion to our enemies is something that our bodies recoil from," she asks, "what should our attitude be to their cries for mercy, the cries that tell us their hearts are breaking, and that they are willing to renounce their past and their role in it?" (15). The makings of a myth begin to unfold before our eyes, since language like this starts not from an empirical base but from a desired goal, which looking backward initiates assumptions that then declare themselves authentic reflections of observed reality. Is the author's search for "remorse and forgiveness after mass atrocity" (15) an expression of a personal wish to create an image of society consistent with particular religious views? Or is it a workable response to a tense political situation? The clash between what is desirable and what is possible gives birth to rival discourses and contrary emphases. In Holocaust testimonies, witnesses eschew ideals and discuss what memory permits them to manage. The political goals of the TRC may be pragmatic, but its ambition for victims (and in some instances their oppressors) is to undervalue internal stress for the sake of a higher ideal. Only a particular way of talking about the world of apartheid could make this possible. For example, to label the gruesome cruelties of its torturers and killers "human rights violations," as Gobodo-Madikizela and others do, is to cloak these brutalities in a civil language that makes the culprits and their crimes seem tolerable to an unwary audience.

The author objects to legal procedures that focus "too heavily on particular individual crimes" (60). Although she does not defend de Kock's acts, she thinks that in his case the law "paid little or no attention to the question of structural and systemic crimes" (60–61). But how is one to charge or prosecute in a court of law or in the public imagination "official policy" as the principal agent of atrocity? By transferring the burden of responsibility for evil to a disembodied institution, we shift much of the guilt for its consequences away from human agents to impersonal forces that lack moral (or immoral) impulses. To revert to our earlier analogy: this would be like blaming Nazi ideology for burning or burying Jews alive and partially justifying the subsequent claims of the accused that they were simply carrying out orders. In the case of the Holocaust, this would be a parody of the truth since explicit orders from Berlin were not required to authorize various individual SS and Wehrmacht excesses against their victims. Neither the TRC nor Gobodo-Madikizela seems willing or able to acknowledge evil as a positive source of fulfillment for those who embraced it not because it was commanded but because it supported their private inclinations. Such an admission would nullify the process of forgiveness and reconciliation, which can only rise from the premise that evil is an absence of good and not an independent power at work in human nature.

Just as the effects of the ghetto and camp experience on those who outlived its assaults could not be meaningfully explored until enough time had passed to allow extensive interviews with surviving witnesses, so, too, the full impact of the apartheid ordeal on its victims and their families cannot be appreciated until testimony can be heard in a setting with no expectations beyond the honest recounting of current feelings and the events that inspired them. It is simply too soon to tell what the ultimate influence of the apartheid ordeal will be on those who outlived it. Efforts to evaluate the situation too early can only lead to unrepresentative suppositions about criminals and their victims, based on one or two examples among thousands, such as the following from Gobodo-Madikizela's volume: "When perpetrators express remorse, when they finally acknowledge that they can see what they previously could not see, or did not want to, they are revalidating the victims' pain — in a sense giving his or her humanity back. Empowered and revalidated, many victims at this point find it natural to extend and deepen the healing process by going a step further: turning around and conferring forgiveness on their torturer" (128). The creeping sentimentalism of this passage may be appealing to those who believe that seeds of virtue deserve more moral attention than flowers of evil, but it offers no evidence other than its own statement that it is valid as a general principle of psychological truth. Auschwitz survivor Jean Améry would have noted wryly that such a position could have been taken only by someone who had never been tortured. I have never encountered a single Holocaust testimony supporting the conclusion that compassion for those guilty of mass murder "is deeply therapeutic and restorative" (129). Those witnesses might argue, following Améry, that only someone insensitive to the gravity of the offense could laud "the desire to be rehumanized by someone who has denied our humanity" (129). Judging from the reports of hundreds of Holocaust survivors, "dehumanization" is an ephemeral condition, triggering a subtle and complex internal division which almost all of those formerly victimized handle through a process of mental partitioning that allows the revival of their humanity without doctrinal guidance. Resentment continues to exist — some would insist that this is a *healthy* response to their past — but it rarely prevails. Phases of memory and not canons of belief release them from the permanent grasp of atrocity and allow them to balance the demands of the normal now and the abnormal then.

Gobodo-Madikizela marvels at the response of two widows — her only specific examples—who publicly embrace and forgive the two policemen who murdered their husbands. She admits that these were atypical responses, but would like to offer them as models for other victims to follow. However, she reveals the deepest source of her inspiration, and that of the TRC, when she confesses, "It is hard to resist the conclusion that there must be something divine about forgiveness expressed in the context of tragedy" (95). The very use of *tragedy* to describe the excesses of apartheid restores human agency to the victims of the ordeal, while the suffering it caused recedes to the orderly domain of Christian faith. But categories of morality and religion such as conscience and redemption, once considered the sturdy bases of civilized Western society, do not thrive in the blighted Holocaust domain. This is a gigantic obstacle for those who seek to rebuild harmony using the same discourse that prevailed before the years of atrocity. If we have the courage and stamina to accept the disheartening news that the Holocaust has disturbed forever easy dreams of human solidarity, then we must seek continuity in a different language, a different attitude, conceding finally the abysmal failure of the prior ones.

Normally we assess information about the past in order to establish a coherent record of how one deed or event leads to another, how, for example, the Nuremberg Laws of 1935 led seven or eight years later to the ashpits of Auschwitz. But as we tread the twisted path leading from one to the other, we stumble across so many barricades and detours and broken bridges that it no longer seems legitimate to call the trail we are following a highway. The ghastly reality of the Holocaust has created a ghostly legacy, one that few Holocaust witnesses would have difficulty recognizing: we no longer imagine physical space and time merely as conditions for progress. When the Holocaust is the subject, the issue of human advance cannot be separated from the idea of a total defeat of the human. One of the most striking features of Holocaust testimonies is the sense of unreconciled *rupture* that emerges from them. The victimized who survived have no cause for celebration because the context of their survival is the death of so many others. They are relieved to be alive and committed to the future and simultaneously haunted by the memories of an unparalleled ordeal of disintegration. To numb those private memories for the chance of embracing an improved communal destiny would be to abandon an authentic burdensome insight for the sake of a hypothetical social and psychological ease. In any event, if we listen carefully to the voices of the victimized, we learn that muting the past is not a matter of choice.

I know of few writers who have better captured the paradoxical duality that governs memory, time, and space after the Holocaust than Auschwitz survivor Charlotte Delbo. In a little known prose-poem called "Kalavrita of the Thousand Antigones," Delbo chronicles the fate of the 1,300 men of the Greek village Kalavrita in the Peloponnesus. In December 1943, while the women and children were locked in the town schoolhouse below, the

Germans took the men to the top of a hill and shot them in a reprisal action against local partisan activity. It is one of the many unrecorded atrocities of the war, and Delbo's tribute is as unfamiliar as the unpublicized crime itself. "Kalavrita" is an artistic expression of Jürgen Habermas's conviction that the Holocaust had "changed the basis for the continuity of the conditions of life within history."[9]

The work begins:

> Right here. This is the path they took. Here it is.
>
> This isn't the earth they trod. These aren't the stones that rolled loose under their feet. This isn't the dry bed of the stream. That was their real path. The real path is underneath the steps, these steps of gold-colored stone cemented down over the real path to preserve its course, to prevent wear to the real path.
>
> The steps of gold-colored stone lead up to a monument. There, up there on the hill.
>
> The real path led them to their death, there, in that ravine on the side of the hill. . . .
>
> The men were climbing the hill. They walked in silence. Soldiers shouted to them to speed it up.
>
> They took a long time to get up the hill. For the women who were locked inside the school, who were hugging their little ones to their bosoms, it seemed they were taking a long time to get up the hill. For the men who were climbing, the path was short. They knew, the men did, that at the end of the path lay death. The way from here to death is always short. And even if the climb was hard, the time was short to them.

For the doomed, ascent is descent and the passage of time signals not its continuity, but its end. The gold-colored stones may soothe the ordeal for later visitors to the site, but for those who were there, like the grieving wife-mother narrator of "Kalavrita," nothing intervenes to placate the pain of her loss. Delbo's lines do more to recapture the inner momentum of the atrocity than the monument on the hill that few tourists ever climb to see. By the end of "Kalavrita," we have experienced a redefinition of time and space, suspended in an eternal duration where the memory of injustice displaces both. The prose-poem ends:

> Farewell, traveler.
>
> When you walk through the village to get back to the road and head homeward, look at the clock on the public square. The time the clock shows is the time it happened that day. Something in the clock's mechanism broke with the first salvo. We haven't had it repaired.
>
> It's the time it was that day.[10]

I would suggest that something in history's mechanism also broke with the first gassing, and that the clock of progress has never been repaired because the gas affected its inner workings and made it irreparable. "It's the time it was that day" is not a formula but a stunning insight into the nature of durational time as it emerges in the testimonies of Holocaust survivors. An event like the Holocaust enjoins us to inhabit several temporal worlds at once.

Delbo's idea of parallel types of memory anticipated by nearly a decade the relatively recent discovery by neurobiologists suggesting that "the brain has two memory systems, one for ordinary information and one for emotionally charged information." The former is easily forgotten, but the latter is engraved on the brain and retained as what I would call a kind of scar tissue in regard to episodes of the Holocaust. In a typical American response, however, researchers speculate that the "emotional memory system may have evolved because it had great survival value, insuring that animals would vividly remember the events and circumstances most threatening to them" and hence use them to protect themselves in the future. The researchers interpret what Delbo intuitively identified as "deep memory" as nature's primitive version of what we in our greater sophistication have transformed into the slogan "Never again!" But whether neurological excitation by atrocity is triggered by a motive to learn for the future or more neutrally simply to "implant information more firmly in memory" is open to dispute.[11] Still inconclusive is the problem of how we separate what we need to believe from what is true.

The inclination to find some way of appeasing deep memory (which recalls atrocities like Kalavrita) by easing it into the more amiable milieu of what Delbo calls common memory (which remembers ordinary events) stems from the discomfort caused by witnessing the constant tension between the two. Delbo's nightmare visions in her Auschwitz memoir of death fastening onto her until she seems really to be dying repeats a theme that surfaces often in survivor testimonies. Today modern technology has made the violent death of others such a familiar sight that it threatens to become part of our own deep memory too, even though we haven't personally experienced it. We do not become victims or survivors ourselves but are offered a chance to share with them the feeling of how abnormal dying can intrude on normal living with such visual and psychological force that confession and forgiveness can do little to erase our sense of the ordeal.

Perhaps it is time to offer a concrete illustration of how this works, to see a witness recalling an episode of atrocity not by dredging it up from a psychically numbed memory but by reproducing it in a rush of revival as vividly as if she were still experiencing the details she is presenting. Rose M. was nineteen at the time, married (because her father thought that a husband would be better able to protect her), living in the large family house with her parents, a little brother, and about a dozen other relatives of various ages. The Germans are rounding up Jews in her village, so the family is spending the last few nights hiding in the woods, but this night it seems safe and they return to the house. They have a concealed bunker, but they are tired and feel that it is too late for an *aktion*, so except for the mother and the mother's half-sister, they all sleep in their own beds. In the middle of the night, they hear trucks stopping outside:

> And when we heard the trucks stop, my husband jumped out from the bed and he looked through the window, he saw a lot of Germans jumping from the trucks with machine guns, so he start yelling, he start yelling, we should go out, and we start jumping through the windows, through the doors, and they were already around our house, and they were shooting, they were shooting. My husband was the first one to run, and he run first, I run after him; then mine father and mine little brother, they woke up, and they jumped through the window, and my father fall right next to the window, he fall. And my brother run after me. So my brother, he always told me in case of something we had to run. Near our house was a big house a Polish family was building, and there was a lot of things, like wood, and things where we could hide under and escape, if we had to escape and fast. So mine brother used to go in all the time to look there where he could hide if he want to hide. I was never there, I wasn't interested in it. So this time I run in and mine brother run after me. When I was running, I was running, the machine guns was shooting, I was around the bullets, all around bullets, I heard them all around me. And I went in in this house, and my brother run right after me, right after me, and he fall, he fell. And I heard right away "Ahhhhh" [imitating her brother] like this, and bullets. And after the bullets I heard this last voice from him. And I hide under the lumber.
>
> Interviewer: You were alone.
>
> Rose M.: Alone. Yeah. In a nightgown. Under the lumber. And I looked at this German like I'm looking now on this television, and I saw him, and he was with a machine gun like this, and he was yelling "One more dog running! One more dog running!" And he was shooting all around, the walls and the floor, the ceiling, every place bullets. And I was laying there, and I said to myself, "Maybe, maybe I should go out and end this misery," because I couldn't take it no longer, I should go out and end it. And then a voice of me said "don't you do it, don't you do it. No way. That's what he wants, he wants to shoot you." And I lay there. And then he went out, and I heard so much screams, God, my God, so much screams, the dogs and screams, human screams, and bullets. It was just like a war zone, exactly like a war zone. . . .
>
> And then when the war stopped, middle of the night everything got quiet, and I fall asleep first, and then when I woke up I heard everything so quiet. I went out from there and it was already morning, I saw already outside the light a little bit, like five o'clock in the morning. And I went to see who fall and I looked, and I saw my brother laying in a puddle of blood, my little brother stretched out just like this [tilting her head back and extending her arms, cruciform fashion], a puddle full of blood.[12]

In a surge of sentence fragments the witness recreates the confusion, the violence, and the terror of the moment, then mimes the climax of her inner vision, the image of her brother's corpse, becoming for an instant that corpse herself. This intimacy with the violent death of another is intrinsic to Holocaust discourse, where the opposition between living and dying vanishes forever and the autobiography of a life coexists with the biography of a death. Incidents like these transform the Truth and Reconciliation Commission's goals into a piece of nostalgia—though we should not underestimate the power of nostalgic memory to reclaim an illusion of restored harmony that most of us find desirable. Whether it is also authentic is a separate matter entirely.

In this instance, as in so many others, the question of justice is moot because the criminals are anonymous. I do not believe Rose M. mentioned the word "justice" once during the six hours of our interview. Who among these faceless murderers could she charge? Of the thousands upon thousands who were guilty of Holocaust atrocities during World War II, a few hundred were put on trial, and most of them were eventually released. Even Kurt Franz, the last commandant of Treblinka, was quietly freed from his life sentence in Germany several years ago. But from the punishment of deep memory there is no liberation. As long as that situation prevails, have we a right to speak of amnesty and reconciliation, to say nothing of forgiveness, for those who imposed this unspeakable burden? In addition to her father and brother, Rose M. watched a cousin and her sister-in-law and five children being murdered by the Germans in a garden potato cellar where they were hiding. Her husband, who escaped to the forest, was subsequently caught by the Gestapo and executed. Some months later she gave birth unattended in a ghetto to a baby boy, who strangled in its umbilical cord because she was too weak to assist it. Her story is by no means unique. But she has carried on with her life, married, established a new family, and managed well, though it is evident from her testimony that her old, dead family has also carried on with her. I suspect that she would have smiled at the proposal that there is an antidote for deep memory named *healing*. The notion that she might embrace and forgive the men who murdered her father and brother, could they be found, in order to reclaim her humanity seems preposterous. Her demeanor and attitude offer not the slightest support to Gobodo-Madikizela's contention that, "If memory is kept alive in order to cultivate old hatreds and resentments, it is likely to culminate in vengeance and in a repetition of violence" (103). Such memories have no motive. They are "kept alive" and refuse to die by their own forlorn gravity. Rose M. subsists on a self-prescribed placebo called *endurance*, and I think the only fitting tribute to her ordeal, and the ordeal of others like her, is that we try to do the same.

7

WITNESSING ATROCITY:
THE TESTIMONIAL EVIDENCE

Some time ago I was asked to examine the videotaped testimony of a woman who survived Theresienstadt, Auschwitz, Flossenbürg, and Mauthausen. Her father was Jewish, her mother was not. She said the Gestapo tortured her mother in 1938 after the November pogrom in an effort to force her to divorce her husband. According to her account, she worked in a Jewish hospital in Vienna, and was deported to Theresienstadt, along with its patients, in October 1941. Since she claims that she was present during the Red Cross visit to the camp, she must have been there at least until June 1944. Soon afterward, she was deported to Auschwitz, where she remained for nine months. Upon arrival she and the women with her were put in a room that was a combination shower and gas chamber. "I was lucky," she insists; "the Germans decided to turn on the water instead of the gas." Five times in four and a half years, she continues, she found herself in similar circumstances, and on each occasion her luck held out — water instead of gas. From Auschwitz, she informs us, she was sent to the main camp at Flossenbürg, where she worked in an aircraft factory. Finally she was evacuated, partly by death march and partly by boxcar, to Bergen-Belsen, where the camp was so overcrowded that her transport was sent to Mauthausen instead. There she lived in a barrack at the base of the quarry. On May 5, 1945, SS guards drove her and her fellow prisoners from their barrack up the steps of the quarry to a gas chamber, where they stood in the sunlight awaiting their fate. Only the arrival of American troops at that very moment rescued them from a horrible death.

The survivor tells her story with such stubborn authority that the well-intentioned but ill-equipped interviewer finds her own few hesitant queries stifled by the overbearing manner of the witness. Subsequently, an enterprising filmmaker prepared a documentary based on this testimony, featuring the survivor. Distinguished members of the community were invited to its premier performance; it was later shown on local TV. No one protested. No one questioned the accuracy of her account. At last, a handful of fellow survivors raised some objections to members of a Jewish organization about her trustworthiness, and that led them to contact me. I should mention that the woman has been speaking about her Holocaust experiences to schools and synagogues and other audiences for nearly 20 years, and it took all that time before someone raised doubts about the details of her story.

How was that possible? I would venture the following: the reverence with which survivors are often held — generally against their wishes — mesmerizes critical consciousness and induces an awed public to accept whatever it hears. How else can we explain the universal acclaim with which Binjamin Wilkomirski's fake memoir, *Fragments,* was received, not only in America, but also around the world? Somehow we continue to perpetuate the illusion, reinforced by Peter Novick's *The Holocaust in American Life,* that Americans are preoccupied with and thus well-informed about the event. Yet if I were to present my opening paragraph to a general audience, not a specialized group, I would wager that fewer than two or three in a hundred — if that many — would find anything to dispute. Incidentally, inquiry at the Department of Documentation in Theresienstadt reveals that a woman of the interviewee's name arrived there from Vienna on June 26, 1943, and was sent via transport to Auschwitz on October 10, 1944. In addition, the Information Center at Flossenbürg confirms that only two days later, on October 12, 1944, she arrived at its subcamp in Bergheim, from where she was evacuated via Czechoslovakia on April 15, 1945, ending up in Mauthausen on April 29th, less than a week before American troops reached the camp, and a day *after* the last gassing took place there.

All this proves is that without an intimate acquaintance with the historical facts by which Holocaust testimonies must be measured, it would be unwise to venture into the field. This is not, however, a judgment on the value of such testimonies, but on the training required to administer or analyze the interviews. Just as trivial books about the Holocaust cannot discredit the serious ones, so exaggerated or untrustworthy testimonies do not compromise accurate narratives that provide particulars about individual experiences in camps and ghettos, in hiding and on the run, that is available nowhere else. None of this should sound new, but perhaps it bears repeating. I am convinced that Holocaust testimonies at their best represent a crucial treasury of reliable texts for understanding the implementation and consequences of the mass murder of European Jewry. Of course, given the atmosphere of skepticism that has always surrounded the portrayal of Holocaust atrocities, discriminating readers and viewers are a sine qua non for the perusal of Holocaust texts of *any* sort. When the typescript of the memoir Adolph Eichmann wrote in prison while awaiting execution is published, the general reader will find it impossible without annotations to distinguish between excuse and truth. For years, the same has been so for the unannotated text of Rudolf Hoess's *Kommandant of Auschwitz*. But I do not find historians ignoring it because of its inaccuracies.

One of the scandals afflicting the reputation of videotaped survivor testimonies is that too many of their critics base their responses more on surmise than on familiarity. In a survey of attitudes toward this material, one scholar with impeccable credentials is cited as arguing that "in the old days the story was how they died. The early accounts captured the life and death of those who died." But now, he continues "the focus has shifted to 'How I survived.' "[1] As I hope to show, this is exactly the reverse of what I have found in the hundreds of testimonies I have examined; only someone who is unversed in the data he is speaking about could have reached such a conclusion. Another scholar of unquestioned repute has followed a similar tactic when speaking of survivor testimonies, but his conclusion too could only be based on a very scanty study of testimonial texts. There is, he is quoted as saying, "a hidden triumphalism in basing the story of the Holocaust purely on the survivor testimonies. They have every right to feel triumphal, to wipe their brows and say, 'We have survived.' But we don't have any right to say 'How wonderful that people survived.' That short-circuits our obligation to understand the Holocaust." Anyone who has patiently studied the survivor testimonies at the Yale Video Archive would know that only on the most superficial level are they about "How I survived." But this scholar's closing inference is even more puzzling. "We don't know," he says, "what those who did not survive had to say. There are other voices we have to hear, the voices of the inarticulate and those who do not wish to speak, and the voices of those who died."[2] But just as the recording of Holocaust history cannot depend on unwritten documents, so the analysis of Holocaust survivor testimony cannot be faulted for not heeding the voices of those unwilling to testify. As for the "voices" of the dead — there are moments when they seem more vividly present in Holocaust testimony than the voices of those who survived to echo their disappearance.

Aeneas returned from the realm of the dead not dispirited but even more resolved to consign defeated Troy to memory and to found a new civilization elsewhere. Myths are made of such dreams, and the Holocaust is no exception. But here the mythmakers are generally not those who returned from the dead, but those who never made the journey at all, who assume that logic and expectation require the narratives of returnees to be driven by a tribute to triumphalism. I fear that such a view reflects more about the mettle of the mythmaker than about the spirit of the witness, and this divergence has led to much confusion about the nature and value of Holocaust testimonies. Of course on their most palpable level they are accounts of a return from near death to life. But these narratives are not one-dimensional; their tensions and their imagery, like most significant literature, challenge us to decipher implicit meanings, to revise our notions of chronology, and to wander through a dark terrain that leads neither to triumph nor to tragedy, but to a far more threatening encounter that stains the historical report with the dye of moral and physical chaos.

Once we have confronted these ordeals, we begin to understand why in many instances it is more accurate to speak not of the feat of endurance but of the ponderous burden of death, even for those who survived. A unique example of this comes from an unexpected source: an American GI, a POW captured in the Battle of the Bulge and gradually shifted southward, away from the advancing Allied troops in the north. His unit ended up in Mauthausen. In the closing weeks of the war, he grew too weak to function:

> At the end of my time in the camp when I was too sick, I was told not to go on sick call. And I asked why and they said, "You don't come back from sick call." And I was pretty sick. So when the Germans made their inspection after everybody had gone to work and found me there, they started beating on me. I crawled out of the barracks and I crawled underneath. . . . That night when I crawled out, some of the fellows in my outfit who were still alive brought me some soup. The next morning they piled me with the dead bodies, and I stayed with the dead bodies until nighttime and they'd bring me back in again, at nighttime. Because they would bury from one end, the oldest bodies first, and they couldn't catch up with the amounts. They were cremating. So they put me with the fresh bodies.[3]

This kind of layering of the living with the dead, a form of death immersion, is a not uncommon image that recurs in many testimonies. Its jolting physical impact nurtured an internalized psychological effect long after this witness's return. As he reports: "It took me a number of years to get straightened out. I didn't dare sleep with my wife after one bad incident where I had a bad dream and she happened to strike me just right. I come to, I was strangling her. So after that, I had separate bedrooms for years so it wouldn't happen again."[4] The very language of certain testimonies seems almost consciously to contradict the illusion that these narratives celebrate survival and the triumphant return to life. A woman who had to surrender her infant to the SS while being deported from the Kovno ghetto tries to reconstruct her reaction at the time:

> Actually I don't recall how long I was on the train because it was a terrible thing to me, because it seemed to me that [I'm] losing everything that

belonged to me and it was a hard fight for us. I was alone, within myself. And since that time, I think all my life I've been alone. To me, I was dead. I died, and I didn't want to hear nothing. I didn't want to know nothing, and I didn't want to talk about it. And I didn't want to admit to myself that this had happened to me. I don't know how long we were going in the train, but to me it was a lifetime. The way I felt is I was born on the train and I died on the train. I actually didn't know why I was there on the train and what was happening to us. I wasn't even alive. I wasn't even alive. I wasn't there.[5]

Normal chronology records a lifetime from the date of birth to the date of death. But the language of this witness allows us to break and shrink that traditional time mold and invites us to imagine an inverse baptism, a ritual whereby one is dipped into a pool of violent death to emerge not forever cleansed but forever soiled. History does not have a discourse for the fierce imprint of the lived-through moment that is also a died-through moment — but testimony does. According to the strict logic of Wittgenstein, "Der Tod ist kein Ereignis des Lebens. Den Tod erlebt man nicht" (Death is not a life-event. Death cannot be lived.)[6] But through the intimacy that the living in the Holocaust shared with unnatural dying, a bizarre paradox arose to contradict Wittgenstein's conviction. Innumerable testimonies include variations on the theme of dying while living, of being dead while still alive, of a memory so coated with the death of others that it introduces a new and startling way of facing reality. It asks us how to assimilate into general consciousness that portion that has been saturated with death. It modifies Freud's belief that no one can imagine his or her own demise. It banishes "triumphalism" from the definitions of survival and substitutes a harsh if not insoluble dilemma in the dictionary of human expectations: how to maintain a hopeful mind and live a civilized existence in an era that has been tarnished by so much mass murder. And of course we need not restrict ourselves to the Holocaust when considering this question.

Holocaust testimonies offer us concrete examples of such tarnished memory, and allow us to conjure up its necrotic features. One witness tells of being sent with his father and his uncle from Auschwitz to a labor camp in Germany called Erlenbusch. After ten months of exhausting work as slave laborers, they were taken in February 1945 with about a thousand other prisoners on a death march toward the west, with Bergen-Belsen as their eventual goal. He recounts one permanently disturbing moment on the journey:

> I'll never forget that day, and that keeps me at night up occasionally. My Uncle Leopold was with me and we were marching and this was a man that used to weigh at one time . . . he must have weighed 280, he was heavy. While we were marching, he was thin, all you could see, bones. If he weighed 70 or 80 pounds it was a lot. And at one point while we were sitting and the Germans said "OK, let's move on!" he couldn't get up. My father was also weak. There were a few people from my hometown, my age, they helped each other, you know, with the walking. And at that point my uncle, he didn't

yell at his brother, meaning my father, he yells at me, "Schlomo, don't leave me here, help me, help me!" In the meantime my father was leaning on me from one side and a friend of mine who's now in Florida is leaning on the other side helping my father, and I'm torn sort of in between, how can I, you know, what can I do? And I hear—we were marching and marching—my uncle still screaming "Schlomo!" and it gets dimmer and dimmer and dimmer, "Don't leave me here. Please. Help me. Help me. Don't leave me." Well, I left him there.

Later on, the SS picked a few boys, young people from that whole big group, and they went back. And they were all dead, they were all shot on the way, and they were put on trucks to be taken someplace, and one guy told me "I saw your uncle [Leopold] there, he was gone. But this screaming and yelling, "Don't leave me here!"—occasionally it's on my mind.[7]

This is as pure an example as I know of the moral enigma I call choiceless choice, which leaves one only with options between the bad and the worse. It marks the defeat of the heroic temperament and charts a kind of enforced behavior that cannot avoid imprinting on memory a vision of unnatural death. Moreover, it rescues from silence, as many of these testimonies do, the voices of the murdered, giving them a rebirth through what we might call their "redeath." Subsequently, the witness must absorb the painful irony that after arriving in Bergen-Belsen his father, starving and physically depleted by the march, collapses and soon dies—but not before refusing to taste, despite his son's pleading, some charcoal-broiled "meat" cut from the flesh of a nearby corpse.

Nowhere but in testimony can we gain a glimpse of the chafing union joining the near dead and the dead with the living, in rare instances literally devouring, in others metaphorically being consumed internally by the substance of those who perished. Had the uncle managed to stay alive and later offered *his* testimony, he would have had to face the memory of his wife and seven children, all of whom were sent directly to the gas chamber at Auschwitz. This episode depicts a pivotal grim principle of the camp universe: no one's survival can be separated from the unnatural death of someone else. One of the unacknowledged victims of these narratives is the notion that survival and non-survival are opposing zones of experience. The nephew who left his uncle behind must find a space in present consciousness for the memory of unnatural death that continues to haunt him. In the absence of other designations, I name it the "coffined self" because it represents the paradox of being dead while still alive. We hear it in the words of the woman who, after telling of giving up her baby, says, "I was dead. I died and I didn't want to hear nothing," and then repeats obsessively "I wasn't even alive. I wasn't even alive." It is clear from these sample testimonies that the wish "to hear nothing" is not fulfilled, since the need to rescue the voices of those who did not return recurs so often as witness memories unfold.

Of course, the historical record also acknowledges these deaths, but the difference between documents and testimonies of destruction is strikingly highlighted by a series of reports from SS-Colonel Karl Jäger, head of Einsatzkommando 3 in the Baltic region. Responding to an inquiry about the number of people executed in Lithuania, his special domain, Jäger submitted a tally stating that as of February 6, 1942, a total of 138,272 persons had been killed, including 55,556 women and 34,464 children. Among the victims were 136,421 Jews, 1,064 communists, 56 partisans, 653 mentally ill, 44 Poles, 28 Russian prisoners of war, 5 gypsies, and 1 Armenian. The inventory reflects the German habit of reducing its victims to statistical groupings, and if we rely solely on these sources, we risk restricting our view of mass murder to the German perspective. Moreover, it strikes me as odd that this well-known document is usually cited without question while testimonies are frequently accused of unreliability. It is therefore heartening to find at least one historian observing about tabulations like Jäger's that, "Numerical information in German contemporary documents often represents estimates or shows a tendency toward being inflated in order to impress superiors in Berlin." He goes on to caution, however, that "Such discrepancies do not invalidate the usefulness of the German sources for the task of reconstructing the scope of the mass murder"[8] — an admonition that might be extended to anyone working with the details of survivor testimony.

Using some of Jäger's material, his superior SS Brigadier-General Walther Stahlecker submitted a map entitled "Jewish Executions Carried out by Einsatzgruppe A," not only in Lithuania but in the whole northern sector under his command. He chose a familiar image to dramatize his message. Next to the number 41,828, signifying those murdered so far in Belorussia, we find drawn a small coffin. From the German point of view, dead Jews were already lost to memory, heirs only to a crude sketch. Moreover, beneath the figure for those executed we find another one, 128,000, preceded by the phrase "Geschätzte Zahl der noch vorhandenen Juden," which a cynic using commercial language might translate "estimated number of Jews still in stock, or available for shipment" — for what purpose we need not seek far to learn. The point is clear — German documents dehumanize their potential victims wherever they mention them, and students of the Holocaust who confine themselves to such documents, crucial as they are, risk limiting the dimensions of the catastrophe to the anonymity that the Germans desired. We have another way of translating "noch vorhandenen Juden," or "Jews who still exist," — we call them "survivors." Their narratives are no substitute for the broader information that documents provide; but their intimacy with the murdered, if not with the murderers, extends the range of our hearing about the Holocaust to include the voices, often literally, of those whom their persecutors had hoped to silence forever.

Like Homer's *Odyssey*, the Holocaust is a story of journeys. Both narratives evoke the peril of forgetfulness. But creatures like Circe and the Sirens who try to hinder Odysseus' homeward voyage tempt him to forget his *future*, not his past—that is, the native land toward which he sails after his departure from Troy. Odysseus' memory is not cluttered with lethal images of corpse-strewn battlefields. But for the survivors of the Holocaust, the situation is otherwise. Their testimonies suggest that the journey "from" is as vivid as and even can overshadow the journey "toward." Perhaps the penchant for viewing their accounts as triumphant returns is fed by the thrust of legends like Homer's heroic tale. The task of Holocaust historians and those who analyze testimonies is to resist the impulse to transform human experience into myth. Asked how she felt when the liberation came, one woman who outlived the catastrophe replied: "I had no desire to live. I had no place to go. I had nobody to talk to. I was just simply lost, without words. I know that everybody is killed."[9] That grim landscape of death, unlike the slaughter at Troy, continues to hover over the future to which lucky voyagers like this one returned.

Another kind of Holocaust testimony is so immersed in the *Todeswelt* of the present that it spares little time for thoughts about past or future. One of the best examples of this tangible universe of dying is found in the detailed diary of Viktor Klemperer, a baptized Jew living in Dresden who officially converted to Protestantism long before the war. To the Nazi regime the conversion was an irrelevant matter; only his "Aryan" wife's unflinching loyalty saved him from deportation. Post-war survivor testimony is of necessity *re*lived, giving us vivid glimpses of deathlife in ghettos and camps from beyond the pale of atrocity, filtered through the mesh of memory. But throughout the Hitler era, Klemperer's often daily entries record *as it happens* the slow stifling of hope as Nazi officials gradually remove the security that sustains the lives of Jews. As energy drains away, the threat of death rushes into the vacuum, and though Klemperer stubbornly keeps working at his various literary projects, he cannot escape the encircling strain of alarm. He captures it in an entry of October 1942: "The terrible thing is the uncertainty, murder sneaking up. No one knows anything, everyone's life is in constant danger, the flimsiest thing is good enough as a pretext for being done away with. Even today we do not know why Ernst Kreidl was killed. We shall also learn nothing about Eger. And always the feeling: Perhaps *I* am next."[10] Klemperer's diaries allow us to share the encroaching peril with its intended victims; that peril reflects a different kind of suffocation, not the instant demise ordained by toxic gas or other forms of execution but the atrophy of the self through a kind of creeping asphyxiation of the spirit. A death *before* death trespasses on Klemperer's regular routines even as he struggles to convince himself that he may be a recording angel destined to survive. He is reminded of his ordeal by the appearance of friends ten years younger than himself who look ten years older; or, closer to home, by the diminishing weight of his wife, whose body shrinks almost weekly as hunger consumes her flesh. Each of them is a visible hint to the other of the radical threat that infiltrates their being. At a funeral in the Jewish cemetery, Klem-

perer notices among the mourners two former acquaintances: "Falkenstein
. . . has changed from a strong man into a shriveled little figure with a pale,
very sunken face" while "broad-shouldered Cohn, who used to collect the
'little winter aid' from us, has become a walking skeleton" (114).

The erosion of physical substance is bad enough. But even more severe is
the psychological deprivation, the loss of mental space that a human being,
and especially an intellectual like Viktor Klemperer, requires in order to stay
alive. As the charnel house of Jewish fate begins to displace the once safe
citadel of his inner self, Klemperer starts to waver in his resolve to retain his
"German" identity no matter what strategy the Nazi regime adopts against
its enemies. Few escaped victims have been able to recall so precisely how
the proximity of death menaced their façade of tranquility:

> My only concern is always to avoid shuddering with the fear of death.
> It shakes me again and again: they will come for me too. It is no longer
> about property — anyone can be murdered. . . . Every time I go to the letter
> box, I think there might be a card summoning me to the Gestapo. . . . I
> would so much like to live another couple of years, I have such a dread of
> just this death, of perhaps waiting for days in the certainty of dying, of
> perhaps being tortured, of being extinguished in absolute loneliness.
> Again and again I save myself by turning to what is now my work, these
> notes, my reading. . . . But the long moments of dreadful fear occur in-
> creasingly often. (104)

Klemperer's candor is a chastening antidote to the celebration of endurance in the face of German oppression that is frequently cited as a model of
heroic resistance. For the diarist, such "endurance" reflects a desperate
deceit; his literary vocation only allows him "to pretend courage to myself"
(105). As his urgent desire to ground his identity in something other than
his Jewish ancestry founders on the absence of alternatives, Klemperer
grows more and more psychologically anonymous, and this proves to be an
insufferable status.

The usual consolations have little appeal for Klemperer as the brutal
realities of German society saturate his environment and finally drown the
floating image of a national dignity that earlier he had been able to use as a
cerebral safeguard against the maelstrom of the Nazi regime. Although he
has long since abandoned the rituals and beliefs of Judaism, most of the
friends he associates with are Jewish (with a few non-Jewish spouses). As they
are slowly but relentlessly deported to Theresienstadt or camps in Poland,
Klemperer's faith in a decent "other" Germany dwindles: "What I find so
much more abominable in all of this than similar things with the Russians:
there is nothing spontaneous about it, everything is methodically organized
and regulated, it is 'cultivated' cruelty, and it happens hypocritically and
mendaciously in the name of culture." Then he adds ironically: "No one is
murdered here" (116). Klemperer's analysis offers a subtle variation on the

testimony of those who outlived places like Auschwitz, since *all* Jews were meant to be murdered *there,* some sooner, some later. But *he* continued to breathe a limited cultural atmosphere. He was able to read and write almost every day despite his dread; he even occasionally was addressed politely by some "Aryan" Germans (a prospect virtually unthinkable for those already inside the camps). Thus the cultivated cruelty he encountered on the "outside" displayed a different demeanor. Klemperer becomes expert in defining the psychological pressures assailing those marked for death but struggling to find the means for staying alive. He is not surrounded by openly monstrous malice but by a population pursuing normal longings while remaining indifferent to the plight of the small number of doomed Jews in their midst.

Klemperer's entries provoke the reader to imagine how the fear of abnormal death through torture or execution seeped into the thinking of the few hundred Jews still in Dresden by mid-1943, most of them in mixed marriages, until this fear became a permanent part of their state of mind. We share his witnessing of atrocity through anticipation rather than memory. If there is undoubted value to the testimonial anecdotes of past Nazi barbarity that we have examined earlier, there is equally challenging imaginative force to Klemperer's "prospective" dread, based on uncertainty rather than remembered experience. He quickly learns that Jewish spouses in mixed marriages are not *necessarily* protected from arrest, as one by one various friends in such unions are summoned to the Gestapo for infractions such as concealing or not wearing their Jewish star, and are never heard from again. Sometimes their corpses are delivered straight from the Dresden jail to the Jewish cemetery; at others, apparently in deference to the "Aryan" spouse, notices are sent to the Jewish Community with the information that the deportee had died from a physical ailment or was "shot while trying to escape."

Klemperer is all the more distraught because he believes none of this. Every time a Jewish friend is called in for questioning, he invents a scenario with which to identify because he finds the mystery and silence behind Gestapo tactics intolerable. These little dramas of expectation give us access to the inner tensions that beset the trapped Jews of Dresden as they awaited their doom: "What torments must he be going through in the cell, must his wife be going through at home. He must expect death every time he hears a footstep outside, she must expect news of death every time the doorbell rings. With all that I myself have only the feeling, the sensation of increasing tension and, more strongly, the apprehension of mortal fear. I cannot help imagining that tomorrow — today — I shall be arrested and Eva [his wife] and I be in [their] situation — it is unimaginably dreadful, not to be compared with any memory of Flanders [the World War I battlefield], or any mortal fear I have ever experienced" (154). The absence of precedent is a key to understanding these narratives about a universe that inverts the normal sequence of existence from birth through life to death. Klemperer's entries induce us to empathize with a spirit adrift in uncharted waters without a compass, in futile quest of a safe and familiar harbor. In spite of his divorce from Jewish traditions, he seems to attend every funeral at the Jewish cemetery in Dresden. Very few of the recently interred, as we have seen, died from natural causes. Yet Klemperer joins the mourners, although his motives remain obscure; perhaps he simply feels obliged to show some courtesy to the dead.

It is unlikely that he hopes the burial ritual may restore some meaningful promise to his blighted spiritual career. Instead, as he wanders with his wife among the new gravesites after one ceremony, he seems vividly aware of the discord between the usual consolations that accompany the loss of a loved one and the "boundless misery" of the present situation of Dresden's Jews. The funerals, he observes candidly, "take place close to the small urn-holes of those murdered outright. By the wall we discovered quite fresh full-sized graves. Numerous double graves, married couples who died on the same day. These are the suicides." He is conscious of the abrupt and abnormal termination of such lives, and this leads him to deplore the language of prayer used by the bereaved to seek solace from a rite that was not designed for death by atrocity. The ancient discourse of the psalms only confirmed his belief that anguish such as theirs required an idiom still waiting to be born. Unlike the mass murders in the east, of which Klemperer has heard only rumors at the time of this entry (August 1942), the individual deaths in Gestapo cells and camps that he learns of have the *appearance* of private dying. But Klemperer knows that trying to assimilate them under this guise is to falsify the truth and to betray the deceased. Speaking, writing, and even thinking "in the exalted tone of someone about to die" (113–114), or, as at the funerals, of someone who has just perished, is to withdraw from reality. The very terms *die* and *death* no longer convey the turmoil of unfolding events.

As the number of air raid warnings mount in Dresden (all false alarms so far), a new danger enters the lives of the city's remaining Jews, and indeed of the entire population. When information on the casualties in nearby Leipzig and other much-bombed German cities seeps through, Klemperer wonders why Dresden has been spared. Of course, he can have no hint of the havoc that lies ahead for the city. And he can speak only for himself, but as the new theme emerges we get a glimpse of how it projects itself onto the surrounding environment and then returns to infect his own inner reality. On New Year's Eve of 1943–1944, he writes: "Everyone in Dresden is full of unutterable fear. There is surely not a soul here who does not feel that he has one foot in the grave" (270). But at the same time, despite increasing visits to the shelters during warnings, raids on Dresden fail to materialize. Klemperer is tempted to nurture a tiny hope that the Allies may have a private reason for preserving the city, an idea he uses as a balance against his feeling of impending doom. His mood resembles the "compartmentalized lives" that many survivors speak of in their oral testimonies when trying to describe the alternating rhythms of their post-war existence. They get on with their routines while at the same time the loss of their families pursues them, in a daily rivalry between normal present and abnormal past. Klemperer is trapped by a tighter timeframe, as two presents contend with each other, allowing him no chronology to ease his pain. He is cheered by the rising number of German military defeats, but admits, "My happiness did not last long." Three of his co-workers in the factory where he is "employed" are suddenly taken away, and he is shaken: "A moment ago I was in constant contact with these three people, and now they are buried. And tomorrow my fate may be the same" (275–276).

The narratives of post-war testimonies and contemporaneous accounts like Klemperer's force us to differentiate between two uses of the not unfamiliar formula that "tomorrow my fate may be the same." After all, this is a conventional response among members of an aging community as they begin to attend the funerals of friends. Only the poverty of language keeps us from distinguishing between the "normal" process of dying and the "abnormal" state of mind that includes the terror of being "taken away." The ancient idea of fate, so casually inserted by Klemperer into his apprehensions about the future, cannot begin to embody the impression he is seeking to convey. It would take a Kafka to draw us into the milieu of unease that continued to consume Klemperer and his fellow Jews even as news of the German collapse at Stalingrad and the Allied invasion of Normandy reached their ears. Klemperer's entry on the momentous day of the landings, June 6, 1944, reads: "I myself remained quite cold. I am no longer or not yet able to hope" (309). It grows clearer and clearer that the heartening events of history cannot erase the scars of disaster already so indelibly stamped on the imaginations of its victims.

If Klemperer's diaries prove anything, it is that during the Holocaust witnessing atrocity was not a transient affair for the victimized. A corollary to this conclusion is that an imagination anchored in a stable present cannot gain access to the uncertainties of that earlier era without suspending that stability. Witnessing atrocity means admitting the immediacy of its threats and temporarily deferring the hope that the future will provide comfort for past or current sorrow. Such a concession will aid us in understanding why a natural pessimism is insufficient to explain Klemperer's less than enthusiastic mood as the Allies move inland in France after the invasion: "Every single thing again and again turns my mind to the endless length of our slavery, to the very long list of those who have disappeared, who are dead, who all hoped to survive. And again and again I tell myself, I too shall not survive, deep down I too am apathetic and quite without hope, can no longer imagine myself back into a human being" (318). We know time proved him to be mistaken, but Klemperer's failure to predict his eventual fate accurately does not discredit the impact on our understanding of his original despair. The vision of attrition, of a self drained by helplessness and humiliation, would fade were it not for testimonies like the ones we have been examining.

Klemperer illuminates the issue when he reflects on "the impotence of memory to fix all that we had so painfully experienced in time" (342). How, in other words, would future generations absorb one axiomatic principle of the Holocaust that "there is nothing more ghastly than the Jewish fear of the Gestapo" (343)? He anticipates the inroads that chronology will make on remembering the atrocity; intuitively, he sees the need for a new version of temporal thought for a post-Holocaust period. Klemperer defines the problem in terms that carry unforeseen implications for a posterity that will have to include unimaginable violence as part of its historical heritage: "When — insofar as we remembered it at all — had this or that happened, when had it been? Only a few facts stick in the mind, dates not at all. One is overwhelmed by the present, time is not divided up, everything is infinitely long ago, everything is infinitely long in coming, there is no yesterday, there is no tomorrow, only an eternity. And that is yet another reason why one knows nothing of the history one has experienced: the sense of time has been abolished; one is at once too blunted and too overexcited, one is crammed full of the present" (342).

Passages like these prompt us to ask, and help us to answer, why the Holocaust continues to haunt consciousness as a kind of perpetual present, refusing to join other crises of national or international scope within the safe and clarifying boundaries of what we call the historical past. War, revolution, famine, even tyranny — each has a predecessor in some earlier time or place; each is a precedented chapter in the long chronology of pain that has always been part of the human condition. But the daily and even hourly anguish that infects a portion of Klemperer's waking and even sleeping hours obliterates temporal sequence. In modern times it bears some resemblance only to the harshest years of the Stalin era, described so vividly by Osip Mandelstam's wife Nadezhda in her reminiscences *Hope against Hope.* Every pore of Klemperer's mind and body seems sensitive to the disaster that threatens to engulf him, even though as a scholar and academic he had devoted his life to understanding prior social and literary traditions. When Klemperer complains that he is "crammed full of the present," we must gloss his comment. The indefinable malaise that permeates Kafka's universe has now been given a local habitation and a name: the German determination to murder all of European Jewry. Such omens of catastrophe cause one to live in the shadow of a canceled future. Primo Levi struggled to express a similar idea in *Survival in Auschwitz* when he wrote "Do you know how one says 'never' in camp slang? '*Morgen früh,*' tomorrow morning."

Testimonies are a principal source for transmitting the disorders of time, place, and language that accompanied the Holocaust experience. A recently published memoir by one who outlasted Auschwitz, Paul Steinberg's

Speak You Only (2000), neatly captures the dislocation of all three as he tries to describe the move from "ordinary" life in the transit camp at Drancy outside Paris to what would lie before him after his deportation: "This lasted twelve days. Twelve days of civilian and almost civil life in that place — Drancy — which, unbeknownst to us, was a chamber leading from the past to what was to be, for almost all of us, death. Not a banal, normal. respectable death; a different death. We probably ought to invent a different word. Decomposition? Putrescence? What term does justice to a physical, psychological, and moral annihilation, often experienced in wretched shame?"[11] After he arrives in Auschwitz, he is more concrete about his aim: "To follow the process, the degradation of human beings before annihilation. The death of feeling, the death of thought, then the death of the man" (62). Like Viktor Klemperer, though with greater literary flair, this memoirist announces the existence of a special death-consciousness that will be a major reminder of his camp ordeal and an urgent if unwelcome bequest to the post-war world.

Different words for different deaths. This remains the lingering challenge as we consider the impact of the Holocaust on contemporary society. More than any other event in recent history, the murder of European Jewry provides a template for the shift in attitude and change of vocabulary that the mass murders of the modern era require. In an age when we seem to spend nearly as much time unearthing corpses as in burying them, the search for evidence of death by atrocity has become a fresh and grisly form of witnessing, consuming more of our imaginative energy than we wish to spare. The Holocaust has gained its "exemplary" status not because of any special priority it has earned as a calamity more terrible than any other, but because it continues to be the most widely researched and publicized crime among several of its kind during the past hundred years. Those who heed its history have been forced to add to the proper ways of life that have always been the goal of reasonable cultures improper ways of death that frustrate those efforts and shrink their chances of success. For most of human history, death was a consequence of life — even death in war, which has long been one of the risks for combatants in military conflicts. But for the victimized in the Holocaust, and for victims of similar atrocities, death was not a consequence of life but a consequence of who they were, of having been a Jew or member of some other group marked for extermination. What I elsewhere call an "alarmed vision"[12] that might anticipate such a possibility did not exist fifty years ago. The unarmed imagination of the world lacked the sort of death-consciousness necessary to foresee the atrocities that lay ahead. Hindsight now allows us to realize how the Holocaust has certified the need for such vision. Not all gifts are gladly accepted, however, and this one has been received, when accepted at all, with a less than cheerful grace. But as witnessing atrocity, much more literally than during the Holocaust, becomes a constant in our daily lives through graphic portrayals by various news media, the earlier catastrophe looms as a paradigm of the savage violence these images inflict on us. Although its motives and details must be differentiated from the ethnic rivalries of our current mass murders, the testimonial evidence about the doom of European Jewry appeals to far more than our interest in the historical past. If embraced, such evidence can condition modern consciousness to absorb some of the darker episodes of present reality, and prepare us to meet if not always to forestall their possible recurrence in the future.

MORALIZING AND DEMORALIZING
THE HOLOCAUST

Twenty years ago, scarcely a conference on the Holocaust could be held without someone solemnly citing these lines attributed to Pastor Martin Niemöller (1892–1984): "When Hitler attacked the Jews I was not a Jew, therefore I was not concerned. And when Hitler attacked the Catholics, I was not a Catholic, and therefore I was not concerned. And when Hitler attacked the unions and the industrialists, I was not a member of the unions and I was not concerned. Then Hitler attacked me and the Protestant church — and there was nobody left to be concerned."[1] In their eager search for lessons to be learned from the mass murder of European Jewry, speakers have seized on Niemöller's words with fervent admiration, even though we have no exact written record of what he said. Moreover, few paid attention to the *details* of the warning, so crucial did its general message seem to be. Subjected to careful scrutiny today, those details reveal how the need for a positive lesson to emerge from the catastrophe of the "final solution" could seduce the critical faculty and lead it to embrace an appeal distinguished by neither logic nor historical truth.

For what had Niemöller actually said? That normally only Jews felt obliged to protest against the mistreatment of Jews, and Catholics against the mistreatment of Catholics? Surely he didn't believe this himself. His parable of indifference may have had rhetorical force, but did it offer insight into the wellsprings of human conduct during the years of the Third Reich? Was the failure to object to Nazi policies a neglect of moral duty or a reflection of positive enthusiasm for the regime? Niemöller's statement never raises that issue, which further reduces its value as a source of practical or spiritual advice. Moreover, although hierarchies of anguish offer little help in understanding the Holocaust, the kind of equivalence of suffering implicit in Niemöller's vision can have unintended mischievous results. Uninformed readers of the pastor's statement could easily assume that Hitler made no distinctions among his victims. From the passage, we might conclude that Hitler's attitude toward the Jews, enshrined in the single term *attack,* was similar to his attitude toward Catholics, Protestants, and union members. Notably absent from Niemöller's list are the other victims of Hitler's hatred who, according to Nazi ideology, did not qualify for Aryan status any more than Jews did. It may not have been Niemöller's intention, but his remarks remain one of the earliest post-war examples of universalizing the Holocaust, of shunning distinctions and suggesting that the hostility to Jews in Nazi Germany was merely another form of discrimination that threatened all dissidents in the Third Reich.

Can we extract from the murder of European Jewry nothing more than the idea that we should worry about our fellow human beings so that when the need arises they will worry about us? The flagrant oversimplification of the Nazi regime's moral and physical reality buried in Niemöller's pseudo-syllogistic thinking is all the more surprising because of its author's own fate. His courage and integrity in opposing the religious policies of the Nazis led to his lengthy imprisonment in a concentration camp, from which he was freed only at war's end. There is, however, no truth, rhetorical or otherwise, to his earnest declaration that when Hitler attacked him and the Protestant church, there was no one left to be concerned. When Niemöller was arrested in 1938 there were millions of Germans, including members of the Protestant clergy, who could have protested. Many of them did not because they were more enthusiastic about their Führer than the fate of a single disenchanted pastor. But Niemöller's implicit reproach to those who failed to take action against the abuse of others misconstrues the reasons for their behavior. Niemöller totally ignores the difference between inferior "them" and superior "us" that was the main psychological allure of "aryan" ideology. Instead, he relies on the traditional principle of universal brotherhood that the theory of a master race was designed to replace. If we find in Niemöller's lament a valuable beacon to guide our own behavior in the future, we repeat his error of approaching the profound evil of the Third Reich with a vocabulary and mental attitude too familiar and conventional to unlock the mystery of that evil's mass appeal.

Certain sayings seem to pass from mouth to mouth like favorite intellectual morsels that are too savory to discard, even though everyone has long forgotten the philosophical recipes that gave them birth. A terser and even more popular "instructive" aphorism about the Holocaust than Niemöller's is the philosopher George Santayana's (1863–1952) admonition that "[t]hose who cannot remember the past are condemned to repeat it."[2] Few who continue to misappropriate this sentiment to foster the study of Nazi genocide know that it appeared in the last chapter of the first volume — published in 1905! — of Santayana's multi-volumed *The Life of Reason*. Santayana wrote this work when America was entering a transition from an idealistic creed to the activism of the Progressive era. The subtitle of his opus is *Phases of Human Progress* and the initial segment is devoted to the topic of "Reason and Common Sense." What could be further from the racial anti-semitism and mass murder that flourished in a corrupted civilization devoted to chaos and unreason? In 1905 Santayana could still cling to the ancient illusion, as he wrote in his Introduction, that "the entire history of progress is a moral drama." For him, "The Life of Reason" would be a "name for that part of experience which perceives and pursues ideals — all conduct so controlled and all sense so interpreted as to perfect natural happiness."[3] The "past" Santayana encouraged readers to remember was one inspired by constructive, not destructive, values; he urged his audience to draw upon the best, not to guard against the worst. Those who failed to do so, he argued, were condemned to repeat not the systematic brutalities of a ruthless social order but the childish gropings of an immature one.

The context of Santayana's assertion makes this perfectly clear. He speaks as a conservative philosopher, not as a modern historian: "Progress, far from consisting in change, depends on retentiveness. When change is absolute there remains no being to improve and no direction is set for possible improvement: and when experience is not retained as among savages, infancy is perpetual. Those who cannot remember the past are condemned to repeat it. In the first stage of life the mind is frivolous and easily distracted; it misses progress by failing in consecutiveness and persistence." Those heedless of the past do not repeat its *horrors*, as many who quote Santayana are intent on proving, but its *monotonies*. They ignore the "plasticity and fertile readaptation"[4] that for the philosopher are the marks of a mature and future-oriented civilization. Retentiveness, then, is a condition of progress for Santayana, not a warning against the continuation of decay. Remembering the past allows the transmission of spiritual continuity, without which civilizations would die away. The pseudo-spiritual unity of the Third Reich led to the murder of millions and the collapse of the nation responsible for that carnage. Santayana's absorption of nineteenth-century Darwinian theory permitted him to celebrate an unlimited future of moral evolution. Post-Holocaust discourse, however, draws on a different kind of biological imagery, imagery that bred a landscape of ruin hardly responsive to the "fertile readaptation" that Santayana called for.

Those who embrace Santayana's formulaic flourish out of context reduce history to a study of action and reaction, as if human decision always controlled external events and all that were required to shape a desirable future was a clear understanding of the defects of antecedent imprudence. According to this didactic reasoning, the devastation of World War I should have prevented the outbreak of World War II, while Napoleon's disastrous campaign in Russia should have alerted Hitler to the folly of repeating the error in his attack on the Soviet Union. But tyrants are driven by the certainty that *their* efforts will succeed even though similar ones in the past did not. History is a poor instructor when the pupil is a stubborn despot who considers himself invincible. A major lesson we learn from history is how little we succeed in learning from it.

Why, then, do we persist in citing Santayana's words as if they offer a clue to our appreciation of a catastrophe as vast and difficult to imagine as the Holocaust, to say nothing about their value in helping us to prevent future ones? Aware of the atrocities during the Nazi era, were we better prepared to prevent similar ones when they erupted in Cambodia, the former Yugoslavia, or Rwanda? The myth sustained by Santayana's language is that some mysterious moral channel links knowledge and memory to good actions, a Socratic principle implicit in the genteel tradition that nurtured Santayana's philosophy but one that bore little relation to the legacy of mass murder. The caution about paying attention to the lessons of history originates in the dubious dual premise that history has lessons to teach and that individuals and nations respond to them in ways that prove beneficial to mankind.

History itself has repeatedly sabotaged the moral force of Santayana's misconstrued idea. Indeed, there is some evidence that certain national leaders who have remembered the Holocaust have been not condemned but *inspired* to repeat it. Former Ugandan dictator Idi Amin was said to have admired Adolf Hitler; he clearly imitated Nazi tactics in his ruthless campaign against his own people. The notion that we learn moral lessons from the past encourages us to expect better even from leaders like Idi Amin, but (as is true of much commentary on the heritage of the Holocaust) this expectation is based more on what is desirable than on what is true. It invites us to discover in the events of history not merely information about the past but comforting advice about possibilities for the future. It has been used again and again in superficial Holocaust discussion as a source of consolation, as a way of finding at least minimal meaning in the desolate spectacle that greeted us at the end of World War II.

This attitude leads to a third and probably the most often repeated refrain from popular Holocaust response: "Never again!" Whether it applies to the destruction of European Jewry or the more general devastation wrought by Nazi Germany, "Never again!" (like its verbal predecessors) implies that there is redemptive value to knowing the details of the Holocaust, since students aware of them would somehow possess the tools for discouraging a recurrence of similar atrocities. But this has always been an untested conjecture; private and political gestures are far more complex than a simple connection between information and deed. I am occasionally asked whether I think another Holocaust is possible, and my answer is always the same: "That depends." Extreme forms of violence are always possible when a leader committed to destroying some part of a population attains power. Mass murder is the result of an unleashed will to destroy; whether or not the criminals are aware of similar prior violations at home or abroad is totally irrelevant. We have had numerous examples since the Holocaust of peaceful groups suddenly turning on their neighbors and viciously injuring or killing them, sometimes because they have been ordered to do so, at others because slumbering frictions have been roused by hate propaganda. The events in Serbia and Rwanda offer convincing evidence that genocidal impulses are unleashed as much by what we might call situational ethics as by inner conviction. Since these are unpredictable until conditions arise that allow them to emerge, slogans such as "Never again!" can do nothing to prevent them. As current history has shown, only direct intervention with force can limit the slaughter. Faith in human virtue has never saved the lives of endangered communities.

Intrinsic to the catastrophe we call the Holocaust is a sense of violation so immense and extreme that the imagination has difficulty encompassing it. It threatens our faith in the stability of social and moral institutions and reminds us of eruptions of mass violence in history that were not subject to the restraints of virtue or good will. Many scientists resist the idea of an infinitely expanding universe because it implies a cosmos without fixed status, obedient to the rules of neither nature, man, nor God, rushing toward extinction at a rate unmeasurable in human terms. Such a vision thrusts the mind into unsettling realms of thought where many prefer not to travel.

The same disquieting intellectual disorder can be generated by the Holocaust, because offspring of morality and religion like conscience and redemption do not thrive in its domain. Yet we persist in pretending that they do, since the alternative to learning from the Holocaust is admitting that the Holocaust has little to teach to those subscribing to the familiar ideals of morality and religion.

Unless we suspend those ideals *in Holocaust discourse,* we risk missing a radical message of that event. The social scientist Jürgen Habermas has expressed the dilemma succinctly: "There [in Auschwitz] something happened, that up to now nobody considered as even possible. There one touched on something which represents the deep layer of solidarity among all that wears [sic] a human face; notwithstanding all the usual acts of beastliness of human history, the integrity of this common layer had been taken for granted. . . . Auschwitz has changed the basis for the continuity of the conditions of life within history."[5] The problem with seeking lessons from the Holocaust is that the inquiry normally proceeds without first acknowledging the abysmal failure during those years of "the deep layer of solidarity among all that wears a human face." Few bonds tied the criminals to their victims; and often, because of the harsh conditions imposed by the Germans, few bonds linked the victims to each other. A clean future cannot be shaped from the clay of Auschwitz and other killing sites; the stained corpses and their residual ashes signify layers of disintegration that are utterly alien to the former "integrity" that Habermas mentions.

"Auschwitz has changed the basis for the continuity of the conditions of life within history." This is a premise from which much Holocaust "learning" might proceed, though the prospect is not very appealing. It does not argue that the continuity of life within history is impossible, but that the foundation on which we now build is made of different and perhaps less substantial material. It reminds us that the crucial issue is not what we learn from the Holocaust but what we must *unlearn* from it. This may deflect the normal momentum of education but it is consistent with the notion that the Holocaust deflected the normal momentum of human experience. The duration of that deflection may be open to dispute but this factor does not alter the insight that portions of reality are *permanently* disrupted — and disruptive. The national habit of reshaping European nightmares to strengthen the American dream does not work with the mass murder of European Jewry, although efforts to achieve this conversion do not abate. We still use the overworked passage from Niemöller, together with Santayana's stereotyped sentiment and the fashionable slogan "Never again!" to inspire civic virtue and social justice, as if exposure to the evils of a dreadful past could spontaneously unlock the secrets of a better future. We knew, and all the world knew, before the Holocaust that love was preferable to hate, that intolerance and discrimination benefited a minority (usually in power) and injured those targeted for bigotry, that we shared in the responsibility for reducing suffering, that endangering ourselves in order to preserve the lives of others was a desirable if often risky endeavor — but none of this made any difference when the safety of Europe's Jews was at stake. The Holocaust requires us to *unlearn* something about the durability of those ideals. This in turn entails a shift in attitude about the absolute value of values themselves, a dose of truth that may be dispiriting to some but need not undermine hope, provided one is willing to explore the possibility that death consciousness may be more helpful than traditional optimism in shaping prospects for a new millennium.

It is difficult to see how an event like the Holocaust could *not* have radically altered the role of hope in human desires. Only indifference, amnesia, or supreme ignorance of the dynamics of history during this period could allow this impulse for designing an improved future to remain unqualified by the ravages of the German "final solution," to say nothing of comparable large-scale atrocities before and since. The philosophical narrator of Tadeusz Borowski's story "Auschwitz, Our Home (A Letter)" expresses an extreme version of the perverse devaluation of the meaning of a single word under the pressure of the deathcamp experience:

> Do you really think that, without the hope that [a better] world is possible, that the rights of man will be restored again, we could stand the concentration camp for even one day? It is that very hope that makes people go without a murmur to the gas chambers, keeps them from risking a revolt, paralyzes them into numb inactivity. It is hope that breaks down family ties, makes mothers renounce their children, or wives sell their bodies for bread, or husbands kill. It is hope that compels man to hold on to one more day of life, because that day may be the day of liberation. Ah, and not even hope for a different, better world, but simply for life, a life of peace and rest. Never before in the history of mankind has hope been stronger than man, but never also has it done so much harm as it has in this war, in this concentration camp. We were never taught how to give up hope, and this is why today we perish in gas chambers.[6]

Borowski wrote this in late 1945 or early 1946, fresh from Auschwitz and Dachau himself, when the ruins of European civilization lay spread about him and he had to wonder if anything of value could be rebuilt from its rubble. The attitude he expresses, with a mixture of irony and cynicism, contains a core of psychological truth, for only after a group of Jews in Sobibor, Treblinka, and the Warsaw ghetto were able to surrender all pretensions to a culture of hope and to embrace instead a culture of despair — the shared conviction that their time to die had come — could they mount the courageous if futile resistance that allowed only a small number of them to survive. The principal result of their admirable gesture is that they became agents in their own death. But their death consciousness just prior to and during their uprisings made them undeluded conspirators against the Nazi threat. In their honesty, they became models for those of us who dwell in less tense but equally urgent times.

For the contemporary mind, grand phrases like "these heroic dead" have always minimized a multitude of political and military outrages that some would call crimes. Rhetoric disguises the ethos of atrocity that intermittently shrouds us while concealing its proper name. This became painfully obvious when Americans were forced to face on their own shores the kind of large-scale senseless killing that other regions of the world have been exposed to for many decades. Niemöller's moral homily and Santayana's misappropriated aphorism, to say nothing of the formulaic "Never again!" drive us to think in a certain way about life and its prospects, but say nothing about absorbing its opposite in our effort to confront a world saturated with unnatural dying. The initial national response to the catastrophe of September 11 was ripe with irony, as audiences leapt to their feet on every public occasion to sing "God Bless America," as if its soaring refrains and the obstinate patriotism they reflected somehow shielded them from the dreadful success of the terrorist attacks. A more genuine reaction to an even greater disaster may be heard in the voice of a Rwandan woman who pleaded after the massacres in her country: "Teach us to live after death." Her entreaty fills an intellectual and psychological void that heirs of the Holocaust have had to face for more than half a century. Although she used words that might have fallen from the lips of a preacher or a member of the congregation petitioning their God for help along the path to salvation, much in the manner of America's favorite anthem, she was actually addressing her existence beneath the shadow of the recent violent slaughter. Hers is no ritualized rubric but a cogent appeal inspired by our corpse-strewn era. Each mass atrocity, including the Holocaust, has tried to shift our consciousness a little closer to the troublesome realm of this secular request about learning to live after death, but we remain reluctant to let it so damage our hope for a better life in this world as to impair breathing within its shrinking frontiers of aspiration. How long can we afford to ignore the fretful uneasiness that lurks behind this façade of reassurance?

During the murderous years of World War II, French novelist Albert Camus warned of the consequences of failing to face this issue. "There is but one freedom," he wrote, "to put oneself right with death. After that, everything is possible."[7] The residual strain of optimism in Camus's outlook at the time may have led him to exaggerate; he probably should have written that "much is possible," since his extreme position has been shattered in the post-war milieu by repeated atrocities. September 11 only seemed to introduce something new to American perception; in truth, profiles of unnatural dying have been present for decades, but at a distance that has made it easy to postpone recognition. We now need to ask what it means to say that we can no longer dismiss the vexations of a far-off terror that has managed to invade our own physical and spiritual terrain. The most urgent challenge at the moment is to find a fruitful attitude toward this unprecedented assault on our sovereignty without lapsing into paralysis or despair, or falling back on tired and irrelevant exclamations of hope like the ones examined earlier. We are finally asked to locate ways — especially in educating a younger generation — of exploring alternatives to the illusion that the promise of American life is eternally available and secure.

Western civilization lacks a discourse for a culture of atrocity. Against the evidence of contemporary history, it resists such labels for the world we live in. Although it is a descriptive rather than a prescriptive summons to awareness, few seem willing to cross its intellectual and emotional borders. Shortly after the destruction of the twin towers in Manhattan and the attack on the Pentagon, countless witnesses were heard to exclaim that "nothing would ever be the same again." People who had "put themselves right with death," who had learned "how to live after death" would not have spoken this way. And as we know, the sense of lasting change lingered briefly and then vanished from public memory, except for those who had been directly affected by the disaster. Unless these intuitions are absorbed into human consciousness, they are doomed to dissipate and join the ranks of urgent-sounding platitudes that displace reflective thought. This is a premise from which all learning, but especially post-atrocity education, ought to proceed.

Defining that dose of reality is the real challenge for Holocaust educators, and the struggle to do so has scarcely begun. "Learning from the past" and "Never again!" now seem meager and deceptive guideposts. How to live after the quantity of violent death that has tainted this century and the last is a question far easier to pose than to answer. We have rituals to ease if not dispel the pain of normal dying, but we have only avoidance to help us face its less graspable companion. It may be that we need a more current and less romantic version of Keats's line about being "half in love with easeful death." The intimacy I speak of is a death consciousness that can have nothing to do with love. The drama of violent destruction that has been played out repeatedly in our era, no matter how different the actors, their motives, and their locale, demands of its audience a mindset tuned to the prospects of several painful truths. The first is that the brutal taking of life is no longer a crime against universal morality but has entered into our experience as a form of personal or national fulfillment, an expression of individual, group, or governmental goals, often "justified" by a language that makes it sound "legitimate" and even "humane." The second is that we seem fated to face it as an almost daily occurrence somewhere on the globe, and unless we choose to exist beneath a bell jar of illusion, we are obliged to find ways, as the Rwandan woman reminded us, of learning to live after it, and perhaps even more urgently, learning to live *with* it as part of the internal landscape of our present existence.

What this would mean is a firm turning away from aversive memory, which is widely practiced amongst private individuals and in public forums, and toward what we might name *contaminated remembrance*, a use of details to imprint on memory the nature of the world that stains us. In so doing, we would implant a gadfly into our power of recall. It is the kind of stimulus W. G. Sebald employed to repeal the amnesia of his countrymen about the massive air raids on German cities during World War II. Appalled by their failure to confront the domestic carnage they had reaped in supporting their Führer with such enthusiasm, Sebald found a language to undo their self-administered immunity by describing the monstrous ruin — many still consider it, with some justification, a misguided and unpardonable onslaught against innocent civilians — caused by the Allied bombing of Hamburg: "Horribly disfigured corpses lay everywhere. Bluish little phosphorous flames still flickered around many of them; others had been roasted brown or purple and reduced to a third of their normal size. They doubled up in pools of their own melted fat, which had sometimes already congealed." Unfortunately, the inclination for anaesthetized consciousness pursues us still; the death-blindness that burdened the Germans even after the war ended is not a unique phenomenon. Aversive memory leads to a bland inattentiveness to the risks (rather than the "glories") of military adventure, a discovery that inspired Sebald to conclude that "a proper understanding of the catastrophes we are always setting off is the first prerequisite for the social organization of happiness."[8] He neglects to add that such understanding may so qualify what we normally think of as *happiness* that we may be obliged to seek a different term entirely.

One of the cruelest ironies of reading atrocity into history is that it succeeds in "undoing" us even as we try—and fail—to undo it. The only antidote is to recoil from the maimed reality that invades our serenity by embracing and acknowledging its existence. This neither negates nor pacifies its contradictions to our civilizing pretensions and the rhetorical flourishes that twist its meaning, but at least it confirms its presence in the spiritual ambience of our lives. This in turn leads to the question of how to resist the crushing pressure of unnatural dying that threatens the sentient contemporary mind. Are we compelled to respond to this now constant pressure with a salutary pessimism that accepts our limits as human creatures and foresees a future that expects us to settle for less than the best? If there ever was a world without atrocity, its contract has expired, and does not seem to be renewable. Perhaps Sebald should have written that a proper understanding of the catastrophes we are always setting off is the first prerequisite for the social *re*-organization of happiness. And after we complete that arduous and distressing task, what are we left with other than what Camus called living within the limits of the possible? As we have heard, this involved "putting oneself right with death," and though Camus had in mind the upcoming slaughter that Germany was about to inscribe indelibly on the world's imagination, he might have been writing about the virus of unnatural dying that continues to infect us a half century later.

Long before they receive lessons in applied morality, students of contemporary history need help in imagining a world where force rather than morality was law. They need to envision a time when, to confine ourselves to a single atrocity among many, men and women were required to dig their own graves and then kneel at their edge or lie down in them waiting to be shot, some of them then to be buried before they were dead. The true enigma of the Holocaust has less to do with the triumph of the spirit than with the near triumph of the wicked, for whom our evil became their good without causing a cataclysm in Western culture or the cosmos. If Germany had won the war, systematic mass murder would have been added to the normal pursuits of everyday existence, and the idea of *civilization* would have been permanently redefined. Superior military force rather than a principle of moral idealism implicit in the universe forestalled the enactment of this loathsome scenario, but it came close enough to realization to raise disturbing issues about human nature that still need to be examined. And we would be deluding ourselves to believe that the Holocaust marked the end rather than a fresh beginning for parallel loathsome scenarios.

As one pain-wracked century slides into another, a capacity for informed mourning would thus seem to be a necessary and legitimate goal of atrocity education. However we view today the legacy of hope and progress left us by the nineteenth century, two world wars, the murder of European Jewry, and other catastrophes of equal horror if lesser scope have dimmed that bequest and counsel us to judge more skillfully the limits of human ambition. For me there is a touch of impiety in seeking to salvage some practical behavioral principles from Nazism's history of mass murder. There may be redemptive value in the study of *ordinary* suffering; however, with atrocities of this magnitude there is none. But if the Holocaust can never be anything other than a story of misery and grief, there is still much to hearten those who continue to be drawn to the topic. Instead of moralizing the event, we need to accept the sufficiency of reclaiming it by recognizing the intrinsic value of documenting the historical record and cherishing the intellectual worth of exploring the sources that establish it. There is enduring educational merit to separating myth from truth by observing how certain cultures manage to wrest a rhetoric of pride from a heritage of shame and twist physical loss into spiritual gain. There is, moreover, something bracing about the way in which writers, artists, memoirists, witnesses in their testimonies, and historians have rejected conventional eloquence and instead found a language and form to express more authentic verbal and visual versions of the disaster. Without their work, we would have no reliable access to unprecedented horrors like the Holocaust. Those who cannot remember the past are not condemned to repeat it, but simply to forget it. Atrocity education is one hedge against such oblivion — an oblivion that is the last refuge of an ignorant mind.

9

REPRESENTING THE HOLOCAUST

More than fifty years after its original appearance in print, Theodor W. Adorno's admonition that "To write poetry after Auschwitz is barbaric" remains a point of dispute for virtually every inquiry into the limits and possibilities of creating a literature about the Holocaust. Few readers know that Adorno's stricture appeared at the end of a long and difficult essay written in 1949 called "Cultural Criticism and Society" which had little or nothing to do with Holocaust literature or the experience it sought to express. He was principally concerned with redirecting the critical intelligence away from "self-satisfied contemplation" so that the "consciousness of doom" that lay heavily upon society could achieve meaningful cultural expression. Rarely has a solitary decontextualized assertion seized the imagination with such authoritative force.[1]

Although the epigrammatic concision of Adorno's maxim lends itself to quotation, this cannot be the sole reason for its continuing appeal. For example, in another essay Adorno also wrote that "All post-Auschwitz culture, including its urgent critique, is garbage,"[2] but few Holocaust commentators ever allude to this equally pungent view. Adorno's aphorism unleashes an anxiety about the potential moral and aesthetic conflict between art and atrocity that threatens the quest for a form and style to represent the unthinkable. His contribution to the abiding challenge is to clear the mind of verbal and metaphysical cant and to remind us that this major disruption in what we used to call civilized behavior cannot be repaired so as to make it seem as if no damage had been done. The breach might not lead to muteness, but it steers us toward fresh premises and perceptions about language and society that future students of art and culture could not afford to ignore.

Perhaps what Adorno really meant to say was that to write poems after Auschwitz the way we wrote poems before Auschwitz was barbaric, because the act would foster a lyric impulse nurtured by denial and pretense. A thread of disenchantment runs through the essay on "Cultural Criticism and Society" that helps to explain Adorno's dissenting judgment about the prospects for an art of the Holocaust. History, and especially contemporary history, had so debased "culture" as both concept and term that its claims in 1949 seemed suspect and overwrought. Since in the past culture, art, and philosophy had "always stood in the life-process of society from which they distinguished themselves,"[3] poetry *after* Auschwitz would have to redefine that "life-process" to include a simultaneous death-process in order to establish some legitimacy. Adorno's initial response to the dilemma—he later modified his view—was to fear that poetry about Auschwitz, instead of seeking an imagery compatible with mass murder, might dislodge from Holocaust literature its vital nexus to the life–death process that was the nucleus of its inspiration.

Israeli writer Aharon Appelfeld agrees with Adorno's warning that to write poetry after Auschwitz might seem barbaric, but he argues that the human need to ritualize grief and pain overrides the summons to silence implicit in Adorno's famous caution. Appelfeld responded to the impasse that Adorno had sketched in his various forays into the theme of art after Auschwitz by insisting that any literary forms emerging from the catastrophe would have to honor *two* impulses, the "desire to keep silence and the desire to speak." The intermediate realm between them, a stylized tension that invaded the very vocabulary of his fictions, supports the principle of what he called "literary nonexpression"[4] that became one of the emblems of his art. Appelfeld's subtle distinction between the inexpressible and the unexpressed allows the inventive temperament to escape from Adorno's plight by inviting it to seek ways of undoing and concealing reality even as it tries to sculpt the shape of its horrifying outlines. All Holocaust art involves a transaction between fact and imagination, between the details of destruction and various techniques for facing or effacing their grotesque features. Not every author discussed in this review would consider such a pact a profitable endeavor; nevertheless, I believe it is the quintessential task for Holocaust art, which includes not only literature but painting, cinema, architecture and, under the enlightened guidance of James Young, the emerging sub-specialty of Holocaust monuments.

In the beginning, however, was not the critical theory but the creative feat. Contrary to the widespread belief that years if not decades had to pass before Holocaust testimony and art would be able to confront the chaos of an unfathomable ordeal, writers and artists were at work well before the war had come to an end, indifferent to what would later become the controversy about Holocaust representation. Perhaps the most substantial achievements during this period were the caustic paintings of Felix Nussbaum, whose *The Damned* (January 1944) and *Death Triumphant* (his last painting, April 1944) — and these represent only two choices among many — mirror the terror and devastation more than a year before it ended. Nussbaum and his wife were deported from Brussels on July 31, 1944, to Auschwitz, where they were murdered ten days later. Even earlier, between 1941 and 1943, Abraham Sutzkever in the Vilna ghetto was composing verses that would later establish him as the world's preeminent Holocaust poet writing in Yiddish. Paul Celan wrote his most famous poem, "Todesfuge" ("Deathfugue") in late 1944 or early 1945; it was first published (in Romanian translation) in 1947. For a long time it was thought that Adorno had this work in mind when he issued his pronouncement about writing poems after Auschwitz, but Celan's biographer John Felstiner conjectures that Adorno was probably still unfamiliar with the poem in 1949, arguing on the contrary that Adorno eventually withdrew his objection *after* reading Celan. "Todesfuge," which Felstiner calls "the *Guernica* of post-war European literature,"[5] did not come out in Germany until 1952. Finally, Nelly Sachs's first volume of Holocaust poetry, *In den Wohnungen des Todes* (*In the Dwellings of Death*), appeared in 1946. Both Sachs and Celan grasped intuitively what Adorno concluded from intellectual reflection — the critical role of the "death-process" in artistic representation of the murder of European Jewry. Neither, however, needed Adorno's theoretical intervention to inspire the trenchant imagery of their art.

Charlotte Delbo finished *Aucun de nous ne viendra* (*None of Us Will Return*), the first volume of her Auschwitz trilogy, soon after her return from recuperation in Sweden in the summer of 1945. It was not published until 1965, although portions appeared in various French journals during the preceding decades. Moreover, two of the most influential Holocaust memoirs were written shortly after war's end, creating their own narrative form and content long before the issue of whether and how the event should be represented became a matter of critical concern. Primo Levi reports that he completed the manuscript of *Se questo è un uomo* (*If This is a Man*, or *Survival in Auschwitz*) within two months of his return to Turin in October of 1945, while Viktor Frankl wrote *Ein Psycholog erlebt das Konzentrationslager* (*A Psychologist Experiences the Concentration Camp*, first translated as *From Death Camp to Existentialism* and later renamed *Man's Search for Meaning*) in 1946. This list could be extended, and should certainly include a curious volume published in Polish in Munich in June 1946 under the title of *Byliśmy w Oświęcimiu* (*We Were in Auschwitz*). It was written by three Polish political prisoners shortly after their liberation by U.S. forces from Dachau-Allach in April 1945 (they had earlier been in Auschwitz). The publisher, Anatol Girs, himself a Polish survivor of Auschwitz and Dachau, bound part of the edition in concentration camp "stripes" cut from the material of original prisoner garments. At least one special copy (which I have seen) had embedded into its cover a piece of rusted barbed wire, as if to forewarn the reader of what lay ahead in its pages. In the preface, the collective authorship introduced a sentiment that Adorno and most of the other authors I have mentioned would endorse: In Auschwitz, they affirm, "We were united by commonplace, pitiless death, not death on behalf of the nation or honor, but death for worn-out flesh, boils, typhus, swollen legs."[6]

Of two of the three authors we know virtually nothing; in America their names—Janusz Nel Siedlecki and Krystyn Olszewski—have slipped into oblivion. The book would probably have suffered the same fate, had not the third member of the triumvirate been Tadeusz Borowski, and had not four of the narratives in this singular volume been translated years later in a collection of stories called *This Way for the Gas, Ladies and Gentlemen*. In an introductory note, Anatol Gils reminds us that one feature of the text is unassailable: "the art in it must be separated from the documentation." Thus the problem of boundaries between Holocaust fact and Holocaust fiction, between history and imagination, so often debated today, was first raised as early as the summer of 1946. Gils insisted on the documentary value of the work, observing rather wryly that perhaps some future artist might "seek in it material for an epic about our era" (1). He may not have recognized that through an ironic narrator disguised as the author's persona, Borowski (at age twenty-three!) had already devised a strategy for transmuting the facts of Auschwitz into a disciplined narrative form. Borowski assaulted the reader's tranquility with a literary subtlety and force that "mere" reportage—indeed, the reportage of his fellow authors—could never have achieved.

In *Words and Witness: Narrative and Aesthetic Strategies in the Representation of the Holocaust*, Lea Wernick Fridman figuratively takes up the gauntlet thrown down by the publisher of *We Were in Auschwitz*. Fridman's modest volume has no pretensions about offering a comprehensive survey of her theme. Instead she wisely limits herself to a reading of selected texts that illustrate the challenge of uncovering "the necessary connections between the experience of historical trauma and its expression." In recent years the term *trauma* has gained widespread favor as a generic description of what Holocaust survivors endured, along with the tendency to view their ordeal within established psychological and often even Freudian paradigms. The terminology of clinical discourse infiltrates Fridman's inquiry too, even though she is aware of the need "to look more carefully at the critical and analytic vocabulary with which we describe and digest our own narrative of extreme experience." Certainly this is true, but it leaves the reader wondering why she was not bolder in following her own advice instead of depending on what she calls "traumatic symptomatology" to illuminate the effects of the historical horror we name the Holocaust. Viewing the murder of European Jewry, the partial destruction of the Roma and Sinti population, the torture and execution of innumerable hostages and political prisoners as a source of "radical traumatic knowledge"[7] risks deflating the details of atrocity through a different kind of verbal suppression. There is a certain irony in the author's search for a language of the unrepresentable when she embraces with no hesitation simplifying rhetorical formulas like "radical traumatic knowledge" and the "narrative of extreme experience." If the Holocaust were nothing more than an extreme experience of history, it hardly merits the global attention it has received for more than half a century.

Since so much has already been written about many of the authors whose works she addresses, Fridman rejects lengthy exegesis and chooses to concentrate instead on the evolution of certain important questions that affect the writing of all Holocaust literature. Chief among these is the crucial issue of finding a voice appropriate to the narrative of atrocity. My instinct was to write "unprecedented atrocity," but this would have violated the premises behind Fridman's inquiry, which begins with a lengthy chapter in which she distinguishes between tales of gothic horror like Poe's and narratives of "historical horror," among which she chooses Conrad's *Heart of Darkness* as a principal and even archetypal example. Some will find this too conventional an inspiration for the literature of the Holocaust. Others will object that a novella drawing on colonial exploitation for its historical base — despite the brooding gloom of its landscape of dark intentions — is too tame a source for imaginative texts grounded in mass murder. In any event, the announcement that "Mistah Kurtz — he dead" ends the journey for Conrad's Marlow, freeing him to return to civilization and his role as storyteller, physically unscarred and wounded only in memory. Kurtz's "the horror, the horror" hints at a ritual catastrophe through the eyes of his private disaster. But when someone exclaims "The Jews — they dead!" — between five and six million of them, to say nothing of the countless other victims of German barbarity — we enter a realm of annihilation undreamt of by Marlow, Kurtz, or indeed the ruthless colonial exploiters whose greed knits together the threads of Conrad's tale. Notwithstanding the suffering and deaths of which they were guilty, the main interest of these exploiters, as with American slavery, was in keeping their victims alive. The will to murder was not an intrinsic part of their scheme. So in an odd way Fridman's insistence on linking the historical horror of the Holocaust and the question of unrepresentability to Conrad's *Heart of Darkness* skirts Adorno's concern that art would be unable to face the death process that lay at the heart of Holocaust darkness.

Nonetheless, Fridman's readings of several texts are suggestive and insightful, especially her analyses of Dan Pagis's poetry and her juxtaposition of Piotr Rawicz's neglected novel *Blood from the Sky* with Charlotte Delbo's memoir *None of Us Will Return*, which she unaccountably says is written as "a stream-of-consciousness novel in the first person plural." This it certainly is not, though the volume, which includes verse and reportage as well as prose vignettes in Delbo's inimitable style, cannot easily be categorized. But both authors were involved in the act, as Fridman puts it, "of grasping violent fact in words," and neither shied away from the challenge. Fridman captures the essence of Delbo's artistic strategy by calling it a "poetic unfolding of consciousness." She is equally precise in summing up Rawicz's technique in her conclusion that "the forms of language and of discourse called upon to speak about historical catastrophe are profoundly connected to the negating character of the experiences they would describe."[8]

Finally, lest readers be misled, one needs to correct a few errors that have crept into Fridman's text. Ida Fink writes in Polish, not Hebrew; Jean Améry (Hans Mayer) was Austrian, not Belgian; and the SS Unterscharführer from Treblinka in Claude Lanzmann's film *Shoah* is named Franz Suchomel, not Schomet.

Moving from Fridman's interpretations to Michael Rothberg's *Traumatic Realism: The Demands of Holocaust Representation* marks a journey from the clear intentions of literary criticism to the complex discourse of cultural theory, but this is by no means an invidious comparison. *Traumatic Realism* is a serious and thoughtful work by an erudite young scholar whose multilingual training allows him to range through sources that are not accessible to many students of Holocaust commentary. In addition, Rothberg is at home not only in literary criticism—his academic base is in an English department—but philosophical inquiry and the theoretical terms of modernism and postmodernism. His book offers an admirable example of the interdisciplinary approach to the Holocaust that the event requires as we learn more about it and the ways various disciplines have responded to its continuing influence. His opening two chapters on Theodor W. Adorno and Maurice Blanchot, which comprise nearly one-third of his text, present one of the most extensive accounts in English of those authors' intricate assessments of the impact of the Holocaust on modern culture. Because of their difficult styles, many readers find Adorno and Blanchot elusive and sometimes inaccessible; to such readers, Rothberg's analysis provides a service of inestimable value. Readers should be forewarned, however, that through an odd kind of literary osmosis Rothberg's own writing in these chapters absorbs some of the abstract quality of his subjects' thought.

Rothberg's provocative readings of major texts by figures such as Charlotte Delbo, Ruth Kluger, Art Spiegelman, and Philip Roth, as well as his assessment of films such as *Schindler's List* and Claude Lanzmann's *Shoah* and an appraisal of the impact of the United States Memorial Museum in Washington on Holocaust culture build upon the tension between the actualities of the deathcamp universe and the efforts to represent them. Art is a mediation between what happened and our striving to envision it. Although labeling the Holocaust an "extreme event" does not begin to capture the nature of its excesses, Rothberg (like Fridman) seems satisfied with this designation. Some might argue that current familiarity with the details of German mass murder is already so extensive that audiences need only the sign of a verbal formulation like "extreme event" to convey what is implicit in those words, but I have seen no convincing evidence that this is true. When the language of criticism skirts the ugly facts of history instead of searching for a way to include them in the process of theory formation, an audience can easily lose a sense of the human (and inhuman) ordeals that generated the need for the theory in the first place. This is one of the limitations of the otherwise stimulating work of Dominick LaCapra, whose influence is vividly felt in several of the volumes under review. If the issue of Holocaust representation is allowed to supersede the immediacy of the experience in the reader's (to say nothing of the critic's) consciousness — and this is often the case in Rothberg's volume — the resulting imbalance between historical and critical truth may be nurtured by a less than desirable sacrifice.

What Rothberg calls "the facts" of the Holocaust become not a source of information and knowledge but the origin of a dilemma, which mere realistic depiction cannot solve. Hence he calls for a "rereading of realism under the sign of trauma." For some readers, that term (trauma) may disintegrate under the weight of its own multiple implications, but Rothberg's intention is to help them over the moral and psychological impasse of mass murder and to reestablish a manageable continuity between the savagery of unimaginable atrocity and the sanctuary of normal behavior. The aim of traumatic realism, he argues, is "to produce the traumatic event as an object of knowledge and to program and transform its readers so that they are forced to acknowledge their relationship to posttraumatic culture."[9]

How does one savor the "other life" of survival, blending what one has lived through with what one has died through, or what has died through one, that defines existence in the wake of catastrophes such as the Holocaust? And after one has absorbed the import of that question for the subject, how does one encourage the "object" group, non-survivors or members of successor generations, to participate meaningfully in that culture of disaster? These are issues that engage chroniclers as different as Ruth Kluger and Charlotte Delbo, Art Spiegelman in his *Maus* volumes, and Lanzmann in *Shoah*. All are concerned with what one can and cannot depict from this universe of destruction, that fringe zone between the inability to describe and the impossibility of knowing fully which Rothberg subsumes under the name of traumatic realism. But not everyone responding to this challenge would agree with Rothberg's assertion that under traumatic conditions "there is a socially shared universe of meaning."[10] Primo Levi has said otherwise, and Delbo herself has written of the limits of solidarity among women in Auschwitz, as one group watched helplessly while members of another were carried off by truck to their death in the gas chamber. Moreover, dozens of witnesses have recorded in their testimonies the feeling of solitude that seized them during the most chaotic moments of atrocity in ghettos and camps.

Other themes in Rothberg's critique of traumatic realism will rouse disagreement from its readers, but this is as it should be: any text worthy of its content cannot expect to elicit merely nods of assent. Rothberg himself disputes the conclusions of some of his predecessors by insisting that his view of coming to terms with the past allows for a continuity if not an equivalence among the traditions of realism, modernism, and postmodernism. Those who favor abyss or rupture as the most valid image for facing the Holocaust will nonetheless be forced to grapple with the ideas of this challenging new addition to the library of Holocaust inquiry. And they will be relieved to hear that while traumatic realism adds to our knowledge of the calamity, Rothberg refuses to twist it into a form of consolation.

Both Lea Fridman and Michael Rothberg recognize the obstacles to representing the Holocaust in literature, but neither disputes the moral or artistic value of embracing the task. Berel Lang's essays in *Holocaust Representation: Art within the Limits of History and Ethics* address in terms relevant to contemporary consciousness the same theme, but with more searching and controversial analysis. Can or should art, he asks, particularly Holocaust art, heed ethical and contextual constraints external to its creation? The question merits the thoughtful consideration that Lang's philosophical temperament bestows on it, even though all readers may not agree with his conclusions. He has firm convictions on the issue, and they offer some valuable cautionary considerations to those involved in what remains a continuing debate.

Logic would seem to dictate that before one can imagine an event like the Holocaust, one must study what it was, its historical actuality, its factual details. But events sometimes have a nasty habit of sabotaging logic, and as I mentioned at the beginning of this essay, artists like Felix Nussbaum and poets like Abraham Sutzkever were plowing the fields of horrific possibility well before historians had established the reality on which their visions were supposed to be based. One would like to believe that in an ordered universe art disposes what history first proposes, that, as Lang argues, a temporal and moral chronology leads from history to art, but in the disordered Holocaust cosmos that was not always the case, and this may prompt some of Lang's readers to pause over his belief that "If ever facts have spoken for themselves, this is the case for the body of fact surrounding the Holocaust."[11] Although Jan Gross has chronicled the "facts" of the 1941 pogrom in Jedwabne, where Polish Christians savagely beat to death some of their Jewish neighbors and burned alive the remainder in a barn, it would be rash indeed to tell those still staring with mute intellectual confusion at Gross's account that its "facts" speak for themselves. Lang is certainly correct in his insistence that "knowing" the details of such an episode is essential for appreciating its causes and consequences, its implications for our understanding of human behavior, but our lingering difficulty in *imagining* those final moments of horror from more than half a century ago says much about the *in*sufficiency, to say nothing of the primacy, of "mere" historical narrative in Holocaust discourse.

Although Lang avoids dogmatic assertion and invariably offers balanced assessments of his concerns, he seems steadfast in his belief that the goal of all Holocaust representation should be to increase our knowledge and understanding of the event. This is a reasonable expectation for works of Holocaust history even though, as Lang admits, Raul Hilberg's views of Jewish behavior during the period and Daniel Goldhagen's of ordinary Germans' attitudes toward Jews have been received with far from universal assent. Similarly, prominent historians like Arno Mayer and Henry Friedlander provide versions of the "Final Solution" and the Nazi euthanasia program that remain in dispute to this day. Thus even historians must filter their facts through the screen of interpretation. Nonetheless, as Lang insists, the core of truth we call "actuality" remains ever-present and imposes a controlling frame for serious historical *and* literary representations of the Holocaust that ought not to be exceeded.

Those who share Lang's view that the Holocaust is "an event as close to sacred, after all, as anything in a secular world is likely to be"[12] may feel more sympathetic to his ideas than those who prefer to see it as one of the unholiest episodes in human history. Lang's usage here exposes a premise and a potential conflict that lies at the heart of his enterprise: it sets limits on the range of language and imagery that is appropriate to its subject. A sacred topic demands restraint and respect in verbal approach that an unholy one might not, and this in turn raises the question of fundamental differences between historical and artistic truth. Poet Paul Celan is less concerned with a search for truth than for words to convey it. If his poems veer between the language and silence that George Steiner explored in some early essays, it is because Celan is convinced that "Writing the Holocaust" — the title of Lang's first essay — is as much a matter of what *can* as what *ought* to be expressed. For Celan, there is no mystery to the unspeakable because he makes it part of the creative process by compelling his readers to experience it through the omission or suppression of speech. If at the heart of Nazi discourse was a moral violation of human exchange, an artist like Celan can explore this vocal corruption by urging us to be wary of any definition of the individual as a creature who speaks. He thus complements the painstaking labor of historians like Raul Hilberg who pierce the silence of Nazi railroad timetables by deciphering the sinister intentions behind their innocent façade of travel information.

Few could quarrel with Lang's distinction between history confronting "the constraints of actuality" and literature dwelling in "the less restrictive domain of possibility."[13] Writers are inclined to invent character, motive, and situation in ways that historians, relying on documents and, less frequently, on eyewitness testimony, are not. But the deeper challenge to both, when the Holocaust is their subject, lies not in the realm of actuality or possibility, but of *impossibility*. Neither form of discourse can draw on traditions that allow for the representation of Jews burned alive, mothers smothering their own infants to maintain silence in their communal hiding places, children brained against brick walls, sons forced to drown their fathers, shooting victims who are only wounded being buried alive in mass graves along with the corpses of the dead, a hunger so intense that it drives decent men to cannibalism — all breaches of normality that challenge the actual and the possible with their cries to be heard — and one is left wondering whether any familiar narrative conventions are equipped to imagine such moral enormities. But I doubt whether readers would turn to historians to find models of writers willing to tackle that task.

One ready to meet the charge was Tadeusz Borowski, whose stories in *This Way for the Gas, Ladies and Gentlemen* Lang uses to illustrate his inquiry into "What space is left for authors who commit themselves to images of a composite event so dense morally and historically as to leave the imagination little room in which to move and act." As mentioned earlier in this essay, Borowski began writing those tales soon after his release from Dachau-Allach in April 1945, long before any moral or historical context for what he had survived had been established. His imagination had all the space it needed, constrained by nothing but memories of his recent Auschwitz experience. His first-person narrators are classic examples of the principle in fiction that one can say *I* without meaning *me*. One is thus bewildered by Lang's assumption that "it is virtually impossible for the reader to decide from internal evidence alone whether these stories are fictional or not."[14] In fact, the ironic tone pervading them distinguishes creator from his creatures and from the outset contrasts the impersonal features of history (or of nature) with disillusioned human response. The story from this volume called "A Day at Harmenz" is a carefully crafted work of art that could not possibly be mistaken for nonfiction by a student of literature. Its inner structure is cemented by imagery of food from start to finish. The opening dialogue begins congenially "Good morning, Tadek. How would you like something to eat?" and the closing one ends nastily, "Okay, Jew, come on up and eat. And when you've had enough, take the rest with you to the cremo." Hunger and food dominate the dialogue and action, alienating or binding together the various characters. What historian could redefine meaning as one of Borowski s prisoners does in this stunning formulation: "Real hunger is when one man regards another man as something to eat"? Far from being mistaken for non-fiction, "A Day at Harmenz" is marked by its unity of tone and imagery as one of the outstanding works of fiction in Holocaust literature.

The odd disparity between Lang's shrewd insight into the moral and philosophical issues raised by writing about the Holocaust and his consistent underrating of the power — or authority — of imaginative literature to translate those issues into the compelling substance of narrative or verse or pictorial representation remains a paradox. Of course, as Lang argues, misleading Holocaust writing abounds, not only by authors of limited talent who abuse their material but also by those who seek to replace shame with dignity, impotence with resistance, horror with laughter (as in Benigni's *Life Is Beautiful*) in order to reclaim from the humiliations of the camp universe an image of heroism more consistent with their own visionary needs. Such bad art does misrepresent the Holocaust, in large part because it is ignorant of its actuality, but these charges cannot be extended to the best of Holocaust representers — Jorge Semprun, Charlotte Delbo, Piotr Rawicz, as well as those whom Lang mentions — who through personal anguish have much more intimate access to the "hard facts" of atrocity than most historians of the subject.

Indeed, one might maintain that their work unintentionally confirms the unimpeachable central tenet of Lang's volume: "Where history figures in artistic representation, the details of historical chronicle have an importance that is absent or much reduced in representations in which specific historical events have no part." And whether we consider it sacred or unholy, this is especially true for an event like the Holocaust. But since the best Holocaust creative work is not based on the reading and interpretation of Holocaust documents but on personal experience, it is difficult to appreciate why Lang would find the moral enormity of genocide at odds with what he calls "the humanizing effects of figurative discourse."[15] Perhaps the problem is with the premise, since the dehumanizing effects of Nazi practices on character and language lie at the heart of the endeavor we name Holocaust literature. When Dante sent his pilgrim through the circles of Hell, he dispatched Virgil, one of the greatest poets of classical antiquity, to enlighten his pupil's mind along the way.

Whether one agrees with Michael Rothberg's conclusions about traumatic realism or Berel Lang's premises about Holocaust literature, each fills his narrative with a strong personal voice that develops a cogent argument on behalf of his ideas. Vivian M. Patraka in *Spectacular Suffering: Theatre, Fascism, and the Holocaust* allows her own critical view to be muffled by citations from so many external sources that her stance frequently seems to vanish from the text. Was it Emerson who said "I hate quotations. Tell me what you know"? In the instance of this volume, it is sound advice. Patraka is so dependent on the opinions of other commentators — I count more than eighty-five instances, in a book of 130 pages — that in many chapters they displace her voice and leave her limited opportunity to shape a coherent vision of Holocaust representation.

As the pun in the book's title, *Spectacular Suffering*, implies, Patraka is mainly concerned with stage representations of the Holocaust. Although she does not raise the issue, she inadvertently invites readers to wonder why the principal achievements in Holocaust literature have been in poetry and fiction rather than in drama. The plays she examines in greatest detail by Charlotte Delbo, Liliane Atlan, Peter Barnes, Joan Schenkar, and Nelly Sachs are neither widely known nor often performed. There is no mention of Beckett, Ionesco, or Pinter, though the influence of Holocaust monstrosity on their dramatic vision can scarcely be doubted, and indeed some consideration of the Theater of the Absurd might have furnished an artistic context for the analysis of Patraka's own authors. Although she draws attention to the experimental value of their works, she devotes a full chapter only to Lillian Hellman's conventional *Watch on the Rhine* of 1940, a "pre-Holocaust" play made popular by Hollywood's film version starring Bette Davis and Paul Lukas. She approaches it together with the "Julia" section of Hellman's *Pentimento* ("Julia" was also turned into a film by Hollywood), but her discussion quickly drifts from the issue of Holocaust representation to the feminist critique that is clearly much more intrinsic to the author's approach: "unlike the aggressively heterosexual text of *Watch [on the Rhine]*, 'Julia' is grounded in a historically specific, sexual, intellectual, and political rapport between two women."[16] This may be so, but it leaves one wondering what that conclusion has to do with the "suffering," "fascism," and "Holocaust" of the book's title.

Of late much reflection on the Holocaust, by which I presume we still mean the murder of European Jewry, has used the event as a point of departure for addressing theoretical topics of only secondary relevance. Some readers may find Patraka occasionally guilty of this, though I think she grounds the main thrust of her argument in a legitimate question: "To what degree can theory, in this case theory about fascist ideology and practice, be theatricalized and performed?" The main problem here is with the terminology, since an expression such as "fascist ideology," favored by East Germany and the Soviet Union before the collapse of the communist empire, hides both the criminals and their victims behind a political label. Patraka adopts this language through most of her text, and as a result much of her commentary remains on a level of abstract exposition. In her effort to construe a theatrical aesthetic of atrocity, she uses what one of her sources calls "horrality" to define "a genre for showing the violated, disintegrating body," and this indeed poses with precision one of the major challenges to all Holocaust writing, one that worried Adorno from the start. Her analysis of the use of dummies and puppets in various plays to represent the body in torment is illuminating, but its effect is diluted by constant allusions to the sexuality of power and the pornography of violence that deflect attention from a character's specific Holocaust ordeal. Yet her incisive reversal of the question that arose in the Vilna ghetto about whether one could perform theatre in a graveyard is ingenious — can one, she asks, "perform a graveyard in the theatre?"[17] — and when she mutes the echo of fascist ideology and pursues concrete applications of this inquiry on the stage, she provides some valuable guidelines for entering the unfamiliar terrain of Holocaust drama.

Patraka shrewdly expands the reference of her question about Holocaust theater so that it might also read "can one install a graveyard in a museum?" Her last chapter addresses the tensions between stage and spectator in the two best-known Holocaust visitor sites in America, the U.S. Holocaust Memorial Museum in Washington, D.C., and the Beit Hashoah Museum of Tolerance in Los Angeles. She wisely decides to consider these fixed locales as performative spaces where the spectator is not a passive vessel for receiving information but an active participant in the dynamic of discovery that propels one through their corridors of potential mutual exchange.

Perhaps because she relies on her own visits rather than on the voices of other critics, Patraka's reflections on these museums represent her most compelling and original commentary on the theme of "spectacular suffering." This does not mean that her views do not contain some lapses. Her assumption that an initial strategy of the Washington museum is to celebrate America's role as liberator of those having survived Nazi Germany's genocidal plans misreads the large photographs greeting visitors as they emerge from the elevator at the start of their journey through the exhibition. What they see are aghast American troops who have stumbled on a camp, stunned by the corpses and the near-dead who occupy a "stage" where what has been "performed" stifles any effort to interact with the "action" before their eyes. If anything, this initial confrontation is designed to sabotage our expectation that American democracy's presumed role in helping bring the Holocaust to an end may provide us with some relief from the burdensome spectacles we are about to encounter.

Patraka offers a provocative "reading" of the challenge of multiple interpretations for visitors to the Washington museum, based on her premise that "witnessing is an active process of spectatorship rather than a passive consumption of pre-narrated spectacles" ([124]; the latter was largely the case with the old photographic exhibits at Yad Vashem). When she moves beyond ideology to an analysis of concrete details of structure and content, even her language changes, pointing without abstraction to "the desecrated realm of the Jewish dead" (128). How much more welcome and effective such phrasing is than her earlier arid allusion to "the enormity of the absent referent" (122). She is equally precise in distinguishing one of the oft-cited weaknesses of the Los Angeles museum, which eschews accretion of detail and provides its visitors instead with "an accretion of information" (129). The drawback of this strategy is its suggestion that "technologies in the current historical moment can reenact the events of the Holocaust in a coherent complete narrative of memory" (129). The attentive reader will carry Patraka's insight further, recognizing the reductive illogic of using mass murder to teach tolerance. One of the many achievements of the

Washington site is that as we wind down its galleries, following the path if not the pattern of Dante's descent into hell, we cannot escape the feeling that "the whole museum is a graveyard" (128). Anxiety in the presence of the barely manageable duplicates the ordeal of those whom the museum is designed to memorialize. The sense of absence and loss that consumes one's visit snares the audience as at a play; Patraka is at her best in analyzing the performative role of the spectator in the presence of this unfolding drama of destruction.

Many critics of the museum in Washington have protested the impropriety of placing a principal site of Holocaust memory in a land whose people never experienced the disaster. Those who raise this complaint overlook the tens of thousands of new citizens who found refuge in America after having survived the catastrophe, to say nothing of the much larger number of their descendants. But equally important, the museum in one of its dimensions could find no better home than the national capital of a country that denied entry before the war to many more thousands of potential victims, thus becoming an indirect agent of their doom. There is thus an implicit connection between the millions of murdered individuals and the monumental failure of U.S. policy to accept a role in saving them when there was still time to limit the oncoming atrocity. Although to a much lesser degree, America shares the guilt of the institutions of church and state in Europe that through cowardice, collaboration or indifference tolerated the deportation and murder of their Jewish countrymen. In one of its guises, the Washington museum looms as a long unacknowledged debt of moral obligation.

Nonetheless, the past that will not pass away disturbs the European mind in ways that most Americans (quite properly) will doubtless never understand. The conflict between private destiny and public response is the theme of Caroline Wiedmer's *The Claims of Memory: Representations of the Holocaust in Contemporary Germany and France*. More than half a century after the event, those two countries in particular wrestle with the memory of their painful past, the one as agent of, the other as collaborator in mass murder. Their stories have been told before, but new documents and information continue to surface, so that Wiedmer's fusion of synopsis and analysis will be helpful to those readers unfamiliar with the tangled history of denial and confrontation that still haunts post-war consciousness in these nations. The painstaking research of Serge and Beate Klarsfeld that resurrects the names of native and refugee Jews from France and the dates of their transports to Auschwitz and other deathcamps establishes with certainty the complicity of the Vichy government in the Nazi plan to exterminate the Jews of Europe. No one has to verify the role of the Nazi regime in mass murder, though films like *The Nasty Girl* (1991) and the variety of memorial sites that are spreading across Germany are constant reminders of the need to counter amnesia.

Although Wiedmer's decision to begin her discussion of French and German representations of the Holocaust with an analysis of Art Spiegelman's *Maus* volumes may seem odd to some readers, her critique of the American text highlights the power of the artistic imagination to enrich and deepen historical narratives of atrocity. Indeed, her subsequent straightforward account of the evolution of memorial sites at Drancy and the Vélodrome d'Hiver, principal locales of deportation for the doomed Jews of France, may seem rather dry after an encounter with Spiegelman's brilliant achievement in visual literature. But the tensions between history and memory that thread through *Maus I* and *Maus II* provide focus for the primary inquiries in *The Claims of Memory*, where Wiedmer searches for "manifestations of the dynamic relationship between personal voice and historical accounting"[18] in local and national efforts in France and Germany to capture for a postwar generation the experience of a criminal past.

Wiedmer depends on her French sources for the majority of her observations on the memorials at Drancy and the Vél d'Hiver, so not much fresh insight emerges from her exposition. Her most valuable comments concern their "evasions," their failure to detail the unspeakable ordeal of the Jews who were interned there or to convey unqualified censure of the wartime French government for its collusion in the roundups and deportations. One would have appreciated a much fuller consideration of the role of such memorials in what the author calls "the working through of traumatic memories in mourning,"[19] since many would disagree that this should be their main function in the first place. Unless a monument contains in its form some clear hint of the specific crimes it is meant to testify to, unless it achieves as a primary office disturbing rather than assuaging memory, it will have failed its principal charge. And when it fulfills its purpose, it may so disable the need to mourn and so frustrate the process of "working through" that those widely esteemed aims may shrink into inconsequence.

The civilized imagination does not readily accept the possibility that atrocities like the murder of European Jewry may so vex the impulse to "work through" them as to sabotage that desire and leave only fragments of moral ruin in its wake. Wiedmer devotes most of her response to Michel Verhoeven's *The Nasty Girl* to a summary of the action, which will be of value chiefly to those who have not seen the film, but in the process she exposes the ease with which efforts at "working through" can be turned into a pantomime of hypocrisy. The attempt to restore balance to the moral equilibrium of society in the German town where the movie is set is paid for, as Wiedmer points out, with the marginalizing of the sole Jewish survivor still living there. The crime against him is further diminished by the information that he had been sent to a camp as a communist rather than as a Jew. The film thus foreshadows the issues that will occupy Wiedmer in the remainder of her volume, as she considers the complex question of how a nation struggles to "memorialize" its own criminal past. Should the post-Holocaust community in Germany, searching for a proper space and adequate form to commemorate the disappearance of the Jews, focus on the victims, the crime, or the general population, who — as in *The Nasty Girl*— chose never to acknowledge or mourn their involvement in the nefarious activities of the Third Reich?

There is no need to rehearse Wiedmer's detailed and thoughtful accounts of Daniel Libeskind's Berlin Museum Extension, or the long and frustrating controversy over a Memorial for the Murdered Jews of Europe in that same city, or the efforts to make an authentic memorial site out of the remnants of the Sachsenhausen concentration camp and its vicinity in Oranienburg. All such enterprises require compromise, since the relevant competitions have long since shown how vain is the hope for consensus, when the subject is so charged with emotional intensity. Perhaps the best one can hope for is a series of localized reminders of the necessity *and* the near-impossibility of *Trauerarbeit* (the work of mourning) for an atrocity that is destined in some circles to remain beyond consolation forever. There are moments in Wiedmer's narrative when one feels that the monumental slaughter of the Nazi era is untranslatable into any single commemoration on a fixed site. The painful truth is that apprehending the Holocaust requires years of patient study, a long journey through history, literature, art, memoirs, human psychology, and countless other disciplines that illuminate its tangled origins and dreadful results. All this means is that it could take a lifetime to grasp and absorb the death time we call the Holocaust, the claustrophobic reign of terror that consumed a people and its culture, its past as well as much of its future, but few have the leisure or will, to say nothing of the energy, to pursue this arduous task.

So we build monuments, hoping for symbolic resurrection and spiritual catharsis. The best of them, like the museum in Washington and Libeskind's Berlin Museum Extension understand the folly of such goals and dismiss them from their agenda. When Libeskind bisected his jagged addition with straight chambers of void, he addressed the need to make "visible and accessible" a huge absence that "is enacted now in the realm of the invisible."[20] But the success of this venture into literal disappearance depends on the educated eyes and sensations of the beholders, and as decades pass and visitors bring with them memories less and less burdened by familiarity with German atrocities, they may be greeted by a mystifying rather than an edifying rendezvous. Can we expect more from the ceaseless search for an imagery to preserve the past than the growth of a system of multiple perceptions, based on the kind of knowledge that viewers bring with them to the sites of memory and commemoration?

In *The Claims of Memory* (1999), Caroline Wiedmer pays generous tribute to the influence of James E. Young's *The Texture of Memory* (1993). In his most recent work, *At Memory's Edge: After-Images of the Holocaust in Contemporary Art and Architecture* (2000), which covers some of the same material as Wiedmer, Young does not mention her book, probably because it was in press and unavailable to him during the writing of his own. It is all the more noteworthy, then, that both begin their studies of Holocaust memory with a chapter devoted to Art Spiegelman's *Maus*. The magnitude of Spiegelman's visual and literary achievement grows with each passing year, and Young's discussion adds considerable insight into the reasons for its acclaim. It becomes a model for the "hybrid forms" and "antiredemptive middle voice"[21] that characterize the work of the figures to whom Young devotes his attention in the remainder of his volume.

Much Holocaust art, whether literature, painting, sculpture, or monument seeks ways to simulate the original loss, pressing the reader or spectator to define his or her role in the encounter between the imagination and the representation of historical truth. More than twenty-five years ago in *The Holocaust and the Literary Imagination*, I predicted the eventual emergence of an aesthetic of atrocity that would do justice to the brutality of the "final solution." More than a decade ago in *Holocaust Testimonies: The Ruins of Memory*, I argued that Holocaust commentators committed to a redemptive mode of inquiry misled themselves and their readers by slighting the lasting disruptive impact of the murder of European Jewry on the religious, philosophical, and artistic quest for closure. In *At Memory's Edge*, Young cogently synthesizes these two views into an "antiredemptory aesthetic" whose practitioners "refuse to assign singular, overarching meaning to either the events of the Holocaust or our memory of them."[22] His acute critique of various American and German exponents of antiredemptory art and architecture provides us with a useful context for the difficult challenge of looking askew, of embracing the negative spaces and cavities without which, as he convincingly shows, Holocaust representation would be deficient.

Young believes that for his second-generation subjects who were born after the Holocaust, history and memory—what happened and how one remembers what happened—exert an equal force on their artistic and architectural visions. He minimizes the fact that those born during the event but at a safe distance from its dangers also depend on the vicarious approach through historical research, testimony, memoirs, and other vital sources for access to the experience of atrocity. In some sense, *all* outsiders to that experience are drawn by the twin magnets of history and memory into the heart of Holocaust darkness. But this does not diminish the originality and force of the work of the second-generation respondents whom Young chooses as candidates for this journey. If many of them are concerned with the theme of "disappearance," the vanished façades of former Jewish businesses (Shimon Attie's "Writing on the Wall," 1991–1993) or a memorial obelisk gradually sinking into the earth until it fades from view (Jochen Gerz' and Esther Shalev-Gerz's 1985 Countermonument "Against Fascism, War, and Violence—and for Peace and Human Rights" in Harburg-Hamburg), this is only to accent the need of the visitor to these sites to move beyond the reassuring presence of visual or structural creations to the twilight zone of absent and hence often forgotten crimes and their victims. Many of the examples in Young's exegesis are inspired by the principle, in Gerz's striking locution, of "Out of sight . . . *in mind*" (142). Instead of reproducing images of the Holocaust, these artists rely on their "after-images," portrayed in photographs or suggested through broken forms, remnants of a missing people and a defunct past that would cling to some internal monitor of remembrance in spectators as a result of their initial encounter with the installations.

Among the most illuminating sections in Young's book are his last two chapters, one devoted to Daniel Libeskind's Jewish Museum in Berlin (what Wiedmer describes as the "Berlin Museum Extension") and the other to Young's personal involvement in the design competition for a "Memorial for the Murdered Jews of Europe." Young's analysis of Libeskind's intentions, coupled with his citations from Libeskind's provocative observations on his own design, provides one of the most discerning commentaries on the problems of Holocaust representation that I know of. A difficult concept for students of the Holocaust to absorb is its violation of temporal reality as a smoothly flowing stream from past through present into the future. In his building, Libeskind claims, he "introduced the idea of the void as a physical interference with chronology." This enables visitors to experience ruptures in time *and* space as they proceed through the Museum. It leads to what Young calls an estrangement from viewers' preconceptions, an essential preliminary for any genuine contact with Holocaust memory. He describes Libeskind's structure as "a negative space created by the Holocaust, an architectural model for absence,"[23] and one is struck by the ease with which such language might be transposed into an exposition of certain Paul Celan poems. (Indeed, the title of Libeskind's unsuccessful proposal for a "Memorial for the Murdered Jews of Europe" — "Stonebreath" — might have been lifted straight from Celan, or from that other celebrated post-Holocaust poet writing in German, Nelly Sachs.)

Young's last chapter is a dramatic and suspenseful account of the prolonged and heated political and cultural struggle to choose an appropriate commemorative monument to the murder of European Jewry for the new capital of a reunited Germany. Since he played an influential role in bringing about a tenuous resolution to the debate, he writes from the center of the maelstrom. But his narrative reaches beyond mere documentation of the difficult process of a nation searching for a manageable memorial gesture toward its own criminal past. By asking his German audience "whether any memorial can ever be more than a ritual gesture to an unredeemable past,"[24] Young focuses the discussion on the magnitude of the atrocity and the irreplaceable loss in its wake. One cannot return from a venture into the void with anything but a sense of disorientation, and this helps to explain the appeal of Peter Eisenman's much revised winning design for the Berlin memorial (according to Wiedmer originally called *Gräberfeld*, Field of Graves, though Young does not mention this title).

Eisenman's "Waving Field of Pillars," with its undulating concrete forms of varied heights, proclaims nothing. The shapes represent blank invitations to visitors to decide where they have been summoned and what direction their sense of uneasiness should lead them in. The paradox of being invited to establish an organic relationship to a past that one can never really inhabit is a theme linking all the volumes under review, though as Young and Wiedmer show, it has proved especially burdensome to the German heirs of the legacy of mass murder. But this does not exonerate the rest of us: a main aim of Holocaust representation is to implicate its audience in the difficult but essential tasks of imagining an absent pain and mourning an unending loss. The rich and diverse results examined in these works are enough to appease Adorno's initial fears that it couldn't—and therefore shouldn't—be done.

10

THE BOOK OF GENESIS IN
THE ART OF SAMUEL BAK

The Book of Genesis begins with the creation of the world and its first
human occupants and ends with the death of Jacob, the last of the patriarchs. A brief coda, the closing words of the narrative, announces the
death of Joseph: "and they embalmed him and he was put in a coffin in
Egypt."[1] But this is not necessarily a melancholy image, since it prepares the
reader for the Book of Exodus where Moses will lead the Jewish people out
of bondage on a journey through the desert toward a Promised Land. The
Torah ends with the death of Moses, but here again the passing of a great
leader is only the harbinger of a more expansive future.

This, however, is only one strain of a multi-layered story. Scarcely has
Genesis begun when an act of disobedience shatters the infinitude of the
initial creation and girdles time with the stricture of mortality. Soon after,
fraternal rivalry initiates a pattern of violence that will become a defining
feature of human history. One of the first inquiries in Hebrew Scripture is
"Where is thy brother Abel?" to which Cain replies: "I do not know. Am I my
brother's keeper?" That question echoes through the centuries to a peace-
seeking civilization still groping for an appropriate response. The ending of
Genesis provides a temporary answer, as Joseph is reconciled with his broth-

ers when he responds generously to their plea for forgiveness. It is one of the many instances of *tikkun,* of healing or repair, that threads through the writings comprising the Jewish Testament. But other events within and beyond Scripture reveal the limited stamina of such a feat, confirming the need to reprise it through the ages.

In an essay called "Tradition and the Individual Talent," T. S. Eliot wrote of the duty to reconsider past literature in the light of later ideas that could not have been predicted by the original artists. The advent of Freud, for example, created an opportunity for new insights that ordained a revising of the critical legacy. Similarly, in his cycle of paintings and drawings called *In a Different Light,*[2] Samuel Bak has shaped a visual universe of discourse that reviews the assumptions of Genesis through the revelations of a later "text" called the Book of the Holocaust—canonically impossible, of course, but intellectually plausible and indeed, in its influence on his work, a source of major imaginative vitality. Bak is not the first artist to note the impact of the involuntary modern voyage of the children of Israel from life to death on prior accounts of the Jewish journey into and back from exile. But he is one of very few to focus so persistently on the importance of this theme. As a result of the Holocaust, a radical shift in thinking about the meaning of covenant has emerged, reducing the nostalgia for a simple renewal of belief to a minor key. In a sense, Bak redraws the lines between man and God, Adam and his Creator, human dreams and divine purpose, time and eternity: the whole spiritual drama that inspires the most crucial moments of Hebrew Scripture. Genesis contains several instances of the suspension of divine compassion following human mutiny. But even more constant is the motif of divine assurance to the Chosen People of protection from their enemies.

To the eye of the contemporary reader, however, a sinister irony pervades the imagery surrounding that promise in the closing lines of the Book of Malachi, the last of the prophets, whose words in the King James version are also among the final ones of the entire "Old Testament" as prepared for a Christian audience: "For lo! That day is at hand, burning like an oven. All the arrogant and all the doers of evil shall be straw, and the day that is coming—said the Lord of Hosts—shall burn them to ashes." When a prophecy designed to comfort ended up confusing the righteous with the wicked, when an innocent allusion to "oven" and "ashes" upset the moral balance, in Malachi's language, for "those who revere the Lord and esteem His name," then the Jewish self was obliged to reexamine both its identity and the bond that joined it to an ancient and honorable religious tradition.

Samuel Bak has chosen a return to beginnings as his point of departure in the series called *In a Different Light.* He imprints on the original template of creation signs of disarray that stain the purity of the pristine scene. Bak literally adopts Eliot's injunction to re-view the work of early masters through the vista of later intellectual and spiritual history by turning to the most monumental representation of Genesis in the annals of art, Michelangelo's paintings on the ceiling of the Sistine Chapel. Bak's idea itself is a tour de force, since art has long played a principal role in shaping our conception of our fate. In a bold imaginative stroke, he redesigns the foremost visual text of the creation, deconstructs its fixed features, and recasts them through the eyes of modernity. Present consciousness requires efforts like these if we are to see clearly the damage done by the ravages of history to standard representations of our numinous past and future. Michelangelo himself adapted a story from Hebrew Scripture to Christianity's vision of the human journey from Creation to the Last Judgment. Visitors to the Sistine Chapel can take in the majestic sweep of this quintessential voyage and the sublime hierarchy implicit in its artistic depiction. Despite the rivalries and conflicts of the early Renaissance, an age of faith saw no reason to question the supremacy of that hierarchy.

But Bak's personal history, together with his evolving artistic growth, furnished many reasons for questioning the assumptions behind both scriptural and Renaissance views of the Creation.[3] For the familiar consolation of extracting hope for redemption from various channels of despair, he substitutes the task of inquiring into the possibilities and impossibilities of re-establishing a meaningful covenant with its original Author. This in turn might illuminate the uncertain destiny of that agreement without ignoring the events that had led to questions about its sanctity. Such doubts rarely entered the minds of the earliest visitors to the Sistine Chapel. The structure of the place reinforced the heavenly hierarchy that defined religious belief of the time. Even today, viewers of the ceiling cannot escape the lofty sensation of having the gaze swept upward to confront the prodigious spectacle of what one Michelangelo scholar has called a metaphor of the universal order and of a fixed and immutable divine design.

When the visual examination of the vast space above finally ends and the line of sight resumes its horizontal vector, it is greeted by the equally colossal Last Judgment. In this encounter with the spiritual plan of the universe, the division between heavenly and earthly zones affirms the preordained journey of the soul from birth to eternity. For these orthodox options of blessing and damnation, Bak substitutes a cyclic view of experience, an alternation between creative action and ruin that is embodied in the imagery and spatial design of his paintings. They reflect the process of redefining the role of the human creature within the framework of modern existence. The troubling questions Bak raises may not be new, but the moral energy behind his inquiries emerges through a highly original metaphorical vision. If the universe was once God's temple and man and woman its noblest worshipers, what has happened to the splendor of the primordial conception? Viewed "in a different light," through the lens of history, the purer aims of eternity seem constantly to have been thwarted by the bloody plunders of time. Such a conflict launches, in the story of the children of Israel, an oscillation between exile and return, and estrangement from and renewed contact with a Deity whose own position in the affairs of His people appears to waver between intimacy and default. To capture this dilemma on canvas is one of the major goals of Samuel Bak's new sequence of drawings and paintings. If according to the artist's view the Holocaust has left us a legacy of Jewish memory in a state of disrepair, the image of the God of the Hebrews has suffered some damages too.

Michelangelo would have been dismayed by the trend of this argument. For him, the honor of mankind lay in heeding and enacting the intentions of divine will. The Sistine Ceiling portrays the newly created Adam and Eve as figures of perfect comeliness and grace. Their distorted features after the expulsion result from a human breach for which their Creator bears no responsibility. Michelangelo's God as He separates light from darkness is an anthropomorphic agent of awesome power whose patriarchal bearing differs sharply from the silhouettes of vacancy with which Bak chooses to replace Him in his various emendations of the Creation of Adam. In his *Life of Michelangelo*, Vasari had called the Adam of the original Sistine painting "a figure whose beauty, pose, and contours are such that it seems to have been fashioned that very moment by the first and supreme creator rather than by the drawing and brush of a mortal man."[4] Bak's blueprints for Adam acknowledge the impossibility of duplicating the chaste gleaming flesh of his model in a post-Holocaust era that has seen so much violation of the body. Any effort to restore its unsullied status would be a naïve expression of nostalgic yearning, a sacrilege against the anguish of time.

Michelangelo's *Creation of Adam* is charged with tension between human expectation and divine wish. The focal point is the narrow space dividing God's resolute finger from Adam's languid hand, awaiting the spark of vitality that will give it life. The symmetrical skill that separates God, in a regal purple cloak, from a naked Adam highlights the one-way transmission of energy from omnipotent divine source to inert human dependent. God's rigid digit is about to animate the flaccid finger of Adam, whose latent virility is proclaimed by the sculptured muscularity of his flesh. If we turn now to Bak's *Adam and Eve*, we discover a composition that accents a changed pictorial reality, based not on the inviolable hierarchical principles enshrined in Scripture but on the muddled continuum entombed in history. The monochromatic tones of the painting, more fiery than bleak, barely distinguish its human figures from the surrounding landscape. A forlorn and weary-eyed Adam resembles the last Jew more than the first Man as he leans in the shadow of a massive brick structure that those familiar with Bak's earlier work will instantly recognize as the wall from a chamber of death. Its solid substance frames and almost visually consumes the thinly outlined profile of Michelangelo's Deity, His former power seemingly drained by the looming edifice behind him. From a rent in God's cloak that is also a breach in the chamber wall peers the sorrowful face of a post-Holocaust Eve, whether victim or survivor we have no way of knowing. Does Adam mourn her loss, or await her return? The principal activity in the canvas is pointing, but the hands represent a trio of skeptical gestures that promise neither union nor even touch. Eve points toward Adam, who does not return her gaze. The hand of God has lost its way; its finger aims not at Adam but at a distant object in the vicinity of twin crematorium chimneys. When God said "Let there be light," did He foresee the ghastly illumination from these flames of death? The observer is left with the challenge of fusing in the imagination the Holocaust story of uncreation with the dazzling instant of human origin portrayed by Michelangelo.

Adam and Eve also prepares us for the ironic merger of sacred and profane narratives that will be a fundamental strategy of many of the paintings from *In a Different Light.* Several metaphors for the idea of divine guidance gone astray vie for our attention in these canvases. Because it was forbidden to look upon God's countenance, a pillar of smoke guided the children of Israel on their journey through the desert. In *Adam and Eve* (and most other variations in the "creation" group), two columns appear as surrogate signs not of a journey to freedom but of a voyage to death. The finger of God points in their direction, but whether to hurl a divine "J'accuse" at those who have corrupted His plan or as a post-mortem decision to include a different kind of darkness in the original design, the distressed viewer is left to decipher. Adding to the interpretive dilemma is the unmistakable image of God's hand crossing a ridge of bricks in a cruciform motion. As if to confirm the artist's intent, just beneath it a gloved piece of wood in the form of a hand is nailed to the brick façade. It is a piercing sign of the need to seek new meaning and guidance after the failure of the Christian doctrine of mercy and forgiveness to forestall the destruction of European Jewry.

All of this is part of the retinal audacity informing the works included in *In a Different Light.* They push our preconditioned eyes to see images in ways other than they were trained to do by established versions of reality. Bak's frequent violation of familiar visual truth finally forces us to reconsider our memories of the historical and spiritual past and the systems of belief that were allied to them. As a result of the Holocaust, the unnatural has displaced much of the supernatural in its impact on modern consciousness. The artist Francis Bacon has said that a painter "has to capture not only the look of things but the emotions they arouse." Bak might add to this advice the corollary that sometimes a painter must undo the look of things in order to discredit the emotions they arouse, so that more valid feelings may infiltrate the vacant space left by the ousted sentiments. Bacon, who once defined man as a potential carcass, continued with "I believe that realism has to be re-invented. . . . This is the only possible way the painter can bring back the intensity of the reality he is trying to capture."[5] Since the Holocaust was unknown to Michelangelo and undreamt of in his perception of reality, Bak had to find a kind of realism that would allow him to imprint on the archetypal version of creation clues to that destruction. This, in turn, would substantially modify our response to Renaissance and other prior visions of human destiny.

Creation of War Time repeats the confrontation between Adam and God, but here God is even less defined, a cutout from the empty space that surrounds His image. A helmeted Adam leans upon a landscape in ruins, the tatters of his rainbow-colored garments summoning up memories of an ancient broken promise from biblical times. In the distance rise the familiar ominous pillars of smoke, haunting the foreground with their echoes of annihilation, while just behind them the curved tops of the Tablets of the Law peek furtively over a low ridge of stone. What fresh covenant will spring from the ravages of war and Holocaust? The sole sign of renewal is the tree that emerges from the silhouette of God's forearm. But the wary spectator will also note that it is adjacent to His hand, nailed to the wall while blood drips from different kinds of stigmata, leaving us with the disturbing fac-simile of a wounded God. Both the painting and its images are inspired by times of violence that form a major legacy to the modern mind. Any renewal or return to creative vigor must be born from the arduous passage through Bak's fragmented landscapes of devastation.

One of the options in the group of creation paintings is to eliminate the figure of God and to leave Adam and the viewer to cope with His temporary disappearance. This is consistent with the view of the Holocaust as a story of the spiritual solitude of Jewish identity on its unwished-for journey to an unpromising land. Variations like *Open Door* and *Adam with His Own Image* violate the symmetry of Michelangelo's model by eliminating half of the cosmic design — the presence of God. In *Open Door* Adam is largely con-cealed, though his forearm, hand, and knee are vividly sculpted from hu-man flesh. But God is totally absent, replaced by a huge installation of a hand composed of rusted metal and segmented stone, a hollow artifact detached from any divine source. In an ironic reversal, the tip of its thumb seems to gain some mortal substance from its proximity to Adam's finger, as if God were now to be remade in the image of man. But there appears to be little prospect for that here, as the giant hand dominates the painting's space as if to crush its content with its monumental weight. What chance will the hidden Adam have to emerge unscathed? Against the symmetrical bal-ance of Michelangelo's vision Bak has inserted an incompatible opposition, leaving the viewer wondering whether the "open door" is a place of exit or of entry. In the nineteenth century, Nietzsche might have viewed this paint-ing as a sign of the loss of contact between the human and the divine, as a hint of the abdication of God, as proof that the fully human could develop only after the withdrawal of divinity from the formation of the natural self. This may be further than Bak is willing to take us, but the imbalance be-tween hands in *Open Door* certainly suggests that Adam may have to seek elsewhere for a reciprocal source of compassion.

One is at least invited to contemplate such a likelihood in *Adam with His Own Image*, where a reclining Adam sculpted from stone but clothed in human garments faces an inverted reflection of himself. Does this signify that after the Holocaust, whose signature chimneys menace the landscape, man is obliged to recreate himself in his *own* image? Is it an endorsement of solipsism, the notion that man can know only himself, or a meditation on the narcissistic impulse, a fatal habit in myth and a hint of vanity in Milton's Eve? It is a question for art as well as philosophy, as the marble Adam indicates. It would take the ingenuity of a modern Michelangelo to carve from the block of stone containing Adam's reflection a human shape consistent with the anguish it has survived. For the artist representation precedes understanding: the large slab before Adam seems to have fallen from the easel behind the block of stone, and in order to transmute himself from marble into flesh, the hand of Adam, or one of his human descendants, will have to become its own instrument of creation.

Without some form of self-definition, the Adam of *Searching* is on the verge of collapsing into a crumbling ruin. Severed hands of wood and stone are pointing in opposite directions, propped up by artificial supports that are detached from any vital source, human or divine. Archeologists of the future will excavate this terrain, only to find remnants of decaying monuments born of an ancient and mysterious creed. Even for the contemporary viewer, the tree and two wisps of smoke fade into the distance, shrinking reminders of the creation and the near ruin of the Jewish people. It is a scene of missed connections, of sphinx-like spectacles, whose icons evoke a search for meaning that is the very theme of the painting. The panorama is presided over by the visible absence of God, a scenario far from Michelangelo's precise portrayal of the vital moment of creation.

Redefining roles for biblical figures is a major goal of Bak's visual foray into familiar episodes from the Book of Genesis. The narrative of creation is soon followed by the story of expulsion from Eden. On the ceiling of the Sistine Chapel, Michelangelo combined in one large panel the sequence from temptation to expulsion. Bak's versions, two paintings and a drawing, omit the former and concentrate on what he calls "banishment." Thus viewers have no chance to see the prelapsarian Eve, one of the most beautiful female figures Michelangelo ever painted. In *Banishment* and *Banishment II*, we glimpse a cowering Adam and Eve whose poses are copied from the Sistine source, but whose fear and pain we can attribute to more than the biblical origin in divine displeasure. Michelangelo's pair are driven from a luxuriant Eden by a colorfully robed angel with a sword; Bak's surrogate angels, with distinctly human features, seem sorrowful themselves. Their metallic wings bind them to earth rather than heaven and their faces are turned away from the supposed objects of God's anger. The background of Michelangelo's panel is open landscape and a boundless sky. Bak's artistic paraphrases offer cramped spaces backed by brick and stone. If we add to

148

this the hand behind the wall that in *Banishment* clasps a rifle, the military shell adjacent to Adam's ossified leg, and the suitcase in the foreground, to say nothing of the floating smoke, we must concede that we are dealing here with a different kind of expulsion, banishment as deportation, a violence that violates the physical integrity of the human couple. In the Book of Genesis, Adam and Eve leave Eden to enter time and face their mortality. In Bak, they enter history to face their potential annihilation. The cloudlike substance in both paintings vaguely resembles the outline of God in Bak's "creation" episodes, but if punishment for sin has culminated in mass murder, then something has clearly gone awry in the accepted scriptural account of divine intention for the Chosen People.

Bak returns us to archetypal moments in that account, inviting us again and again to see them in a different light — through the lens of subsequent darkness. The story of the patriarchs, of Abraham, Isaac, and Jacob, the founding fathers of the people of Israel, and especially of their various contracts with God, are the subject of several paintings in the series, and each one bids us to reinterpret their legendary significance through the experience of contemporary consciousness. Without rejecting their importance in the history of the Jewish struggle for identity and the emergence of a unified community, Bak drafts variations on key biblical settings that provoke review of long established religious truths.

For example, *Dress Rehearsal* offers a version of the Akedah (the binding of Isaac) rendered with an oriental splendor whose glowing colors remind us of the panels on the Sistine Ceiling. Both father and son are blindfolded, cut off from the divine authority that in *Genesis* presided over the scene. Instead, in a sardonic reversal of roles, Abraham himself seems the determined author of the unexplained act of violence, while distressed angels weakly seek to impede the deed. Their burdensome wings do not identify them as supernatural messengers, and they seem prepared to dispute rather than to intervene as heavenly delegates. No ram quivers in a nearby thicket as a surrogate victim. The former agents of God are now like sad-eyed human creatures, Hebrew sages with useless pinions, no rivals to the power of Abraham's mighty scimitar (not the expected knife). In this "dress rehearsal," a holy ritual of sacrifice is metamorphosed into a pagan rite of slaughter. The clash of cultures raises the question of how and why "sacrifice" ceased to be the operative word in the narrative of Jewish suffering, to be replaced by the anti-redemptive term *annihilation*.

Bak's variation on the Akedah contains a visual mutation on the original story that casts it in a different and unsettling light. No figure in the painting is looking at its most intrusive and disorienting image. Blinded by its blaze of colors and dramatic action, we are in danger of missing it ourselves. Father and son have their eyes shielded, and the angels turn their back to it, as though acknowledging its anomalous presence would further complicate their already difficult task. But one angel has its wings pinned to the image's surface, the arrow (if we notice it) drawing our eyes away from Abraham's menacing weapon to the even more sinister brick chimney rising beyond the upper margin of the canvas. Was the aborted sacrifice of Isaac only a "dress rehearsal" for the vaster killing of the children of Israel in a later age? How is one to construe the covenant that grew out of Abraham's devotion to God in the unholy light of the ensuing carnage? The arrangement of the principal actors in Bak's version, the human confusion that reigns in the absence of divine guidance, the infidel implications of some of the costumes — all conspire to unsettle our view of a scriptural episode that has long troubled commentators because of its pitiless test of a father's divided loyalty. For Bak, the history of the Holocaust has provided fresh reasons for re-examining this ur-text on the role of faith and deliverance in the continuing saga of the Jewish people.

Robert Alter has observed that "the literary prose of the Bible turns everywhere on significant repetition, not variation."[6] Visual equivalents of this stylistic idea abound — Monet's numerous Water Lilies come instantly to mind. They may be seen as artistic reactions to the biblical admonition to be fruitful and multiply, duplicating the initial act of Creation through the renewal of forms. If they resemble each other, as they do in the example of Monet, they signify no lack of invention but are rather forceful reminders that a view reveals more of its beauty through subtle shifts in perspective. Since surfaces, colors, and the play of light varied on the single pond that Monet observed, multiple versions could only enhance the attraction of his subjects — that is, when they were seen "in a different light." When Samuel Bak addresses the more painful theme of time in a half dozen paintings from his cycle, the landscapes are similar though not identical. Each contains a version of a tree, newly uprooted, or as a dead trunk, intact or sliced and dissected — all reminiscent of that tree and its fruit "whose mortal taste," as Milton wrote, "brought death into the world, and all our woe / and loss of Eden." Bak imitates the original creative moment in a re-creation that appears to substitute a statuary Adam for God to rectify an omission from the primordial design. When God created day and night, He meant them to exist within a context of eternity. In *Creation of Time,* Bak introduces a complex paradox for our contemplation: insofar as the human creature is a victim of mortality, time conquers man; but as the artist renders a permanent portrayal of that dilemma, art subdues time. The clock face made from a slab of tree rings may be Bak's reminder that the best way to rectify the absence of infinity is to understand time and use it wisely. But the stone Adam's pointing finger recalls another legacy, the missing figure of Michelangelo's mighty anthropomorphic God. The aging tree rings seem a humble substitute for that absent presence.

If the main question in this sequence of paintings is the preservation of roots, one is compelled to ask which roots form the principal source of the Jewish chronology. In *About Time,* the effigy of Adam, or his descendant in the guise of Everyman, receives silent counsel from two faces amid a land-scape suffused with hues of blood and fire. It is easily the most ominous painting in the "time" group. The tree is a fallen, segmented column of wood, surmounted by an intact column of stone topped by a flag of drifting smoke that summons us to a sinister phase of Jewish destiny that time has wrought beyond the frontiers of biblical narrative. Adam is little more than an outcropping of rock; the human faces before and adjacent to him appear to warn and instruct him about the direction he must take if he is to inter-pret and repair the ruins of time. Here, as in many of the paintings in this series, biblical and historical vistas collide, and the idea of creation slides into a version of re-creation. The imagination is constantly assaulted by the need to reconstitute its vision of experience, using a mixture of ingredients from an ever-changing physical and spiritual reality. Adam's advisors in *About Time* seem to represent an ancient sage and a modern confidant, perhaps a Holocaust survivor, and the challenge before Adam — and before us — is to find a way of reconciling their respective views.

Before one can "be" what was seen, one must first see what has been. Bak's paintings demand a seeing beyond mere looking, until sight gradually glides into insight, an agenda for internalizing the artistic encounter that helps to explain the process of how one can be what was seen. We first meet Bak's figures in a painting; they possess their own dramatic truth, based on their understanding of what has been. Then we confront the artist's view of his creation, both intentional and subconscious. Finally, we contend with our own perception of both, embracing contradictions where we cannot reconcile them and often struggling to accept an ultimate ambivalence that may be contrary to our expectations about the role of art in its representa-tion of the human scene. Another related group of canvases from *In a Different Light* challenges our sense of "knowing" by enacting in their very content the disputes between tradition and modernity, faith and skepticism, the disruptions of history and the certitudes of eternal truth. The silent exchange in *Conversation* pits a marble angel, more Roman than biblical in bearing, against a human face emerging from a brick structure that could easily be the remnant of a crematorium chimney. A monumentalized past greets the ruins of the present and leaves us wondering whether any mutual basis for discourse can be found. The key image is in the painting's center, the partially obscured solemn face of a camp inmate, touching the fragment of cloth that was once his prison garb. For the moment his memories eclipse the talk above his head. How can this messenger of God defend himself against the account of destruction that will fall from his interlocutor's lips? Will a time come for the Holocaust too, when monuments will be the only vestiges of its terrible history? Will the future one day provide a pillar shape for the chimney equivalent to the columns that link the angel to a holier edifice, the makeshift temple that we associate with his own fragmentary form? Or will the memory to which the survivor clings resist efforts to monumentalize the evil of annihilation, acknowledging that this grotesque parody of angelic influence in human affairs will never find a visual equivalent to restore equilibrium to its intrinsic disarray? In many ways, Bak's paintings pay tribute to the countermonument movement in modern Germany, where many architectural attempts to commemorate the event we call the Holocaust have shunned the idea of public memorials that project order and hence consolation in their conventional designs.

Bak's *Day and Night* clarifies some of these issues. Against the background of countryside ravaged by fire, Bak constructs a domestic façade that fails to conceal the conflagration, or to hinder the eye from witnessing its devastation. Its reality seems to have eroded much of the substance of the angelic figure guarding the entrance to the scene of the disaster. Despite its raised palm, the former spiritual deputy now full of vacant space seems powerless to prevent the solitary traveler, perhaps a deportee surrounded by his meager belongings, from penetrating the blazing landscape to meet his fate. Beyond the façade looms a crucifix, once the herald of salvation, which has been redrawn as a gallows, the threshold of death. The traveler is totally oblivious to the ghostly messenger from heaven, whose contours vanish before our eyes. The indifference of flesh to spirit resembles the opposition between day and night. The man seems puzzled rather than solaced by the fallen wing beside him. The rungs of the truncated ladder offer descent as an alternative to ascent, but it is not a hopeful omen and certainly no means of escape. The mélange of imagery is held together by slender threads of sense, as if the whole edifice of fractured shapes were about to topple in the absence of solid foundations to prop it up. We experience the dearth of sturdy forms as testimony to the disappearing unity once celebrated by symbols of transcendence.

Daylight and nighttime themselves are tainted by the pink and purplish shades that dominate this canvas. We are faced with a reflected incandescence, as the main sources of illumination are hidden from view. Lacking a familiar internal principle of structural coherence such as that which a conventional commemorative monument might possess, *Day and Night* stimulates the consciousness and imagination of the viewer to embrace a cardinal principle of art associated with the Holocaust—in representing this painful theme the act of creation must contain within its vision of the human scene some evidence of the deed of destruction too. Form and chaos, longing and disillusionment thus vie for our regard, the resulting tension invading us with an anxiety and sense of turmoil that are twin legacies of the subject to which Bak devotes so much of his artistic energy.

One of the few anomalous themes of *In a Different Light*, highlighted by *Reflecting*, is the dilemma of the angels, laid-off actors in the drama of God's universe who are left to ponder the reasons for the loss of their usual employment. They are poised on a promontory surrounded by the waters that once, as a sign of God's displeasure with His creation, drowned all living creatures with the exception of Noah and the voyagers on his ark. They seem pensive and disconsolate, gazing into opposite sides of a pier glass that mirrors the double entendre of the painting's title. They meditate on their own images as if wondering what to do next, like stranded messengers cut off from any possibility of completing their intended mission. Seated beneath the arching remnants of a proverbial rainbow, a breached semi-circle deprived of its luminous promise, they portray the dilemma of a world that appears to have lost contact with its heavenly source. Their princely purple robes are sad but vivid reminders of their erstwhile task, the earthbound ladder behind them a diminished echo of the spiritual purpose they once pursued between the human and the divine. Is the longing for a semblance of their former selves a sign of angelic nostalgia or a disenchanted critique of our surrender to the illusion that once infused them with vital meaning?

If there is a hint of the subversive in Bak's visual response to this query, an impatience with orthodox solutions, a desire to test our consciousness with the heritage of deprivation we all share, it is nothing more than a frank admission that for him the salves to heal the wounds of Holocaust time have yet to be contrived. This is the theme of *Lost Homes,* where not only the departed Jews but the angel too seems orphaned from his original habitat. He stands behind a ghetto wall, adjacent to a fatal brick pillar: is he the last victim of the disaster that has already consumed the people to whom he once carried messages of divine inspiration? Bearded Jew with a Christ-like visage but lacking a visible audience, he points to a hole that may be a sign of his own spiritual disrepair. That space may be the void left after the withdrawal of divine presence, but also an indication of the vacuum created when human evil tore the moral fabric of the universe. Whether it represents what the incursions of men have wrought or the deflection of God has allowed, the motif of the hand with extended finger once devoted to acts of creation now imposes on the viewer the responsibility of interpreting the spidery emptiness of its challenge.

The viewer is aided in this endeavor by the cluttered foreground of *Lost Homes.* The telephone pole with its disconnected wires, half gallows and half arrested crucifix, proclaims the temporary triumph of death over resurrection. Those dangling wires touch a sloping roof painted with the gray stripes of the jackets worn by camp inmates. The facades of houses like these are used in many Bak paintings to evoke the ruined Jewish Vilna of his youth. Their empty windows stare with eyeless dismay in recognition of a vacancy different from the one to which the angel draws our attention. Were their inhabitants walled in, or walled out? And from what? Are we asked to lament an absent God, or mourn an absent people? The wall appears to loom as a barrier between the two, an image of the hurdle separating death from transfiguration that remains an abiding legacy of the Holocaust. A lowering sky presides over the scene, which is illuminated by a hauntingly unnatural light. Both nature and the supernatural seem displaced by these icons of catastrophe.

But I do not think that the artist means to abandon us with a merely dismal prospect. Bak's most remarkable contribution to the evolution of a post-Holocaust sensibility is the tenacity with which he fashions through visual encounter a *point of view* for absorbing the intellectual and spiritual consequences of the destruction of European Jewry. The atrocity that undid one version of creation, evident in his blasted landscapes with their smoke-tainted skies, laid the foundations for a fresh way of seeing, one more sympathetic to the nature of modern reality. We might call it a principle of collateral perception, which then must grow slowly into a collateral mode of thought. It is an empirical rather than a theoretical process, spurring viewers to regard the tensions between biblical and historical narratives with a double vision that sustains simultaneously in a delicate inner balance the claims upon our imagination of creation and decay. They are engaged in perpetual strife, but the beguiling appeal of the paintings from *In a Different Light* to enter into their world of ambivalent duality prevents a victory for either side. At the original instant of creation, God forced the darkness over the deep to recede to allow for the formation of our known cosmos, replacing the "waste and wild" of chaos with a human universe from which emerged the covenantal narrative of the Jewish people. Bak's cycle shows how through the Holocaust those ancient powers of discord have sought to retrieve their primordial rights by trespassing on the world that displaced them. His art captures the resultant stress, leaving to his audience the chore of deciding how it affects or afflicts their consciousness and their lives.

Adam and Eve.
Crayon and oil on brown paper by
Samuel Bak, 2000.
IMAGE COURTESY OF PUCKER
GALLERY, BOSTON, MASS.

Creation of War Time.
Oil on canvas by Samuel Bak, 1999.
IMAGE COURTESY OF PUCKER GALLERY, BOSTON, MASS.

Open Door.

Oil on canvas by Samuel Bak, 1999.

Adam with His Own Image.

Pencil and oil on paper by Samuel Bak, 2000.

Searching.
Oil on canvas by Samuel Bak, 1999.
IMAGE COURTESY OF PUCKER GALLERY,
BOSTON, MASS.

Banishment.
Oil on canvas by Samuel Bak, 1999.
IMAGE COURTESY OF PUCKER
GALLERY, BOSTON, MASS.

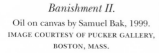

Banishment II.
Oil on canvas by Samuel Bak, 1999.
IMAGE COURTESY OF PUCKER GALLERY,
BOSTON, MASS.

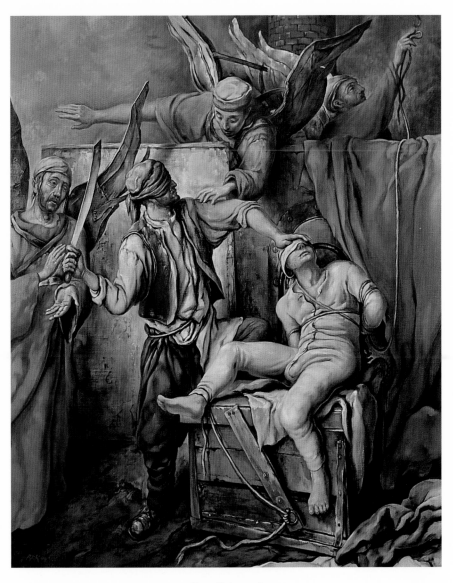

Dress Rehearsal.
Oil on canvas by Samuel Bak, 1999.
IMAGE COURTESY OF PUCKER GALLERY, BOSTON, MASS.

Creation of Time.

Oil on canvas by Samuel Bak, 1999.

About Time.

Oil on canvas by Samuel Bak, 1999.

Conversation.
Oil on canvas by Samuel Bak, 1999.
IMAGE COURTESY OF PUCKER GALLERY,
BOSTON, MASS.

Day and Night.
Oil on canvas by Samuel Bak, 1999.
IMAGE COURTESY OF PUCKER
GALLERY, BOSTON, MASS.

Reflecting.
Oil on canvas by Samuel Bak, 1999.
IMAGE COURTESY OF PUCKER
GALLERY, BOSTON, MASS.

Lost Homes.
Oil on canvas by Samuel Bak, 1999.
IMAGE COURTESY OF PUCKER
GALLERY, BOSTON, MASS.

NOTES

1. THE PURSUIT OF DEATH IN HOLOCAUST NARRATIVE

1. Jean Améry, *At the Mind's Limits: Contemplations by a Survivor of Auschwitz and Its Realities*, trans. Sidney and Stella P. Rosenfeld (New York: Schocken, 1986), 15.

2. Joshua M. Greene and Shiva Kumar, eds., *Witness: Voices from the Holocaust* (New York: Free Press, 2000), 173–174. Testimony of Renee H.

3. Ibid., 174–175. Testimony of Hanna F.

4. Charlotte Delbo, *Auschwitz and After*, trans. Rosette C. Lamont (New Haven: Yale University Press, 1995), 257.

5. *The Buchenwald Report*, trans. and ed. D. A. Hackett (Boulder, Colo.: Westview Press, 1995), 372.

6. Jorge Semprun, *Literature or Life*, trans. L. Coverdale (New York: Viking, 1997), 13.

7. Jorge Semprun, *The Long Voyage*, trans. Richard Seaver (New York: Grove, 1964), 93.

8. See Elie Wiesel, "The Death of my Father," in *Legends of Our Time* (New York: Avon, 1970).

9. Semprun, *The Long Voyage*, 197.

2. ANNE FRANK REVISITED

1. *Lodz Ghetto: Inside a Community under Siege*, comp. and ed. Alan Adelson and Robert Lapides (New York: Viking, 1989), 419–420.

2. Anne Frank, *The Diary of a Young Girl*, ed. Otto H. Frank and Mirjam Pressler, trans. Susan Massotty (New York: Doubleday, 1995), 281.

3. *Lodz Ghetto*, 425.

4. *Diary*, 321.

5. *Lodz Ghetto*, 426.

6. Anne Frank, *Diary*, 196.

7. From "Diary of Janina Heshele," trans. Azriel Eisenberg, in *Children in the Holocaust in World War II: Their Secret Diaries*, ed. Laurel Holliday (New York: Pocket Books, 1995), 70–71.

8. Anne Frank, *Diary*, 196.

9. Ibid., 147.
10. Ibid., 246.
11. Ibid., 73–74.
12. Cited in Ralph Melnick, *The Stolen Legacy of Anne Frank: Meyer Levin, Lillian Hellman, and the Staging of the Diary* (New Haven, Conn.: Yale University Press, 1997), 2.
13. Ibid.
14. *New York Times Book Review* (June 15, 1952), 1.
15. Ibid.
16. Ibid.
17. Ibid., 22.
18. Anne Frank, *Diary*, 332.
19. Patricia Hampl, *New York Times Book Review* (March 5, 1995), 1.
20. Jan Romein, *Het Parool* (April 3, 1946).
21. *Forward* (March 17, 1995), 1.
22. Alvin H. Rosenfeld, "Anne Frank — and Us: Finding the Right Words," *Reconstruction*, II, 2 (1993), 88.
23. Willy Lindwer, *The Last Seven Months of Anne Frank*, trans. Alison Meersschaert (New York: Pantheon, 1991), 63.
24. Ibid., 74.
25. Ibid., 104–105.
26. Anne Frank, *Diary*, 196, 281.
27. Ida Fink, *A Scrap of Time and Other Stories*, trans. Madeline Levine and Francine Prose (New York: Schocken, 1987), 32.
28. Lindwer, 84–85.

3. LIFE IS NOT BEAUTIFUL

1. The full interview of October 27, 2000, may be heard at www.theconnection .org. Click on "archive," then enter "Art Spiegelman" in the search engine.
2. I am grateful to Geoffrey Hartman for pointing out this connection.
3. See Ida Fink, *A Scrap of Time and Other Stories*, trans. Madeline Levine and Francine Prose (New York: Schocken, 1987), 107–109.

4. FRAGMENTS OF MEMORY: A MYTH OF PAST TIME

1. See Stefan Maechler, *The Wilkomirski Affair: A Study in Biographical Truth*, trans. John E. Woods (New York: Schocken, 2001). Since the appearance of Maechler's volume, Wilkomirski was forced to submit to a DNA test during judicial proceedings against him. This confirmed that he was born in Switzerland to a Swiss father (who is still alive).
2. Jonathan Kozol wrote: "This stunning and austerely written work is so profoundly moving, so morally important, and so free from literary artifice of any kind at all that I wonder if even I have the right to try to offer praise." *Nation* (October 28, 1996), 24.
3. See Maechler, 119 and 333n23.
4. See Peter Novick, *The Holocaust and American Life* (Boston: Houghton Mifflin, 1999).
5. James Park Sloan, *Jerzy Kosinski: A Biography* (New York: Dutton, 1996), 207–209, 214–218, 220–221. Wilkomirski's publishers, on the other hand, seem not to have considered the issue worth discussing.

6. Ibid., 108. For example, Kosinski told me that he wrote the epilogue (which was removed from all subsequent reprints) at the last minute only after his editor insisted that he do so, though there is evidence that the epilogue had been written even *before* he submitted the manuscript to Houghton Mifflin. See Sloan, 215–216.

7. Kosinski, *The Painted Bird*, 2nd. ed. (Boston: Houghton Mifflin, 1976), xiii–xiv. This volume also restored some details of sexual violence and promiscuity that his publisher had insisted on deleting from the original edition, though they had already been included in the Pocket Books paperback version of 1966.

8. Ibid., xxiii.

9. Kosinski, *The Painted Bird*, revised ed. (New York: Bantam, 1972), n.p.

10. Binjamin Wilkomirski, *Fragments: Memories of a Wartime Childhood*, trans. Carol Brown Janeway (New York: Schocken, 1996), 3. Subsequent citations included in text.

5. WOUNDED FAMILIES IN HOLOCAUST DISCOURSE

1. See the documentary *Diamonds in the Snow*, written, directed, and produced by Mira Reym Binford. Available from The Cinema Guild, Inc., 1697 Broadway, Suite 506, New York, NY 10019-5904 (tel. 1-800-723-5522).

2. Nechama Tec, "A Historical Perspective: Tracing the History of the Hidden-Child Experience" in Jane Marks, *The Hidden Children: The Secret Survivors of the Holocaust* (New York: Ballantine, 1993), 287.

3. Nechama Tec, *Dry Tears: The Story of a Lost Childhood* (New York: Oxford, 1984), 109.

4. Yehuda Nir, *The Lost Childhood: A Memoir* (New York: Harcourt Brace Jovanovich, 1989), 26.

5. Ida Fink, *A Scrap of Time and Other Stories*, trans. Madeline Levine and Francine Prose (New York: Schocken, 1989), 37.

6. Ibid., 37–38.

7. Rachel. G. Holocaust Testimony (HVT-139); Fortunoff Video Archive for Holocaust Testimonies, Yale University Library (hereafter cited as Fortunoff Archive).

8. Menachem S. Holocaust Testimony (HVT-152), Fortunoff Archive.

9. Edith H. Holocaust Testimony (HVT-47), Fortunoff Archive.

10. Ely M. Holocaust Testimony (HVT-1170), Forunoff Archive.

11. Charles Taylor, *Sources of the Self: The Making of the Modern Identity* (Cambridge, Mass.: Harvard, 1989), 36.

12. Zezette L. Holocaust Testimony (HVT-100), Fortunoff Archive.

13. Carl Friedman, *Nightfather*, trans. Arnold and Erica Pomerans (New York: Persea Books, 1994), 5.

14. Isaiah Spiegel, "Bread," reprinted in Lawrence L. Langer, ed., *Art from the Ashes: A Holocaust Anthology* (New York: Oxford, 1995), 253.

15. *Lodz Ghetto*, 348–349.

16. Reprinted in Langer, *Art from the Ashes*, 578–579.

6. MEMORY AND JUSTICE AFTER THE HOLOCAUST AND APARTHEID

1. Bernd Naumann, *Auschwitz: A Report on the Proceedings Against Robert Karl Ludwig Mulka and Others Before the Court at Frankfurt*, trans. Jean Steinberg (London: Pall Mall, 1966), 218. Information in the brackets was added by the author.

2. Ibid., 404–405, 412–413.

3. See my "The Pursuit of Death in Holocaust Narrative" chapter one in this volume.

4. Cited in Antjie Krog, *Country of My Skull: Guilt, Sorrow, and the Limits of Forgiveness in the New South Africa* (New York: Random House, 1998), 143.

5. Cited in Lyn S. Graybill, *Truth and Reconciliation in South Africa: Miracle or Model?* (Boulder, Colo.: Lynne Riemer, 2002), 45, 32.

6. Ibid., 84, 49–50.

7. Ibid., 53.

8. Pumla Gobodo-Madikizela, *A Human Being Died That Night: A South African Story of Forgiveness* (Boston: Houghton Mifflin, 2003), 15.

9. See chapter 8, note 5.

10. Charlotte Delbo, *Days and Memory*, trans. Rosette Lamont (Marlboro, Vt.: Marlboro Press, 1990), 87, 108. Other sources suggest a figure of nearly 700 victims. See Mark Mazower, *Inside Hitler's Greece: The Experience of Occupation, 1941–1944* (New Haven, Conn.: Yale University Press, 1993), 179.

11. *New York Times* (October 10, 1994), C1, C11.

12. Rose M. Holocaust Testimony (HVT-1638), Fortunoff Archive.

7. WITNESSING ATROCITY: THE TESTIMONIAL EVIDENCE

1. See Michael Kenney, "Remaking the Holocaust?" *The Boston Globe*, Living Arts Section (January 3, 1996), 58.

2. Ibid.

3. Testimony of Herbert J. in *Witness: Voices from the Holocaust*, ed. Joshua M. Greene and Shiva Kumar (New York: Free Press, 2000), 173.

4. Ibid., 227–228.

5. Testimony of Bessie K. in *Witness*, 109, 111.

6. Cited in Jorge Semprun, *Literature or Life*, trans. L. Coverdale (New York: Viking, 1997), 201.

7. Testimony of Sol. See "Survivors: Testimonies of the Holocaust" CD Disc 2 (Los Angeles: Steven Spielberg and Survivors of the Shoah Visual History Foundation, 1999).

8. Jürgen Matthäus, "Assault and Destruction," in *Hidden History of the Kovno Ghetto* (Boston: Little, Brown, 1997), 24n21.

9. Testimony of Hannah F. in *Witness*, 218.

10. *To the Bitter End: The Diaries of Viktor Klemperer: 1942–1945*, trans. Martin Chalmers (London: Weidenfeld & Nicolson, 1999), 148. Ernst Kreidl was arrested by the Gestapo late in 1941. A telegram to his "Aryan" wife from the SS in Buchenwald announced: "Ernst Kreidl deceased this morning May 22nd [1942], letter follows." Robert Eger was also arrested by the Gestapo, together with his "Aryan" wife. She was detained and released a few weeks later (she had a brother in the SS), but in January 1943 she was notified that her husband had died of "myocardial infarction" in the "Auschwitz camp."

11. Paul Steinberg, *Speak You Also: A Memoir*, trans. Linda Coverdale with Bill Ford (New York: Henry Holt and Co., 2000), 62.

12. See Lawrence L. Langer, "The Alarmed Vision: Social Suffering and Holocaust Atrocity," in Arthur Kleinman, Veena Das, and Margaret Lock, eds., *Social Suffering* (Berkeley: University of California Press, 1997), 47–65.

8. MORALIZING AND DEMORALIZING THE HOLOCAUST

1. Because the text was never written down but only overheard, numerous versions exist. The version cited here has been called the "exact text of what Martin Niemöller said" and appears in *Congressional Record*, 14 (October 1968), 31636.

2. George Santayana, *Reason in Common Sense*, vol. 1 of *The Life of Reason, or the Phases of Human Progress* (New York: Scribner's, 1905), 284. The line is incorrectly quoted in one of the epigraphs to William L. Shirer's *The Rise and Fall of the Third Reich* (New York: Simon and Schuster, 1960).

3. Ibid., 1, 3.

4. Ibid., 284, 285.

5. Quoted by Saul Friedlander in his "Introduction" to Saul Friedlander, ed., *Probing the Limits of Representation: Nazism and the "Final Solution"* (Cambridge, Mass.: Harvard University Press, 1992), 3.

6. Tadeusz Borowski, *This Way for the Gas, Ladies and Gentlemen*, trans. Barbara Vedder (New York: Penguin, 1976), 121–122.

7. Albert Camus, *Notebooks 1942–1951*, trans. Justin O'Brien (New York: Knopf, 1965), 151.

8. W. G. Sebald, *On the Natural History of Destruction*, trans. Anthea Bell (New York: Random House, 2003), 28, 64.

9. REPRESENTING THE HOLOCAUST

1. Theodor W. Adorno, "Cultural Criticism and Society," in *Prisms*, trans. Samuel Weber and Sherry Weber (London: Neville Spearman, 1967), 34.

2. Adorno, "Meditations on Metaphysics," in *Negative Dialectics*, trans. E. B. Ashton (New York: Seabury Press, 1973 [1966]), 367.

3. Adorno, *Prisms*, 23.

4. Aharon Appelfeld, "After the Holocaust," in Berel Lang, ed., *Writing and the Holocaust* (New York: Holmes & Meier, 1988), 89, 85.

5. John Felstiner, *Paul Celan: Poet, Survivor, Jew* (New Haven, Conn.: Yale University Press, 1995), 26.

6. Janusz Nel Siedlecki, Krystyn Olszewski, and Tadeusz Borowski, *We Were in Auschwitz*, trans. Alicia Nitecki (New York: Welcome Rain, 2000), 3.

7. Lea Warnick Fridman, *Words and Witness: Narrative and Aesthetic Strategies in the Representation of the Holocaust* (Albany: State University of New York Press, 2000), 128, 129.

8. Ibid., 109.

9. Michael Rothberg, *Traumatic Realism: The Demands of Holocaust Representation* (Minneapolis: University of Minnesota Press, 2000), 108, 109.

10. Ibid., 140.

11. Berel Lang, *Holocaust Representation: Art within the Limits of History and Ethics* (Baltimore: Johns Hopkins, 2000), 11.

12. Ibid., 17–18.

13. Ibid., 37.

14. Ibid., 37, 38.

15. Ibid., 68, 70.

16. Vivian M. Patraka, *Spectacular Suffering: Theatre, Fascism, and the Holocaust* (Bloomington: Indiana University Press, 1999), 83.

17. Ibid., 42, 88, 99.

NOTES TO PAGES 137–150

18. Caroline A. Wiedmer, *The Claims of Memory: Representations of the Holocaust in Contemporary Germany and France* (Ithaca, N.Y.: Cornell University Press, 1999), 30.
19. Ibid., 69.
20. Ibid., 128.
21. James E. Young, *At Memory's Edge: After-images of the Holocaust in Contemporary Art and Architecture* (New Haven, Conn.: Yale University Press, 2000), 40.
22. Ibid., 10.
23. Ibid., 175.
24. Ibid., 222.

10. THE BOOK OF GENESIS IN THE ART OF SAMUEL BAK

1. For this essay I have used Robert Alter's *Genesis: Translation and Commentary* (New York: W.W. Norton, 1996).
2. *In a Different Light: The Book of Genesis in the Art of Samuel Bak* (Boston: Pucker Art Publications, 2001; distributed by University of Washington Press). Copies may also be obtained from the Pucker Gallery, 171 Newbury St., Boston, MA 02116 or (contactus@puckergallery.com). Many of Samuel Bak's paintings may be viewed on the Gallery web site at www.puckergallery.com.
3. Bak and his mother survived the Vilna ghetto. His father and four grandparents were shot by the Germans at Ponary, a wooded suburb of Vilna. See his *Painted in Words: A Memoir* (Bloomington: Indiana University Press, 2001).
4. Cited in Carlo Pietrangeli et al., *The Sistine Chapel: A Glorious Restoration* (New York: Harry N. Abrams, 1994), 105.
5. The citations from Bacon appeared on wall placards accompanying an exhibition of his paintings at the New Tate Gallery in London in the summer of 2001.
6. Alter, xxvi.

INDEX

LAWRENCE L. LANGER

is Professor of English Emeritus at Simmons College in Boston. His books
include *The Holocaust and the Literary Imagination* (1975); *Versions of
Survival: The Holocaust and the Human Spirit* (1981); *Holocaust Testimonies:
The Ruins of Memory* (1991), winner of the National Book Critics Circle
Award; *Admitting the Holocaust* (1995); and *Preempting the Holocaust* (1998).